Roberta Johnson Hinds

D1707471

THE GRANDMOTHER.

THE GRANDMOTHER

A Story of Country Life in Bohemia

By BOZENA NEMEC

TRANSLATED FROM THE BOHEMIAN

WITH A BIOGRAPHICAL SKETCH OF THE AUTHOR

By FRANCES GREGOR, B.L.

CHICAGO

A. C. McCLURG AND COMPANY

1892

28/1/02

~~1311E 51~~

~~A. 154894~~

BH

BIOGRAPHICAL SKETCH OF THE AUTHOR.

Bozena Nemec was born in Vienna, February 2, 1820. Her father, John Pankel, was equerry to the Duchess of Zahan, the owner of the large Nachod estates. The Duchess spent most of her summers in the castle at Nachod, where she was visited by many distinguished people from all parts of Europe, and even from England. Most of the incidents related in THE GRANDMOTHER are based on fact, for the Princess of the story was the Duchess of Zahan, and Barunka, none other than the author Bozena Nemec. The Duchess early recognized Bozena's talents and did not a little to encourage and aid her in her education. The life at the castle had also much influence upon the young girl.

Bozena's father was a great lover of music and literature, and tried to awaken the same taste in his children. He loved them all; but Bozena on account of her talents was his favorite child, and she in turn clung to her father with great devotion. In after years she said, "Father could do with me what he wished. When he turned his beautiful eyes to me and said, 'Go, my Bozenka, do this or that,' I would have jumped into the fire for him." This love was the source of much of her inspiration.

It was quite different with the mother. Theresa Novotny was a woman who in no way rose above the common mass of woman kind. She loved her husband and her children; she was an excellent house keeper; but city life in Vienna had changed the bright peasant girl into a stiff lady of few words and of great austerity in morals and behavior. The smallest fault was sharply reprimanded; and for severer punishments, which were by no means rare, the children were expected to thank her.

Bozena looked upon this as something fearful, and never could be induced to do it, although she knew that a much harder whipping was sure to follow her refusal. She said: "Although at times my feelings urged me to submit, my feet would not move from the spot, and my lips refused to utter the words of repentance."

Bozena's education as regards books was begun when she was but four years old. Her mother brought her a card from the market, upon which were the letters of the alphabet in large, black print. Giving her the card she said: "Here Bozenka, since you can learn songs you can learn your letters."

Her first teacher was an "uncle," as he was called,— though in reality he was uncle to no one. It was said of him that he knew how to do more than eat bread. Bozena said: "I went to show him my card and he offered to teach me. I soon learned the letters and how to put them together to form words. At the same time I learned to write, using for this purpose the large lead buttons upon his coat and vest. In the summer we studied but little. He went about with me and taught me the names of flowers and trees and the habits of insects."

When Bozena was six years old she was sent to school in another village, where she was to live with her god-mother. She had never heard anything good of schools, and had every reason to be afraid. At home they often said to her: "Just wait; when you get to school, they'll teach you to mind!" The old servant trying to comfort her would say: "Dear child, it cannot be otherwise. Teaching is torturing; every one must bear it. When I went to school I was thrashed like rye." Bozena, in her recollections says: "The first morning, when I awoke at Chvalin, I thought I was the most unhappy creature in the whole world. Weeping I arose and weeping I dressed myself. At the breakfast table my godmother said to Aunt Agnes: 'When you go to the market, take Bozena with you to school; she has already been announced.' My heart seemed to be held in a vise, and my tears were ready to fall; yet I feared to cry before my godmother. Aunt Agnes took the basket, and putting my satchel over my shoulder started with me for school."

On the way, Bozena refused to go on and begged to stay at home one day longer. Much persuasion and considerable force were required before the old aunt succeeded in getting her into the school room, but her fears were soon dispelled by the kind, pleasant school master. In this school she remained six years, and it was this teacher, as she afterwards acknowledged, who laid the foundation of her future culture and taught her to love her neighbor, her country, and her God. She kept his memory green in the pretty tale of "The Schoolmaster."

When Bozena left school, she lived at Chvalkovitz in the family of the steward of the manor. As her stay here had much influence upon her life, some account of her surroundings will not be out of place. She said:

"The steward was a good friend of my father's, and that was why I was placed in the family. He was a man in middle life, the most learned of all the officers, indeed, of the whole neighborhood. He had a fine library, and that not merely for ornament. Shakespeare and Goethe were his favorite authors. He was well versed both in the classics and in modern literature. He read French and English and always took the best journals. He was also very fond of gardening. Although he wished well to the Bohemians, his own sentiments were those of a true German. He was a good, jovial man, an admirer of beauty, fond of good living, hospitable, and agreeable to all. His influence could have been exerted much for good, had his domestic relations been different.

"His wife, who was several years his senior, was in no way congenial to him. She had been maid of honor to the Princess, and when young must have been beautiful; but now her black hair and her sky blue eyes were her only remaining charms. This, however, was not the cause of the trouble. She and her husband were not adapted to each other. She was a bigoted Catholic, while he was a

Protestant who hated priests. She could bear no reflections upon the nobility; the time she had spent in 'the
castle she regarded the most delightful period of her life,
and her husband tormented her for this with the most bitter irony.

"Then, too, he preferred Bohemian cookery, while she
prepared everything according to an Austrian cook-book.
When he would not eat, her eyes filled with tears as she
said: 'Aber, August, es ist ja gut, iss nur.' To which he usually replied: 'Ich glaub's, liebe Netti, habe aber keinen ap-
petit.' Then he smiled grimly, arose, drank a glass of
wine, and went into the fields,—a sure sign that something
was wrong. These fits grew more and more frequent, until not a day passed when he was not under the influence
of liquor, and at such times he indulged in the most cutting remarks, causing intense suffering to his wife. I
often came upon her kneeling with hands upraised before
the crucifix, and weeping bitterly. I pitied her, but on
other occasions I was sorry for him. He wanted to enjoy life, but something ailed her all the time; she was
swathed in flannels from one end of the year to the other.
When she went to bed, she was dressed like a driver ready
to start for Amsterdam.

"He read late at night and early in the morning, and
when thus engaged no one dared disturb him. His wife
was very jealous of him, and in her turn succeeded in in-
flicting on him as much wretchedness as he on other occasions caused her. They had three children, and it
grieved him much that they were not at all bright. As I
was there for study, I often went to him to ask a question,
to have something explained, or to change my book, and
he always did everything for me with the greatest pleasure. When I had read a book through, I was obliged to
tell him its contents, and he explained what I had not
understood. Some evenings I read to him; in short, I became his pet and at once aroused the jealousy of his wife.
Later it was worse."

She describes the house as follows: "The manorhouse had, indeed, been renovated, but upon the old foundation, so that it was half old and had lost none of its somber appearance. It lacked not in dark underground passages nor in fearful tales of ghosts, so that I was almost dead with terror when I was obliged after dark to cross from the apartments of the servants to our own rooms. The way led through a long, dark corridor, lighted by high gothic windows, through which the light of the moon came in, making fantastic shapes upon the walls. It was said that a white lady haunted the passage, also one of the family of Dobren, who had been murdered there and who walked about in his shroud, from his room to the chapel, carrying his head under his arm.

"And my chamber! I was lost in it. It was high, dark, with tall windows and oaken blinds. The doors were of the same material, with heavy iron bolts which I always closed for the night. But one becomes accustomed to everything;— I, too, soon felt at home in the old manorhouse, and looked upon myself as one of the ' ladies of the castle ' of whom I had read so much."

A young and beautiful castle maid must also have her knight, and so far as is known there were two such knights, who lived in the castle above. Of these she speaks:

" The one was a youth about seventeen years of age, a relative of the lord of the castle. He was a good boy, but somewhat foolish, handsome, but with no expression in his face. We were good friends, but when I was told that he was in love with me, that was the end of our friendship.

" The other knight was quite different. He was no longer young, being about thirty-six years of age. He was dark, well built, but small. His face had something satanic in it, but was not repulsive. His forehead was high, his hair, dark brown; he had handsome white teeth, his eye — that was demoniac. He could look dreamily, lovingly, so that all the young women were in love with him. When he fixed his eye upon any one, which he often did, he was irresistible. The person was like a bird charmed by the eye of its destroyer.

"He was a strange man. At times he was a great spendthrift, then again he was the most exemplary of men. Now he laughed at the whole world and no sentiment was sacred to him; and yet I saw the time when he was entirely overcome by his own feelings. He seemed cold, and yet he was the most passionate of men. He was a man of the world, experienced in all the ins and outs of society. Although fond of gay company, he himself was never gay. He was passionately fond of dancing, but was never carried away by the excitement. While he danced, his face was paler than usual, but his eyes betrayed the fire within.

"He had no respect for women. I never saw him kiss the hand of any lady, nor give a compliment to any of them. He held our mistress for nought; she was the butt of all his wit. He ruled the house; the steward liked him, and the rest of us were afraid of him. Whenever he fixed his eyes upon me, I trembled, and yet I was never angry; I was the only one whom he loved; before me he wept like a child, but that was much later. At this time he had regard for my youth and treated me with great consideration, and severely reprimanded any one who dared utter a word of double meaning before me."

Bozena remained in this family only two years, but the instruction she gained in that short time was invaluable to her. Under the direction of the steward she had read many excellent books, and what he had not given her she took and read secretly. She had been placed there to learn German, music, and needle work. Music she soon gave up, when her instructor told her she had no talent for it. As for her needle work, her teacher found her very careless and often reprimanded her severely; but she bore his censure meekly, knowing that it was well deserved.

Her time was spent among books, and she lived in an ideal world whose inhabitants were the heroes and heroines of novels, poems, and dramas. When she returned home she continued her reading, borrowing books from the castle library.

Her life at home was quiet, but full of ideals and aspirations. She looked forward to the future as to a new world that had wondrous treasures in store for her.

But her dreams were cut short by her marriage, in 1837, to Joseph Nemec, an officer of finance in Kosteletz. It was a marriage without love, entered into at the wish of her father. How she regarded this step may be judged from her own words.

" The years of my girlhood were the most beautiful of my life. When I married I wept over my lost liberty, over the dreams and beautiful ideals forever ruined. . . Woman's heart is like wax, every picture is easily impressed; but what does it all avail? Now everything seems to me pale, tame, and cold, and lead seems to course through my veins. I could weep over myself, when I consider my condition."

Although Madame Nemec looked upon her marriage as entirely unhappy, it was not without some redeeming features. Her husband was a very estimable man, beloved of many friends. He was, moreover, a man of culture, an ardent patriot, and had his wife been an ordinary woman they might have lived happily together. But what she lost in her marriage she tried to make up in her literary life.

While Madame Nemec had always taken a deep interest in all things pertaining to her country, and her early education had been in the Bohemian language, she knew nothing of the literature of her native land until the family moved to Polna, where she became acquainted with the writings of Tyl.* She had already written some tales, and now, roused by patriotic enthusiasm, she composed the beautiful poem, *To the Bohemian Women.* This and several other poems and tales gained her much popularity, so that when, in 1841, the family moved to Prague, she was received with open arms into the circle of young

---

* One of the earliest novelists of this period in Bohemia.

authors. The chief of these were Erben, Tyl, Chelakov-sky, Nebesky, and Chejka.

The last named gentleman proved of the greatest ser-vice to her. He saw that she was introduced among the most cultivated ladies, provided the way for some culture in art, and induced her husband to engage for her a Bohe-mian teacher, which he not only willingly did, but him-self began to study the language. These were happy and profitable days for the author, but they were of short dura-tion. In 1845, her husband was again transferred, this time to Domazlitz (Taus).

A new field of labor was now open to her. She found abundant material to work up, and during this time she wrote: *Pictures from Domazlitz, Fables, Karla,* and *The Mountain Village.*

Madame Nemec's experience at Domazlitz was some-what singular. She delineated the life of the people so faithfully that some of the tradesmen, imagining that she was holding them up for ridicule, tried to rouse the people against her. Charles Havlichek* took her part, and so ably defended her in the papers that the people turned to her with greater love than before. She tried to instruct them through conversation, read to them, and lent them books, and they appreciated her kind labors, followed her from village to village, until the police inter-fered, thinking that she was propagating ideas hostile to the government. While at Domazlitz, she contracted the dread disease, consumption, so that her future work was done under great disadvantages.

In 1847, M. Nemec was transferred to Neumark, on the Bavarian frontier. Here his wife's health was considerably improved. She wrote: "I feel much better and am be-coming fleshy; perhaps it is because my life in these mountains is so peaceful. We sent the two elder boys to Domazlitz to school, and I am very lonesome; you know I live only in my children. O, heavens, soon the world will claim them and then my heart shall yearn for them

* One of the patriots who fell a victim to Austrian intolerance.

in vain!" This peaceful life at Neumark was of short duration; in 1848, they were transferred to Nymburg.

The same year came the stormy times when the revolutionary wave swept over Europe. Bohemia, too, was involved; and M. Nemec, as an ardent patriot, could not look on with indifference. In a letter dated at Nymburg we read: "Believe me, no one here knew what to do. All, Germans as well as Bohemians, wanted to go to the assistance of Prague. I wept for my husband as already lost, but was resigned, sending him in God's name to fight for his country." As might be supposed, she, too, was not silent; for all faithful Bohemians were carried away by enthusiasm, imagining that the time had come for delivering the great mass of their countrymen from servitude, and for securing for all constitutional rights. At this time she wrote *Peasants' Politics* which gives a very good idea of the way the countrymen looked upon the constitution, and the rights and privileges promised them.

The active part Madame Nemec and her husband took in the revolution did not remain overlooked by the government. In 1849, M. Nemec was transferred to Liberetz, the following year to Hungary, and in 1853, he was placed upon the retired list with a pension of three hundred and fifty florins. This was a great blow to the family, and from this time poverty was added to the numerous ills against which they had to struggle. The same year they lost their son, Henry, and Madame Nemec, broken down by her afflictions, was taken seriously ill.

After this the family lived mostly in Prague, M. Nemec being closely watched by the police. He engaged in some literary labors and held various positions on the staff of some of the newspapers. But the amount thus earned was so small that the family were reduced to great want. A small collection was made for them; but the hosts of friends that had surrounded the promising author in the days of her prosperity scarcely showed themselves in her adversity. A few remained true, but they were not able to assist her. Her difficulties, too, were increased by her reckless generosity. This was a trait of her whole family and is well described in the story, in the scene where Grandmother relates to the Princess her journey from Silesia to Bohemia. Add to this her open and confiding nature, and it may easily be seen that she was often made the dupe of selfish, designing persons. She believed in them and shared with them all she had, whether it was much or little. Thus, when the collection spoken of above was given her, she immediately divided it with a young man who was just then in the house and who had awakened her sympathy by the recital of his own trials and financial difficulties. This, too, was one of the causes that often disturbed the domestic harmony of the Nemec family.

The year 1861 was the darkest of her life. Eager to seize any opportunity whereby she might relieve herself from eating the bitter bread of charity, she accepted the offer of a publisher at Lytomysl to give her her board and twelve florins for every thirty-two pages of manuscript which she should write. She accordingly moved to that city; but the publisher treated her most cruelly. Not only did he refuse to give her the price agreed upon, but he went so far as to order the hotel keeper not to give her any food at his charge. As she had come from Prague almost penniless, she was obliged to live on bread and water until she could receive assistance from her husband. Her expenses ranged from four to eight kreutzers a day. She returned to Prague shortly after, completely discouraged and broken down both mentally and physically, and died the following year. She was buried in the old cemetery of Visehrad, and several years later the ladies of the American Club erected a suitable monument over her grave.

Her husband lived till 1869. Her son Charles is a professor in the Agricultural College at Tabor, Jaroslav fills a similar position in the Real School at Odessa, and her daughter, Dorothea, is a teacher in Jincin, Bohemia.

The two motives that guided Madame Nemec in her work were her patriotism and her love for the common people. While at Domazlitz she wrote to a friend: "The common people, they are my joy; I feel refreshed whenever I grasp the hard, rough hand of one of these women."

In reply to the advice given in the *Prager Zeitung*, that all should learn German as fast as possible and thus end that eternal strife between the two nationalities, she says:

"Yes, that would be well, only that by so doing we should become estranged from the greater part of our nation, which looks to us for guidance and light." This is the key note to her whole life and work. She loved the common people and labored to elevate them. She knew that she could reach their hearts much more quickly through their mother tongue than through another language, and for this reason she wrote in Bohemian, although she had been better educated in the German language. Then, too, she longed to see her nation strong, great, and free, and many fervent words were spoken and written by her to arouse the educated women to greater earnestness in its behalf.

As regards religion, Madame Nemec believed in the essential principles of Christianity, but was an enemy to priestcraft and superstition. Writing from Domazlitz she said:

"The ruin of several villages here is that accursed Jesuitism. Not far from here are two priests of that order, and you have no conception of the evil they have done! They have imposed upon the people, stupefied them, led them into poverty, so that they walk about bewildered like so many wandering sheep. And no one dares touch that hundred headed dragon!"

While a child, it was her custom to pray before the picture of Christ.

"While praying, I did not turn my eyes from it, and I gazed so long that it ceased to be a mere picture. Christ seemed to be before me in reality; to him I prayed, to him I made known my wants, asking for his help and guidance. My father praised me, said that I was pious, held me up as an example to the other children, who performed their devotions carelessly, often dozing or pushing each other; they did not see before them the living Christ!"

Madame Nemec was not the worshiper of mere culture. In one of her letters is the following:

"You say that you desire nothing so much as culture. Believe me, if you knew the nature of culture here (in Germany) as it is exhibited in its results, you would be astonished. Above all things I desire to protect my children against this culture. I know not what to think! My highest aspirations, too, were to gain culture; and yet to-day I have the conviction that more precious than all learning is simplicity of manner and purity of heart. I see here among the cultured a contempt for worthy senti-ments; I see the conceptions of virtue perverted or up-rooted, and this not only among individuals, but through-out society. Domestic happiness, sincere love and tender-ness, these are unknown. This culture of which the wealthy boast forms a deeper and deeper abyss betwen the learned and the unlearned, the rich and the poor, and who is there to reconcile these opposites?"

The works of Madame Nemec were collected and pub-lished, in 1862, in eight volumes, and again, in 1875, in six volumes. THE GRANDMOTHER is without question her best work, but *The Mountain Village* is also a novel of much excellence. As a story, it is superior to the former, since it has a more developed plot; but as a picture of Bo-hemian life, it is too local and restricted. The other works consist of shorter stories, tales and fables, and *Recollections from my Life in Hungary*.

Since the days of Madame Nemec many authors have arisen, and a great deal has been written that has been re-ceived with much favor by the public. As novelists, Mrs. Caroline Svetla, Alois Jirasek, Benes Trebisky, and, per-haps, some others are superior to Madame Nemec; but as a faithful artist of Bohemian country life,— one that saw and was able to reproduce the salient characteristics of the country people,— she has no equal; and her works will ever be regarded as a precious legacy to her people.

THE GRANDMOTHER.

CHAPTER I.

IT was long, long ago, when last I gazed on that dear face, kissed those pale, wrinkled cheeks, and tried to fathom the depths of those blue eyes, in which were hidden so much goodness and love. Long ago it was when, for the last time, those aged hands blessed me. Our Grandmother is no more; for many a year she has slept beneath the cold sod.

But to me she is not dead. Her image, with its lights and shadows, is imprinted upon my soul, and as long as I live, I shall live in her. Were I master of an artist's brush, how differently, dear Grandmother, would I glorify you! but this sketch — I know not, I know not how it will please. But you used to say, "Upon this earthy ball, not a soul that pleases all." If, then, a few readers shall find as much pleasure in reading about you as I do in writing, I shall be content.

Grandmother had three children, a son and two daughters. For many years the older daughter lived with relatives in Vienna; when she married, the younger took her place. The son, a mechanic, worked at his trade in a small town in Bohemia, while Grandmother dwelt in a village upon the borders of Silesia. Her family consisted of herself and Betsey, an old servant who had been in the family ever since Grandmother could remember.

Grandmother did not live the life of a recluse; all the people of the village were to her brothers and sisters; she was to them a mother, a counsellor, and a friend. No christening, wedding, or funeral could go on without her. The course of her life was so even, her days were so busy and happy, that she desired no change — she would have been content to live thus forever.

This even course of life was disturbed by a letter. Grandmother often received letters from her children, but none ever came before, fraught with such momentous questions for her to solve. It was from her daughter in Vienna, who told her mother that her husband had obtained service in the household of a certain princess, whose estates were but a few miles distant from the village where Grandmother lived, and that he was to be at home with his family during the summer only, while the princess lived in the country, and therefore it was their earnest desire that Grandmother should come to live with them. Indeed, no excuse would be accepted, as both she and the children had set their hearts upon it and were eagerly looking for her arrival.

Upon reading this letter Grandmother burst into tears. She did not know what to do. She loved her daughter, and her heart yearned towards her grandchildren whom she had not seen; on the other hand, the good people of the village were very dear to her, and it was hard to break away from all the old associations. But blood is thicker than water. After much tossing up of the matter, her maternal instincts came to the aid of her convictions, and she decided to go. The old cottage, with all it contained, was given over into the care of Betsey with these words: " I don't know how I shall like it there; and perhaps, after all, I shall die here among you."

A few days after this a wagon stood at the door of the cottage. Wenzel, the driver, placed upon it Grandmother's large flowered chest; her feather-beds tied in a sheet; the spinning wheel, to her an indispensable piece of furniture; a basket, contain- ing four top - knotted chickens; and a bag with a pair of party - colored kittens. Last, but not least, came Grandmother herself, her eyes red from weeping. It was no wonder that she wept; for around her stood the villagers, who had come to bid her farewell, and followed by their blessing she rode slowly to her new home.

What bright anticipations, what rejoicing at The Old Bleachery,—for thus the people called the iso- lated house that had been assigned to Grand- mother's daughter, Mrs. Proshek, as her home on the estates of the princess. Every few moments the children ran out to the road to see if Wenzel was coming; and every passer by heard the won- drous news that Grandma was coming. The chil- dren kept asking each other, " How do you sup- pose Grandma will look?"

They knew several grandmas, whose images were curiously confounded in their little heads, and they could not decide to which of them their own could be compared.

At last the long expected team arrived. "Grandma's come!" shouted the children in a chorus. Mr. and Mrs. Proshek rushed out to meet her; Betty, the maid, followed carrying the youngest child, and behind her came the three children accompanied by the two dogs, Sultan and Tyrol.

The wagon stopped at the gate, and Wenzel helped a little old woman to alight. She was dressed in the garb of a peasant, having her head wrapped up in a large white kerchief. This was something the children had never seen before, and they stood still, their eyes fixed upon their grandmother. Mr. Proshek welcomed her cordially, her daughter embraced and kissed her, and Betty presented the dimpled cheeks of Adelka to be kissed. Grandmother smiled, called the child " her own sweet fledgling," and signed her with the cross. Then she turned to the other children and said: " O my darlings, my little ones, how I have longed to see you! " But the children, with downcast eyes, stood as if frozen to the spot, and uttered never a word; and not until they were ordered by their mother would they step forward to be kissed, and even then they could not recover from their amazement. They had known many grandmothers in their life, but never one like this; they could not turn their eyes from her; they walked round and round and examined her from head to foot.

They wondered at the curious little coat, with its full pleating, like organ pipes, behind; the green linsey-wolsey petticoat, bordered with a wide ribbon was an object of great admiration; they were pleased with the flowered kerchief that was tied beneath the large, white head shawl. They sat down upon the ground that they might examine better the red wedge - shaped insertion in her white stockings, and also her black slippers. Willie touched the pretty patchwork on her handbag, and the fouryearold Johnny, the older of the two, slyly raised her white apron; he had felt something hard beneath it, something hidden away in her large outside pocket, and he wanted to know what it was. Barunka, the oldest of the children, pushed him away, whispering: "Wait, I'll tell on you! you want to feel in Grandma's pocket!"

That whisper was a little too loud, it would have been heard behind the ninth wall; Grandmother noticed it, and turning from her daughter she put her hand in her pocket and said: "Well, look at what I have here!" She placed upon her lap a rosary, a jack - knife, several bits of crust, a piece of twine, two horses and two dolls made of ginger-bread; these were for the children. As she distributed them she said: "Grandma brought you something more." Thus speaking she took from her handbag some apples and Easter eggs, and set the kittens and chickens at liberty. The children shouted with delight. Grandma was the best of all grandmas! "These kittens were born in May, are four colored, and will make excellent mousers. These chickens are so tame that if Barunka teaches them, they will follow her about like puppies."

The children then began to inquire about this and that, and soon were on the best of terms with Grandmother. Their mother rebuked their end-less questioning; but Grandmother said: "Never mind, Theresa, we are happy in each other's love," and so they had it their own way. One sat in her lap, another stood upon a bench behind her, and Barunka stood before her, intently gazing into her face. One wondered at her snow-white hair, another at her wrinkled forehead, and the third cried: "Why Grandma, you have but four teeth!" She smiled, smoothed down Barunka's dark brown hair, and said: "My child, I am old; when you grow old, you, too, will look different." But they could not comprehend how their smooth, soft hands could ever become wrinkled like hers.

The hearts of the grandchildren were won the first hour, for Grandmother surrendered herself to them entirely. Mr. Proshek won her love by his frankness and the goodness of heart that beamed from his handsome face. One thing, however, she did not like, and that was that he could speak no Bohemian. What little German she had ever known she had forgotten, and yet she so longed to have a talk with John. He comforted her some by telling her that although he could not speak the language, he understood it quite well. She soon perceived that two languages were used in the family: the children and the maid spoke to Mr. Proshek in Bohemian, while he replied in German, which they understood. Grandmother hoped that in time she, too, would be able to understand it; and in the meantime she would get along as well as she could.

Another thing that did not quite suit her was the appearance of her daughter. She had expected to find her as she was when she left home, a bright, cheerful peasant girl; and now she saw before her a stately lady, in city garments, of stiff manners and few words. This was not her Theresa! She observed, too, that their domestic life was quite different from that to which she had been accustomed; and although, for the first few days, she was surprised and delighted, she soon grew tired of the new ways, and had it not been for the grandchildren, she would have packed up and returned to her own little cottage.

Mrs. Proshek, it is true, had some city notions; but she was not to be disliked for this, for on the whole she was a very estimable woman. She loved her mother dearly, and the departure of the latter would have grieved her much. She was not a little disturbed when she perceived that her mother was becoming homesick; and guessing the cause, she said to her: "Mother, I know that you are used to labor, and that you would not be content here, if you had nothing else to do than to go about with the children. Should you desire to spin, I have some flax up in the garret, and if the crop is good I shall soon have much more; still I should prefer to have you see to the housekeeping. My duties at the castle, together with my sewing and cooking, occupy all my time, so that the rest must be left entirely to the servants. Now, if you will be helpful to me in this, you may manage everything your own way." "That I will gladly!" replied Grandmother, overcome with joy. That very day she climbed up the ladder into the garret to see about the flax, and the next day the children watched the process of making thread upon the spinning wheel.

The first thing of which Grandmother assumed full charge was the baking of bread. She did not like to see the servants handling "the gift of God" without any reverence or ceremony. They never signed it with the cross, either before or after taking it out of the oven; they handled it as if the loaves were so many bricks. When Grandmother set the sponge, she blessed it, and this she repeated each time she handled it until the bread was placed upon the table. While it was rising no gaping fellow dared come near it lest he should "overlook" it and make it fall; and even little Willie, when he came into the kitchen during baking time, never forgot to say: "May God bless it!"

Whenever Grandmother baked bread, the children had a feast. For each one she baked a little loaf filled with plum or apple sauce; this had never been done before. They, however, had to learn to take care of the crumbs. "The crumbs belong to the fire," she used to say as she brushed them up and threw them into the stove. If one of the children dropped a bit of bread, she made him pick it up, saying: "Don't you know that if one steps upon a crumb, the souls in purgatory weep?" She did not like to see bread cut uneven, for she used to say: "Whoever does not come out even with his bread will not come out even with people." One day Johnny begged her to cut his slice from the side of the loaf, as he wanted the crust, but she said: "When one cuts into the side of the loaf, he cuts off God's heels! But whether it be so or not, you must not get into the habit of being dainty about your food." So Master Johnny could not indulge his appetite for crusts.

Whenever there was a piece of bread that the children had not eaten, it always found its way into Grandmother's pocket; and when they happened to

go to the water, she threw it to the fishes, or
crumbled it up for the birds and ants. In short, she
did not waste a crumb, and ever counseled the children: " Be thankful for God's gift; without it there
are hard times, and God punishes him who does
not value it." Whenever one of the children
dropped his bread, upon picking it up he was
obliged to kiss it. This was a kind of penance; and
whenever Grandmother found a pea, she picked it
up, found upon it the chalice, and kissed it with
reverence. All this she taught the children to do.

If at any time a feather lay in the path, she
pointed to it saying: " Stoop down, Barunka!"
Sometimes Barunka was lazy and said: " O Grandma, what is one feather!" But Grandmother at
once reproved her. " You must remember, child,
that one added to another makes more, and a
good housewife will jump over the fence for a
feather."

The larger of the two front rooms was used by
Mrs. Proshek as her bed-room. Here on occasions of domestic festivals the family used to dine
or take their lunch. In this room they had modern
furniture; but Grandmother did not like it here. It
seemed to her impossible to sit comfortably in those
stuffed chairs with their carved elbows, when one
had to be constantly on one's guard lest they should
tip over or break in pieces. Once, only, had she
made the experiment. When she sat down and
the springs gave way, she was so frightened that
she almost screamed. The children laughed at her
and told her to come and sit down again, assuring
her that the chair would not break; but she would
not try it again. "O go away with your rocker,

who wants to sit in it? it may do well enough for you, but not for me." She was afraid to place anything upon the polished stands, lest they should be rubbed or scratched; and as for the large glass case that held all sorts of bric-a-brac, she declared that it was a nuisance; for the children were sure to knock into it and break something, and then get a whipping from their mother. Whenever Grandmother held Adelka, she sat by the piano, and when the little girl cried, she always quieted her by striking some of the keys; for Barunka had taught her to play with one hand the tune to the words, " Those are horses, those are horses mine." * While she played she kept time with her head. Sometimes she remarked: " What things people do invent! one would think a bird were shut up in there; it sounds like the voices of living creatures."

Grandmother never sat in the parlor unless she was obliged to do so. She liked best her own little room, which was next to the kitchen and the servants' apartments. Her room was furnished according to her own taste. By the side of the large stove that stood in the corner was a long bench. Next to the wall stood her bed, at whose foot was the large flowered chest. On the other side was a small bed, where Barunka slept; she had obtained this privilege as a special favor from her mother. In the middle of the room stood the large basswood table, the legs of which were bound together by braces that served as foot-rests. Above the table hung a dove made of an egg-shell and pleated paper; — this was to remind one of the Holy Ghost. In the corner stood the spinning wheel and distaff.

* A popular peasant song.

The walls were decorated with several pictures of saints, and above Grandmother's bed was a crucifix adorned with garlands. Inside of the double window were some flower pots with sweet balsams and musk, and on the sides there hung little linen bags of medicinal herbs, such as linden blossoms, elder blossoms, and the like.

The table drawer contained Grandmother's sewing, a bundle of sacred hymns, the prayers of the Holy Passion, some spinning-wheel cords, and a blessed candle which was always lighted when a thunder storm was coming up.

What the children liked the best in her room was the large flowered chest. They loved to examine the blue and green roses with brown leaves upon the red background, and the blue lilies with red birds among them; but they were the most delighted when she opened the chest. The inside of the cover was lined with pictures and prayers,—all brought from the various shrines to which people made pilgrimages. On one side of the chest was a small drawer, and what treasures were in that! Family documents and letters from her daughters in Vienna, a small linen bag full of silver dollars sent by her children for her betterment, but which out of joy and gratitude Grandmother never spent. In a small wooden box, there were five strings of garnets, with a silver coin on which was engraved the picture of Emperor Joseph and Maria Theresa. When she opened that box,—and she always did so whenever the children asked her,—she would say: "See, my children, these garnets were given me by your grandfather for my wedding, and this dollar the Emperor Joseph himself gave me. That was a good man, may the Lord grant him eternal glory! Well, when I die all this will be yours," she added, as she closed the box.

"But, Grandma, how was it that the Emperor gave you that dollar? Tell us about it," said Barunka.

"Remind me of it some day, and I will tell you," she replied.

Besides these things Grandmother had in that side drawer two rosaries that had been " touched " (by sacred relics), streamers for her caps, and usually some delicacy for the children.

At the bottom of the chest were her clothing and linen. All those linen petticoats, aprons, coats, corsets, and kerchiefs lay there in the best of order, and on the top of all were two stiffly starched caps, with large bows behind, that were called "doves." These things the children were not allowed to touch. Still, when Grandmother was so disposed, she raised one article after another saying: " See, children, this petticoat I have had for fifty years; this coat was worn by your grandmother; this apron is as old as your mother; — and all as good as new; and you spoil your clothes in no time. That all comes because you do not know the value of money. Do you see this silk coat? it cost a hundred Rhine dollars; but in those days they paid with bank-notes." Thus she went on, and the children listened as though they understood it all.

Mrs. Proshek wished her mother to wear city garments, because she thought they would be more suitable; but to this Grandmother would not listen. She said: " The Lord would surely punish me, if I, an old woman, should begin to grow worldly.

Such changes of fashion are not for me; they would not suit my old age." Thus she remained faithful to the "good old ways;" and soon every thing in the house went according to her will, and no one thought of disputing her word.

CHAPTER II.

IN the summer, Grandmother rose at four, but in the winter, at five. The first thing she did was to bless herself and kiss the cross upon her rosary. This rosary she always carried with her, and at night placed it beneath her pillow. Then she dressed and said her prayers, sprinkling herself with holy water; this done, she sat down to her spinning, and sang morning hymns as she worked. Her own sleep, poor old lady! was not good; but she remembered how sweet it used to be when she was young, and so was always glad to let others enjoy it.

After she had been up almost an hour, a light step was heard, one door squeaked, then another, and in a moment more, Grandmother stood at the kitchen door. At that instant the geese sneezed, the hogs grunted, the cows lowed, the chickens shook their wings, and the cats, coming from somewhere, rubbed themselves against her feet. The dogs jumped out of their kennel and at one bound were by her side; if she had not been careful, they would have knocked her over and scattered the grain which she had for the poultry. She was very fond of all these animals, and they seemed equally fond of her. She could not bear to see any creature harmed, no, not even a worm! She would say: "What is injurious to man, or must be killed for food, with God's will kill it, but let it not

suffer needlessly." The children were never allowed
to look on while a creature was killed, lest by
pitying it they should make it die hard.

Once, however, her wrath was roused against
the two dogs, Sultan and Tyrol. There was
cause! They had dug into the ducks' house and
before morning had killed ten ducklings, — bright
yellow ones and full of promise. When, the next
morning, Grandmother discovered this, her hands
fell to her side. There was the old goose, frightened and cackling, and with only three ducklings
left of the large brood that she had hatched out,
when they were deserted by their own truant
mother. At first she suspected the raccoon of the
deed, but she soon discovered by the tracks that it
was the dogs. The dogs, those faithful watchers!
She could scarcely believe her eyes. And yet they
came out and wagged their tails as if nothing had
happened. "Away from me, you wretches!
What had those ducklings done to you? Are you
hungry? Indeed, you're not; you have done this
out of pure willfulness. Away, out of my sight!"
The dogs dropped their tails and sneaked off to
their kennels; Grandmother, forgetting that it was
yet early, went into the bed - room to tell her
daughter of the misfortune.

When Mr. Proshek saw her pale face and tearful eyes, he thought that the burglars must have
broken into the store - room, or that Barunka was
dead; but when he heard the whole story, he could
scarcely refrain from smiling. What were a few
ducklings to him! He had not "set" them; he had
not seen them break through their shells; he did
not know how pretty they were as they swam in

the water, at times hiding their little heads and showing their pretty pink feet, — to him they were nothing but so many roasts. For all that, he arose and went to administer justice. Taking the heavy horsewhip from its hook, he proceeded to give the dogs something that they would not be apt to forget. When Grandmother heard the noise, she placed her hands upon her ears; but she said: "It can't be helped, they must be made to remember it!" When, however, an hour later, they still stayed in their kennels, she went out to see if they were harmed. "What's gone is gone, and after all they are only dumb brutes," she said as she looked inside. The dogs moaned and crawled to her feet upon their bellies, looking so mournful that she said: "Now you are sorry, are you not? See, thus it happens to such rascals; remember it." And they did remember it. Whenever the duck-lings wabbled about the yard, the dogs hung their heads and skulked away, and this seeming peni-tence again won them Grandmother's favor.

When the poultry was fed, Grandmother called the servants, if they were not yet up. After six o'clock she went to call the children. She rapped gently upon Barunka's forehead — the soul is thus awakened the soonest — and whispered: "Little maiden, it is time to arise?" She helped her to dress and then went to call the rest of the little ones. If she found them awake and lounging about in bed, she spanked them, saying: "Up, up, the cock has marched twice around the yard, and you are still in bed. Are you not ashamed?" When they were up, she helped them to wash, but she never could learn how to dress them. These curiously made clothes, with all their straps, hooks, buttons and buckles, were beyond her comprehension. As soon as they were ready, they knelt before the picture of Christ and said The Lord's Prayer. Then they went to breakfast.

In the winter, when there was no regular work to do, Grandmother sat in her room with her spinning; but in the summer, she took her work into the orchard, or into the yard, where stood the large linden, or she went out walking with the children. During her walks she gathered herbs, which she dried and put away for future use. In all her life she had never had a physician. She also used to get a large supply of herbs from an old dame who came from the Sudetic mountains. When the herb-dame came, she was always entertained at The Old Bleachery. She brought the children a bunch of sneezewort, and the housekeeper fragrant herbs and moss for the window sills.* But the children enjoyed most the wonderful tales which she related about a certain prince, named Rybercol, that great hero that played such pranks upon those mountains. Somewhere, hidden away in the forests, lived a princess named Katharine, and Rybercol was in love with her. His journeys to and from the princess were marked by great horrors. When she called, he rushed to her with such delight that everything that came in his path and hindered his progress was destroyed. Trees were broken and torn up by the roots; the roofs of houses and barns were carried away by the hurricane caused by his headlong speed; great boulders were hurled down

* In Bohemia the windows are double, and the space between them being quite large is filled, in winter, with moss and ferns.

the sides of the mountain, destroying cottages, and
at times killing the inhabitants; in a word, his
pathway was marked by destruction as if the hand
of the Lord had passed over it in vengeance.
Although this prince rushed to his beloved with
such joy, she did not allow him to remain, but after
a time drove him away, when he wept so hard that
all the streams overflowed and there was danger of
an inundation.

The herb-dame brought each year the same
herbs and the same stories; but they always seemed
new to the children, who looked for her coming
with eager anticipation.   As soon as the meadow
saffron was seen in the fields, they said: "Now the
herb-dame from the mountains will come;" and if
her arrival was delayed, Grandmother would say:
"What has happened to our Granny?   I hope she
has not been afflicted with illness, or that she is not
dead!"   Thus she was the constant theme of conversation till she again made her appearance in the
yard, with the large basket upon her back.

Sometimes Grandmother took the children out
for long walks, either to the gamekeeper's or the
miller's, or wandered about with them in the woods.
There the birds sang sweetly, the ground was
covered with leaves, making a soft bed, the air was
fragrant from the lilies of the valley and the violets,
and there they could gather primroses, wild pinks,
thyme, and those beautiful Turk's cap-lilies. The
last was the favorite flower of the pale Victorka,
who brought it to the children whenever she saw
them gathering flowers.   Victorka was always
pale, her eyes shone like two live coals, her hair
hung over her shoulders in disorder, her clothes

were soiled and ragged, and she never spoke to any one. There was a large oak on the borders of the forest, where Victorka used to stand for hours, her eyes fixed upon the mill - dam. At twilight she used to go to the edge of the dam, and seating herself upon an old stump gaze into the water, and sing long, long into the night.

One day, as the children heard her singing, they asked: " Grandma, why doesn't Victorka ever have any nice clothes, and why doesn't she speak to any one ? "

" Because she is crazy."

" And what is it to be crazy ? " again asked the children.

" For example, Victorka doesn't speak to any-one, goes about ragged, and lives in the woods both summer and winter."

" In the night, too ? " asked Willie.

" Certainly. Don't you hear her as she sings every night by the dam ? After that she goes to sleep in the cave."

" And isn't she afraid of Jack - o' - the - lantern, or of the waterman ? " asked the children in great surprise.

" Why there is no waterman," said Barunka, " Papa said there isn't."

In the summer it was quite unusual for Victorka to come to the house to beg; but in the winter she came like the raven, rapped on the door or window, and stretched out her hand. As soon as she received a piece of bread or something else to eat, she hastened away without saying a word. The children, seeing the bloody tracks left on the ice by her bare feet, called to her: " Victorka, come here

Mamma will give you some shoes, and you can
stay with us." But she heeded them not, and in a
few moments was again out of sight.

On summer evenings, when the sky was clear,
Grandmother used to sit with the children upon the
bench under the old linden. While Adelka was
small, she sat in Grandma's lap, and the rest of the
children stood at her knees. It could not be otherwise, for as soon as she began to speak, they looked
right into her face so as not to lose a single word.

She told them about shining angels that dwell
above and light the stars for the people, and about
guardian angels, who protect children, rejoicing
when they are good and weeping when they are
bad. The children then turned their eyes to the
thousands of bright lights that shone in the heavens,
some small, some large and of various brilliant
colors.

"I wonder which one of those stars is mine?"
asked Johnny one evening.

" God alone knows," replied Grandmother; " but
think, could it be possible to find it among those
millions?"

" I wonder whose are those beautiful stars that
shine so bright?" asked Barunka.

" Those," replied Grandmother, " belong to people whom God especially loves, His elect, who have
accomplished many good works and have never
displeased Him.

" But, Grandma," again asked Barunka, as the
sad tones came to them from the dam, " Victorka
has her star too, has she not?"

"Yes, but it is clouded. But come, let us go in;
it is time to go to bed, for it is quite dark. Let us

pray ‘Angel of God, Guardian Mine.’ ” They entered the house, and Grandmother blessed them with holy water and tucked them up in their little nests. The little ones fell asleep at once, but Barunka often called her Grandma, saying that she could not sleep. She came, took her granddaughter's hands in her own, and began to pray with her, and they prayed until the girl's eyes were closed.

Grandmother's bedtime was ten o'clock. She knew the hour by her eyelids — they felt heavy then. Before she retired, she examined all the doors to see if they were locked. She called the cats and shut them up in the garret, lest they should come into the bed rooms and choke the children. She put out every spark of fire, and placed the tinder box upon the stove. Whenever a storm appeared to be brewing, she got out the blessed candle, and wrapping a loaf of bread in a white napkin placed it upon the table, while she admonished the servants: “Now, don't you forget, should a fire break out, the first thing to be saved is the bread; for then a person doesn't lose his presence of mind.”

“But the lightning won't strike,” objected the servants.

This answer she did not like at all. “Only God, who is omnipotent, knows that. What do you know about it? Besides one never loses anything by being careful.”

When all was in order, she knelt before the crucifix and prayed. This done, she blessed herself and Barunka with holy water, placed the rosary under her pillow, and commending herself to God's care fell asleep.

CHAPTER III.

SHOULD a traveler, accustomed to the busy hum of city life, wander into the vale where stands the isolated house of the Proshek family, he would think: "How can these people live here during the whole year? During the summer, when the roses are in bloom, it may be pleasant enough; but how dreary it must be in the winter!" Yet the family had many pleasures, both in summer and winter. Love and content dwelt under that humble roof, and the only sorrows that visited them were the frequent departures of the father, or the illness of some member of the family.

The house was not large but pretty and cosy. The front part was ornamented with a grape vine, and the garden was full of vegetables, roses, and mignonette. On the north-eastern side was an orchard, and beyond that a meadow stretching out clear to the mill. Close to the house stood a large pear tree, whose branches spread themselves over the shingled roof, beneath the eaves of which the swallows built their nests. In the middle of the large yard stood the linden, where the children used to sit in the summer evenings. On the south-eastern side were the stables, sheds, and other outbuildings, and behind them grew shrubbery clear to the dam.

Two roads went past the house: one a wagon road, by which a person could travel up the river to Riesenburg castle, and thence to Red Hura; the other led to the mill and along the river to the nearest village, a short hour's distance. That river is the wild Upa, that flows from the Riesenburg mountains, plunging over rocks and rapids, and wandering about through narrow valleys, till it reaches the level plain, where without any further hindrance it flows into the Elbe.

Its banks are always green, in places precipitous, and often covered with dense shrubbery.

In front of the garden there was a stream of water, across which there was a foot bridge leading to the oven and the drying house. In the fall, when the drying house was full of prunes, apples, and pears, Johnny and Willie were often seen running across the bridge; they were always on the lookout lest Grandmother should see them. That, however, helped them little; for as soon as she entered the drying house, she knew how many prunes were missing. "Johnny, Willie, come here!" she called, "it seems you have been taking some of my prunes?" "Oh, no!" protested the boys, while the tell-tale color mounted to their faces. "Don't tell any falsehoods; don't you know God hears you!" They remained silent and she knew all. The children wondered how she found out everything, and how she could tell by their noses whether they spoke the truth. They were afraid to deceive her.

When the weather was warm, she took the children to the river to bathe; but she never allowed them to go in deeper than their knees, lest they should be carried away by the force of the current and drowned. Sometimes she sat down with them on the bench from which the servants rinsed the clothes, and allowed them to paddle their feet in the water, and play with the little fishes that darted about in the stream. Dark leaved alders and willows bent down over the water, and the children were fond of breaking off twigs, throwing them into the water, and watching them as they floated farther and farther down the river.

" You must throw the twig well into the current, for if it remains near the bank, its progress will be hindered by every herb and every root," said Grandmother.

Barunka broke off a twig and threw it into the middle of the stream; when she saw that it floated in the middle of the current, she asked:

" How will it be, Grandma, when it comes to the lock? can it go any further then? "

" It can," replied John. " Don't you remember how, the other day, I threw one into the water at the very lock; it turned and turned, and all at once it was under the lock and floated under the trunk, and before I passed the mill-room, it was in the stream and floated down the river."

" And where does it go then? " asked Barunka.

" From the mill it floats to Zlitz bridge, from the bridge to the channel, from the channel down across the dam around Bavirsky hill to the brewery. Below the rocks it will press its way across rough stones beyond the school-house, where you will go next year. From the school-house it goes to the large bridge thence to Zvoli, from Zvoli to Jarmirn and then to the Elbe."

" And where will it go then, Grandma? " again asked the little girl.

" It will float far down the Elbe until it reaches the sea."

" Oh, dear, that sea! Where is it and what is it like?"

" Oh, the sea is wide, and far away, a hundred times as far as from here to town," answered Grandmother.

" And what will happen to my twig?" sadly asked the child.

" It will be rocked upon the waves, till they cast it ashore; many people and children will be walking there, and some little boy will pick it up and say: 'Little twig, whence came you, and who cast you into the water? Probably some little girl sitting near the river broke you off, and sent you afloat.' The boy will take the twig home and plant it in his garden. It will grow into a handsome tree, birds will sing in its branches, and it will rejoice."

Barunka heaved a deep sigh. In her interest in Grandmother's story she had forgotten all about her petticoats; they dropped down into the water and had to be wrung out. Just then the gamekeeper came along and seeing her plight laughed at her, calling her a waterman. She shook her head and said: " There is no waterman."

Whenever the gamekeeper passed by, Grandmother called: " Stop in, sir, stop in; our folks are at home." The boys ran, seized him by both hands, and led him to the house. Sometimes he objected, saying that his pheasants were hatching, that he had to see to them, or that he had some other business on hand; but when Mr. and Mrs. Proshek happened to see him, willing or unwilling he was obliged to come in.

Mr. Proshek always had a glass of good wine for any welcome guest, and the gamekeeper belonged to that number. Grandmother brought some bread and salt and whatever else they had, and during the conversation he forgot that his pheasants were hatching. When he recollected himself, he cursed his thoughtlessness, and seizing his gun hastened away. In the yard he missed his dog. "Hector! Hector!" but no Hector appeared. "Where in the deuce is that brute racing?" he scolded. The boys ran out, saying that they would fetch him, that he was somewhere with Sultan and Tyrol.

The gamekeeper sat down upon the bench under the linden to wait until the boys brought his dog. Then he started, but stopped once more and called to Grandmother: "Come up our way, my wife is saving some guinea eggs for you." He knew well the weak points of housewives. Grandmother assented at once. "Give your wife my regards and tell her we will come." Thus they always took leave of each other with some pleasant word.

The gamekeeper used to go, if not every day, certainly every other day past The Old Bleachery. This he did year in and year out.

The other person that one would see every morning at about ten o'clock, on the walk leading to Proshek's house, was the miller. That was his hour to see about the locks. Grandmother used to say that the miller was a good man, but somewhat of a rogue. This was because he was very fond of teasing and cracking jokes at the expense of others. He never laughed himself, but his face was drawn

out into a mischievous grin. His eyes from
beneath his pendent eyebrows looked cheerily into
the world. He was of medium height and thick-
set. He wore light-gray trousers the whole year
round, at which the children marveled greatly,
until one day he told them it was the miller's color.
In the winter, he wore a long cloak and heavy
boots; in the summer, a grayish blue jacket and
slippers. On week days, he wore a low cap
trimmed with fleece. In rain or shine his trousers
were turned up, and he was never seen without his
snuff box. As soon as he was in sight, the children
ran to meet him and went with him to the lock.
On the way he teased the boys. Sometimes he
asked Johnny if he could reckon how much a penny
roll would cost, when wheat was two Rhine dollars
a bushel. When the boy answered correctly, he
would say: "You're a trump! Why, they could
appoint you squire to Kramolna!"* He would
give the boys snuff, and when they sneezed hard,
he smiled grimly. Whenever the miller came,
Adelka hid behind Grandma's petticoats; she
could not yet speak plainly, and he teased her by
asking her to repeat after him quickly, three times
in succession, "Our gable is of all gables the most
gabley." The poor little girl almost cried when she
could not say it. To make up for this, he would
bring her, sometimes a basket of strawberries,
sometimes almonds, or other delicacies, and when
he wished to flatter her, he called her "little
linnet."

Another person who used to go regularly past
The Old Bleachery was Long Moses, the watch-

---

* A small hamlet that never had a squire or justice.

man from the castle.   He was tall and slender like
a pole, with dark sinister looks, and was wont
to carry a bag upon his shoulders.   Betsy, the
housemaid, told the children that he carried disobedient boys in that bag, and from that moment,
whenever Long Moses made his appearance, they
turned crimson and were as still as mice.   Grandmother was angry and forbade the girl to tell any
more such stories; but when Vorsa, the other servant, said that Moses was a grabber, that everything that he could reach clung to his fingers,
Grandmother did not say anything to that. Indeed,
he must have been a bad man, that Moses, and to
the children he remained terrible, even if they no
longer believed that he carried children in the bag.

In the summer, when the nobility lived in the
castle, the children often saw some beautiful princess on horseback, with several lords following in
her train.   The miller seeing this once remarked to
Grandmother: "It appears to me like the whip of
God (a comet) dragging its tail behind."

" With this difference, my dear miller: the whip
of God announces evil to the world; the nobility,
when they show themselves, bring us profit," replied Grandmother.   The miller turned his snuff
box, smiled grimly, but made no reply.

Christina, the innkeeper's daughter, frequently
came over in the evening to visit Grandmother and
the children.   She was as pretty as a pink, spry as
a squirrel, and happy as a lark.   Grandmother called
her Smila, because her face was always radiant
with smiles.

Christina came on a run, just for a word; the
gamekeeper stopped in; the miller came for a mo-

ment; the miller's wife, when once in a great while she undertook to come to The Old Bleachery, brought her spinning; the gamekeeper's wife generally brought her baby; but when the stewardess from the manor honored the Proshek house with her presence, Mrs. Proshek would say: "To-day we shall have company."

On such occasions, Grandmother took the children and went away; she had not the heart to dislike anyone; but this lady was not agreeable to her, because she held her head higher than her station warranted. One day, when Grandmother had been but a short time at her daughter's and was unacquainted with the customs of the family and those of the neighbors, the stewardess, with two other ladies, came to make a call. Mrs. Proshek happened to be out, and Grandmother, according to her custom, after asking the ladies to be seated brought bread and salt and invited her distinguished guests to partake of her hospitality; but the distinguished guests politely informed her that they were not hungry, and then gave each other a significant glance, as much as to say: "You old-fashioned granny, do you think we are only so, so?" As soon as Mrs. Proshek entered the room, she saw that a mistake had been made; and when the ladies were gone, she told her mother never to offer bread and salt to such people, as it was not the custom among them.

"Theresa," spoke up Grandmother quite put out, "who will not accept bread and salt from me is not worthy to cross my threshold; you yourself may do as you please, but do not come to me with any of your new fangled notions."

Among the annual visitors that came to the Old Bleachery, the peddler Vlach was one of the most welcome. He came with a one horse wagon, which was loaded with delicacies: such as almonds, raisins, figs, perfumeries, oranges and lemons, and toilet soaps. Mr. Proshek bought up a large supply both in the fall and in the spring, and for this reason the peddler always gave the children a package of candy. This pleased Grandmother, who would say: " He is a clever man, this Vlach; still, I don't like his haggling ways of bargaining." She preferred to trade with the medicine vender, who also came twice a year. She always bought a bottle of Jerusalem balsam for wounds, and added to the price a large slice of bread.

She always had a hearty welcome for the wire drawer and the Jew peddler. They were the same ones each year, so that they seemed to belong to the family. But when the Gypsies appeared near the village, she was alarmed and quickly took some food and carried it out to them; for she said: " It is for one's own advantage to see them clear to the cross roads."

The most welcome visitor, both to the children and to the rest of the family, was Mr. Beyer, the gamekeeper of Marshendorf, from the Sudetic mountains. He came every year as the overseer of the wood that was floated down the Upa river. Mr. Beyer was tall and slender, his body being composed apparently of bone and muscle only. He had a long face, a sallow complexion, large, bright eyes, a Roman nose, brown hair, and a long mustache which he was in the habit of stroking. The gamekeeper of Riesenburg was thick - set, with a florid complexion, a short mustache, and hair always in order; Mr. Beyer's hair was parted in the middle and hung down below his coat collar. The children noticed this at once. The gamekeeper of Riesenburg walked with an easy gait, Mr. Beyer, as though he were stepping over precipices. The former never wore such heavy boots as the latter, and his gun straps and munition bag were finer and newer than Mr. Beyer's. In his cap he wore blue jay's feathers, while Mr. Beyer's green felt hat was decorated with feathers of kites, hawks, and eagles.

Thus looked Mr. Beyer; but the children liked him as soon as they saw him, and Grandmother declared that children and dogs never made any mistakes as to who were their friends; and she was right. Mr. Beyer was very fond of children. Johnny was his pet,— naughty Johnny, who was generally called a scamp; but Mr. Beyer said he would make a good, sturdy youth, and that should he take a fancy to forestry, he himself would undertake to instruct him. The gamekeeper of Riesenburg, who usually came to The Old Bleachery to see his brother of the mountains, would say: "Indeed, if he should wish to be a gamekeeper I myself would take him; for very likely my Frankie will be one, too." But Mr. Beyer objected to this; he said: " Brother, this would not do at all; here he would be too near his home; and, besides, it is always well for a young man to learn the difficulties of his calling. You foresters and gamekeepers here below have an easy time; you don't know what hardship is." Here he began to depict the hardships of his lot. He spoke of great storms of wind and snow in the winter time, of dangerous

paths, of precipices, of tremendous snow drifts and
fogs. He related how he had been many a time
in danger of losing his life, when his foot slipped
upon some precipitous path; how many times he
had lost his way and wandered about for two or
three days without a mouthful of anything to eat,
not knowing how to find his way out of the laby-
rinth. "On the other hand," he added, "you
dwellers in the lowlands have no idea how beautiful it is in the mountains, in the summer. As soon
as the snow melts the valleys become green, the
flowers burst into bloom, the woods are full of song
and fragrance, and all seems as if an enchan-
ter's wand had passed over it. Then it is a pleasure and a delight to wander about in the woods for
game. Twice a week I ascend the Snowcap
(Snezka), where I see the sun rise and this God's
world spread out before me in a grand panorama;
and forgetting all my hardships I think, after all, I
would not remove from the mountains."

Mr. Beyer often brought the children stones of
various crystalline forms, and told them about the
caves in the mountains where such specimens were
found; he brought them moss as fragrant as violets;
he loved to describe to them the beauties of Rybercol's garden, into which he had wandered once,
when he was lost during a fearful snow storm.

As long as Mr. Beyer was with them, the boys
did not leave his side. They went with him to the
dam, watched the floating of the logs, and took a
ride upon the raft. When he was getting ready to
leave, they could scarcely restrain their tears; and
with Grandmother they accompanied him part of
the way, helping to carry the generous luncheon

with which Mrs. Proshek provided him. "Next year, God willing, we shall see each other again. Farewell!" Thus they parted, each wending his way homeward. For several days nothing else was spoken of but Mr. Beyer, the wonders and terrors of the Riesengebirge, and the happy time when he would come again.

CHAPTER IV.

BESIDES the holidays, Sundays were looked forward to with great pleasure; for then the children could lie abed as long as they pleased, Grandmother, who called them, being at the village at early mass. Mrs. Proshek, and her husband when he was with them, attended high mass; and when the weather was fine, the children went with them to meet Grandmother. As soon as she was in sight, they ran to meet her and shouted as though they had not seen her for a year. On Sundays she did not appear to them the same as on week days. Her face was brighter and more loving, and she was dressed a great deal better. She wore fine black slippers, a white cap of which the stiffly starched strings were tied behind in a bow resembling the wings of a dove; indeed, it seemed as though a dove sat on the back of her head. The children remarked that on Sundays Grandma was very beautiful.

As soon as they met her, each wanted to carry something. One got the rosary, another her handkerchief; and Barunka, being the eldest, carried the handbag. This, however, gave rise to disputes, for the inquisitive boys wanted to see what was in it, which Barunka would by no means allow. It always ended in a quarrel, when Barunka turned to Grandmother, asking her to give the boys a good scolding. Instead of this, she opened the bag and gave them some apples or some other dainty, and good humor was at once restored. Mrs. Proshek would sometimes say: " Mother, why do you always bring them something? " but she replied: " Indeed, that would be strange, if I brought them nothing from church! We were no better." Thus the old custom was kept up.

Grandmother was usually accompanied by the miller's wife, and sometimes by some gossip from Zernov, the village nearest the mill. The miller's wife wore long petticoats, a basque, and a silver cap (a cap heavily embroidered with silver thread); she was a short, buxom woman, with pleasant black eyes, a short flat nose, smiling lips, and a pretty double chin. Sundays, she wore small pearls around her neck; on week days, garnets. She always carried a long, round basket of wicker work, in which she had such spices and herbs as are usually used by good housewives.

A short distance behind the women was seen the miller with some friend. When it was warm, he carried his light gray coat on his cane over his shoulder. On Sundays his boots were blacked clear to his ankles and ornamented at the top with a tassal, which the children greatly admired. His trousers were tucked into his boots, and on his head he wore a high cap of lamb's fleece, one side of which was adorned with a row of bows made of blue ribbon. The other neighbor was dressed in the same way, except that the long coat with deep folds behind and large lead buttons was green instead of gray, the miller's favorite color.

The people going to high mass welcomed them as they came from divine service, and they returned

their salutations. Sometimes they stopped to inquire how this and that neighbor was, what
had happened at the village, and what at the
mill.

In the winter, one rarely met any of the Zernov
people going to the town church, for the path on
the mountain side was steep and dangerous. They
went then to Studnic or to Red Hura, to either of
which places the path was more passable. In the
summer one did not mind the bad road; this was
the case especially with the young people. On
Sunday morning, the path across the meadows to
the town was never empty. Here, one could see
an old lady in a fur lined cloak, with a kerchief
upon her head, and beside her an old man leaning
upon his staff; one could see that he was old, for
his hair was fastened down with a comb, a custom
kept up by very old men. There, one could see
women in white dove-caps, and men with fleece-
lined jackets, hurrying across the foot bridge to the
valley to overtake the others. From the hill above
could be seen maidens frolicking about like fawns,
and behind them young men like deer. Here, a
white, puffed sleeve glances between the trees, then
the bushes catch a floating streamer from the shoulder of some maiden, and then again one sees the
bright colors of the embroidered jacket of some
youth, till at last the whole happy company finds
itself on the green plain below.

Coming home, Grandmother changed her
clothes and then hurried about the house to see if
anything had been neglected during her absence.
After dinner, she lay down to rest a few moments.
She usually fell asleep, and when she awoke she

wondered how it happened that her eyes closed ere she was aware of it.

In the afternoon she usually took the children to the mill, and that half day seemed to them a great holiday. The miller had a daughter of the same age as Barunka; her name was Mary, but she was always called Manchinka. She was a good, playful child.

In front of the mill, between two lindens, was a statue of St. John of Nepomuk, and there the miller's wife, Manchinka, and the Zernov women usually sat on Sunday afternoon. The miller generally stood before them, telling them some news while he turned his snuff box in his fingers. As soon as Grandmother and the children were seen coming, Manchinka ran to meet them, and the miller slowly followed with the women. The miller's wife, however, turned to the house to get something ready for those dear little ones, "so that they will behave," as she said. Before they reached the house, a table was already prepared for them either under the windows in the orchard or on the little island. They had a generous supply of buns and honey, bread and butter, and cream. In the summer the miller generally brought a basket of fruit, but in the winter they had dried apples and prunes. Coffee and similar beverages were not yet in common use; in the whole neighborhood only the Prosheks drank coffee.

"How good of you to come to see us," said the miller's wife, offering a chair to Grandmother. "Why, if you did not come it would not seem like Sunday; and now accept of the bounty that God has given."

Grandmother, who ate but little herself, begged her hostess not to trouble herself so much, at which the good lady only laughed. " You are old, and it is no wonder you eat so little; but children — oh, heavens! they have stomachs like ducks. Just look at our Manchinka! I never knew the time when she was not hungry." The children's smiling faces confessed that she was right.

When the children got another bun apiece they hastened behind the barn, for when they were there, no one worried about them. There they played ball, horses, colors, and similar games. The same company waited for them each Sunday,— six children, of different sizes, like the pipes of an organ. They were the children of the organ grinder from the flax mill. When he moved there with his family, the inn keeper built them a cottage having one living room and a kitchen. The father went about with his hand organ, and the mother after finishing her own work went among the neighbors, doing chores for a little food. They had nothing in the world but those six " pandores " — as the miller called the organ grinder's children — and some music. For all that, no great want was seen in the family. The children's cheeks were like roses, and at times an odor came from the flax mill that made the mouth of the passer-by water and long for roast chicken. When the children came out with greasy and shiny lips, the neighbors thought: " What in the world are those Kudernas roasting? "

Once Manchinka came from the flax mill and told her mother that Mrs. Kuderna had given her a piece of hare, and that it was so good, " just like almonds."

"A hare!" thought the mother, "where would they get a hare? I hope Kuderna hasn't taken to poaching; he'd get himself into trouble if he did."

When Celia, Kuderna's eldest daughter, came over with the baby — that girl always carried a baby, for a little one came to the flax mill each year — the miller's wife asked her: "Cilka, what did you have good for dinner, to - day?"

"Oh nothing, only potatoes," replied the girl.

"What! nothing but potatoes? Manchinka said your mother gave her a piece of hare, and that it was very good."

"O, I beg you to excuse me, that wasn't a hare, that was a cat; Daddy got it at Red Hura; it was fat like a pig. Mammy fried out the grease, and Daddy will rub himself with it; the blacksmith's wife told him to do it when he began to cough, so he should not get consumption."

"God save our souls!" exclaimed the horrified woman, spitting with disgust.

"Oh, but you don't know how good they are! but squirrels are better still. One day Daddy met the forester's apprentice carrying three squirrels which he had shot for his owl; he asked him for them, because he had heard that their flesh was better than that of hares, since they live on nothing but hazel nuts. The apprentice said it was so, and gave them to him. Daddy took them home and skinned them. Mammy roasted them and cooked some potatoes, and we had a very good dinner. Sometimes Dad brings us crows, but they are not very good. But not long ago we had a feast! Mammy brought a goose from the manor. The girl killed it in stuffing it with meal rolls to fatten it, and the lady would not eat it; so they gave it to us, and we had meat for several days and lard for a long time." Here the girl's story was interrupted by the miller's wife, who said: "Go, Go, I feel the cold chills creeping over me. Mary, you godless child, don't you ever dare eat meat at Kuderna's again! Go quickly and wash yourself, and don't touch anything." Going on like this, she pushed Celia out of doors.

Manchinka cried, and assured her mother that the hare was good; the mother said nothing more, but showed her disgust by spitting. The miller came, and hearing what had happened turned his snuff box and said: "Well wife, what are you scowling for? who knows on what the girl may thrive! Tastes differ; I don't know but I should like to invite myself to Kuderna's for a good squirrel dinner."

"You'd better keep such stuff to yourself!" scolded the wife. The miller closed his eyes, and a mischievous smile played about his lips.

Not only the miller's wife, but other people also had a feeling of repulsion toward the Kudernas, and all because they ate cats and squirrels, which nobody else ate. But to the Proshek children it was all the same whether their friends from the flax mill had crow pie or pheasants for dinner, if only they came to play with them behind the barn; and they willingly shared with them their food, glad to see them happy. Celia, who was ten years old and had the care of the baby, placed a bun in its chubby fists, laid it down in the grass, and went to play with the rest; or she sat down and braided from plaintain stalks little caps for the boys and baskets for the girls. When they had played till they were tired, the whole company rushed into the yard, and Manchinka announced to the mother that they were very hungry. The mother was not at all surprised at this news, and fed them all, even those whose lips were repulsive to her on account of the squirrels. The miller, however, always teased her, and when the children came in he began: " I don't know what is the matter, I feel a pressure upon my breast. How is it, Celia, haven't you a piece of hare at your house? Couldn't you —— "

His wife coughed and went away. Grandmother shook her finger at him saying: " What a rogue you are, sir! if I were your wife, I would give you roast crow with peas." The miller turned his snuff box, closed his eyes, and smiled grimly.

When they sat in the garden, the foreman of the mill usually joined their party. They discussed the morning's sermon, told what the announcements had been, for whom prayers had been said, and whom each one had seen at church; from this their conversation drifted to the crops, the flood, storms and hail, weaving and bleaching linen, how the flax was this year, till at last they came to discuss soldiers and the prison. The foreman was very talkative, but towards evening as the farmers began to come in with the grist, remembering the rule, " first come first served," he was obliged to go to the mill, while the miller went to see what was doing at the inn.

In the winter, the children spent the whole afternoon on top of the large oven that was built in the corner of the room.* The servant had her bed

---

* In all country houses, in Bohemia, there is a large brick structure in one corner of the living room, which is a stove and oven combined.

there, and Manchinka, her dolls and playthings. When the children were all together, the oven was full, the niche in the corner that served as a step being occupied by the dog. On the top of that oven a wedding was celebrated every Sunday. The chimney sweep was the groom, and Nicholas served as the priest. Then there was eating, drinking, and dancing, until somebody stepped on the dog's tail. The dog yelped and the conversation in the room was interrupted. The mistress of the house cried: " See here, you youngsters, don't you break down that oven for I must bake to-morrow!" But they were already as still as mice. Then they played " Father and Mother." The stork brought a baby to the young bride. Adelka was the nurse, Johnny and Willie, the sponsors, and the baby was named Jack. Now they had the christening festival; all sorts of wonderful dishes were served, and this time the dog, too, was a guest, so that they might make up with him. Jack grew up and his father led him to school. Johnny was the schoolmaster and taught him to spell. But one pupil! — that wouldn't do; they all had to study, and therefore they agreed to play school. As no one brought the prescribed task, the master got angry and ordered each to receive two blows upon the hand. Seeing no help, they submitted; but the dog, who also was a pupil, and didn't know anything at all except to snuff at things, was to receive in addition to the two blows a dunce card upon his neck, which was done at once. But as soon as the card was fastened, the offended brute jumped down from the oven with a great noise and rolled about the floor, trying to rid himself of the sign of shame. The

foreman sprang from his bench, Grandmother
almost screamed from fright, and the miller, shaking his snuff box at the children, exclaimed: "By
Gemini! let me come there, I'll — " and turning his
box he smiled, but not so that the children could
see him.

" That reprobate of ours surely was to blame!"
said Grandmother. " I must take them home before the whole house is torn down!"

This, however, the miller's wife would not allow; they had not finished their conversation about
the French war and those three potentates. Grandmother knew them all; she had had great experi-
ences, she understood army life,— every one believed her.

" Grandmother, who were those three ice war-
riors that the Russian sent against Bonaparte?"
asked a handsome youth with a pleasant face.

" I should think you could guess that," quickly
replied the foreman. " They were the three months,
December, January, and February. In Russia, it
is so cold that people are obliged to wear some
covering over their faces to keep their noses from
freezing off. The French soldiers, not being accustomed to this cold, froze to death as soon as they
came. The Czar, knowing this, drew them on
into the country, until they could not return. Oh,
he is a crafty one, that Czar!"

" Grandmother," asked another," you knew the
Emperor Joseph personally, did you not?"

" Of course I did! Why I spoke with him, and
he gave me this dollar with his own hand," she
replied as she showed them the dollar that hung on
the string of garnets around her neck.

" And may we ask how it happened, and when?" asked several of the bystanders at once.

Just at this point there was a lull in the noise upon the oven, for the children hearing this question were at once attentive, and jumping down begged Grandmother to relate this story, as they had never heard it.

" But both the miller and his wife have heard it," objected Grandmother.

" A good story will bear repeating," said the miller, " so just go on."

" Well, then, I will begin; but you children must be perfectly quiet."

The children obeyed, and did not lisp another syllable.

Grandmother began as follows:—

" When the Novy Ples (Joseph-hof) was building, I was a young girl. I come from Olesnic,—do you know where Olesnic is? "

"I do," said the foreman, "it is in the mountains, beyond Dobruska, on the Silesian frontier, is it not? "

" Yes, it is there. Not far from our house was a cottage, where dwelt the widow Novotny. She made her living by weaving woolen blankets. Whenever she had a good supply on hand, she took them to Jarmirn or Pilsen to sell. She used to be at our house a great deal, and we children would run to her cottage several times a day. Father was sponsor to her son. As soon as I was able to do any hard work, she would say to me, when I came over: ' Come, sit down at the loom and learn to weave; some day it may be of use to you. What one learns in youth may serve one in old age.' I was always eager to work, so did not need to be told twice. I soon understood the trade so well that I could weave a whole blanket without assistance. At that time, the Emperor used to come quite often to see the new city, and he was the constant topic of conversation with the villagers. Whoever had the opportunity of seeing him felt greatly honored.

" On one occasion, when the widow was going to town, I asked mother if I could go with her, as I wanted to see the Novy Ples, too. As she was to have a heavy load, mother readily consented, saying: 'Yes, go; you can help her carry the blankets.' The next day we started in the cool of the day, and before noon were in the meadow before the Ples. There we sat down upon a pile of timber and began to put on our shoes. The widow said: ' Alas! where shall I go to sell my blankets?' Just then we saw a gentleman coming from the Ples directly toward us. He carried something in his hand resembling a flute; from time to time he put it up to his face and turned round and round.

" 'O look!' I said to the widow. ' That must be some musician; he is playing on a flute and dancing to his own music.'

" 'You foolish girl, that is not a flute and he is no musician. Most likely that is some gentleman whose business it is to oversee the building; I often see them walking about here. He has a sort of tube, in that tube a glass, and he looks through that. They say he can see a great ways, and everywhere, and whom and what he wants.'

" 'Oh, Mrs. Novotny, if he saw us when we were putting on our shoes!' I said.

" ' Well, and what if he did? That isn't anything to be ashamed of,' she replied.

" While we were thus talking, the gentleman reached our side. He had on a gray coat and a three cornered hat, beneath which was his cue with a bow at the end. He was quite young and handsome as a picture. ' Where are you going and what have you there?' he asked, as he stopped near us. The widow said she was taking her work to sell at Ples.

" ' What kind of work?' he further asked.

" ' Woolen blankets, sir; they make good coverlets for soldiers; perhaps you might like one,' said she, quickly opening her bundle and spreading out the blankets one by one. She was a good woman, this widow, but when she tried to sell anything she was extremely talkative.

" ' Your husband makes these, does he not?' asked the gentleman.

" ' He used to make them, dear sir: but at harvest time it will be two years since he made his last blanket. While he worked, I sometimes helped and so learned the trade, and now I find it very profitable. I always tell Mandie: ' Only learn, Mandie; what you once learn, not even a *gendarme* can take away from you.'

" ' Is she your daughter?' again asked the gentleman.

" ' No, she is not mine, but our sponsor's child. Do not think she is too small; she is stout and willing to work. She made this blanket all herself.' He tapped me on the shoulder and gave me a look of approbation. In all my life I never saw such beautiful eyes; they were as blue as the corn flower.

" ' And you have no children?' said he, turning to her.

'I have one son,' she replied. I send him to school to Rychnov. The Lord gives him the gift of the Holy Ghost, so that learning is to him as play; he sings well in the choir. I'm trying to save a few groschen, so that I can send him to study for the priesthood.'

" ' But suppose he refuses to be a priest?'

" ' O sir, he will not refuse; George is a good lad,' replied the widow.

" In the meantime I had been looking at the tube and wondering how he looked through it. He must have noticed this, for all at once he turned to me and said: ' I suppose you would like to know how one looks through this telescope, is it not so?' I blushed, but dared not look at him. The widow Novotny spoke up: ' Mandie thought that that was a flute, and that you were a musician. But I told her what you were.'

" ' And you know it?' he asked smiling.

" ' Well I do not know your name; but of course you are one of the men that come here to oversee the workmen, and you look at them through that tube, is it not so?'

" The gentleman laughed till he held his sides. Then he said: ' The last, mother, is correct.' Then he turned to me and said: ' If you wish to look through this tube you may do so.' Then he placed it to my eye, and Oh, dear people, what wonders did I see! Why, I saw into people's windows, and could see what they were doing as if they were close by; and way off in the fields I saw people working as if they were but a few steps from me. I wanted the widow to look, too; but she declared it was not proper for an old woman to play with such things.

" ' But that is not for play, that is for use,' said the gentleman.

" ' Well, perhaps it is, but it is not for me,' and she could not be induced to look through it. Then I thought that I would be so glad to see the Emperor Joseph, and because the gentleman was so kind, I told him whom I'd like to see.

" ' What do you care about the Emperor? ' he asked, ' Do you like him?'

" ' Of course I do; why shouldn't I like him, when everybody speaks well of him and praises his goodness. Every day we ask God to bless him and his wife, and grant them a long reign.'

" He smiled and asked: ' Would you like to speak with him, too? '

" ' God forbid! where would I turn my eyes? ' I replied.

" ' Why, you are not afraid to look at me, and the Emperor is only such a man as I?'

" ' O, sir, it is not the same,' spoke up Mrs. Novotny. ' His Lordship the Emperor is after all his Lordship, and that is something to say. I have heard that when a person looks the Emperor in the eye, he is seized with fever and ague. Our alderman spoke with him twice, and he says it is so.'

" ' Very likely your alderman has a guilty conscience and cannot look any one in the eye,' he replied and at the same time wrote something upon a slip of paper. He handed it to Mrs. Novotny, telling her to go to the Ples, to the provision house, where she would sell her blankets and get her pay when she showed them that paper; then turning to me he gave me this silver dollar, and said: ' Take this as a keepsake from the Emperor Joseph. Do not forget to pray for him and his wife, for prayers coming from earnest hearts are acceptable to God. When you get home, tell your friends you spoke with the Emperor Joseph.' With these words he turned and hastened away.

" Overwhelmed with joy and surprise we knelt down, not knowing what we did. Mrs. Novotny scolded me because I had been so forward, but she also had been bold enough. But who would have thought that it was the Emperor! We comforted ourselves, however, by thinking that if he had been offended he would not have made us presents.

" When Mrs. Novotny came to the magazine she got three times as much for her blankets as she asked.

" We almost flew home, and when we got there, there was no end of telling about it, and everybody envied us. Mother had a hole punched through the dollar, and I have worn it on my neck ever since. Many a time I have been in need, but I would never part with my dollar. A thousand pities that the sod covers that good man! " added Grandmother softly, as she finished the story.

" Yes, indeed, a thousand pities! " echoed the listeners. The children, after learning the history of the dollar, turned it from side to side, for now it had acquired a new interest to them, and Grandmother, because she had spoken to the Emperor, was regarded with even more reverence than before.

At the mill the week began on Sunday evening,

5

for then the peasants came in with their grist. The rumbling of the wheels was heard; the foreman went about the mill room, examining all with a practiced eye; the workmen hurried from basket to basket, upstairs and downstairs; while the miller stood at the door welcoming his customers with a pleasant smile, and offering each a pinch of snuff.

In the summer, the miller's wife and Manchinka accompanied Grandmother over to the inn. When there was a dance there, they generally stopped at the gate, where they were joined by several of the women from the village, and all remained for a while to watch the dancers. To enter was impossible on account of the crowd standing at the door; even Christina, when she took beer out to the gentlemen sitting in the orchard, was obliged to hold the glasses high over her head for fear they should be knocked out of her hands.

"Do you see these gentlemen?" said the miller's wife as she made a gesture with her head toward the orchard, where sat several of the men from the castle and tried to detain Christina whenever she brought them beer,— "do you see them! Yes, indeed, that is a lass such as doesn't grow upon every bush. But do not imagine that the Lord had her blossom out for such as you, that you might ruin her beautiful life."

"No danger!" said Grandmother, "Christina is too sharp for them. She knows how to dispose of them at short notice."

Grandmother was right. Just then one of those gentlemen, perfumed so strongly that he could be smelt ten yards off, whispered something in her ear; she laughed as she replied: "Unload your wares, sir, unload; we will not buy!" Then she hastened into the dancing hall and with a smiling face put her hand in the large, hard palm of a stalwart youth, who placed his other arm around her waist and led her off to the dance, unmindful of the call, "Christinka, some more beer!"

"That one is dearer to her than the castle with all its lords and treasures," smiled Grandmother, as she bade the miller's wife good night, and then with the children slowly wended her way homeward.

Once in a fortnight, or in three weeks, when the weather was fine, Grandmother would say: "To-day we will go to the gamekeeper's to spin." The children spoke of nothing else until they had started on their journey. Behind the dam the way led on the steep side to the bridge, beyond the bridge clear to Riesenburg; the path was shaded by rows of tall poplars. Grandmother, however, preferred the way along the river to the mill. There was a high hill above the saw-mill, where much mullein grew, which Barunka was fond of gathering for Grandmother. From the saw-mill the valley grew narrower and narrower, until the river was confined in a narrow trough, and flew quickly over the large stones that obstructed its path. The hills here were covered with evergreens, whose dense foliage cast a dark shadow upon the valley below. This was the path Grandmother took with the children, until they reached Riesenburg fortress, whose moss covered ruins projected above the dark wood.

A short distance from the fortress, above an underground passage, through which it was said one could go a journey of twelve miles, but into which no one ever ventured on account of the damp and foul air, was built an arbor having three gothic windows. When the gentlemen from the castle went out hunting, they stopped here to eat their second breakfast. To this arbor the children directed their steps, climbing up the steep banks like chamois. Poor Grandmother got up the steep place with the greatest difficulty, all out of breath and catching hold of every shrub. "Oh, you're too much for me!" she exclaimed as she scrambled to the top.

The children took her by both her arms and led her into the arbor where they seated her in a chair. The air here was cool, and the outlook beautiful.

To the right of the arbor, could be seen the ruins of the fortress; below the fortress there was a vale in the shape of a crescent, the top and bottom of which were closed in by evergreens. On one side of those hills there was a chapel. The murmuring of the water, and the song of the birds were the only sounds heard in this solitary place.

John recollected the story of the strong Ctibor, the shepherd of Riesenburg. It was down in the meadow below that his master caught him carrying a large tree upon his shoulders. When he was asked where he had got it, he confessed that he had stolen it from the forest. His master, pleased with his candor, not only forgave him, but invited him to come to the fortress, saying that he would give him as much provision as he could carry. Ctibor was so greedy that he took his wife's nine ell feather-bed cover and went to the fortress, where they filled it with peas and hams. The knight liked him on account of his strength and frankness, and when there was a tournament in Prague, he took him along. Ctibor overcame a certain German knight whom no one else could conquer, and on that account was knighted by the king.

This tale delighted the children, and from the time that the old shepherd related it, the fortress and the meadow acquired a new interest for them.

"What is the name of the place where that chapel stands?" asked Willie.

"That is Bousin. If God grants us good health, we will go there sometime when there is a pilgrimage there," replied grandmother.

"What happened there, Grandma?" asked Adelka, who could listen to such stories from morning till night.

"A miracle was performed there; don't you remember how Vorsa related it?"

"We don't remember at all. Please, Grandma, tell us about it."

"Well, then, sit down quietly upon the benches and do not lean out of the windows lest you fall and break your necks." After thus admonishing them, Grandmother began her story:

"Beyond this hill and these woods are the villages of Turyn, Litobor, Slatina, Mecov, and Bousin. In olden times they all belonged to one knight named Turynsky, who lived in Turyn castle. This knight had a wife and one child, a pretty little girl, but alas! deaf and dumb, which was a great grief to her parents.

"Once as the little girl was wandering about in the castle, she thought she would like to go to Bousin to see how the lambs were doing and how much they had grown since last she saw them. You must remember that at that time there was neither village nor chapel here. There was only the farm and the farm house where dwelt the steward and such servants as were needed to do the work. All around there was nothing but woods, in which were many wild beasts.

" Turynsky's little daughter had often been to the farm, but she had ridden with her father. Now she thought, simple child: 'I'll take a little run and I'll be there.' She followed her eyes, thinking one way as good as another,— she was young and ignorant like you. When, however, she had gone a long time, and no farm was in sight, she began to be alarmed; she thought: 'What will my father and mother say when they find out that I have left the castle?' She turned and hastened back toward her home. When one is alarmed, especially such a child, one becomes confused very easily. She lost her way and went neither to the castle nor to the farm, but into a dense forest where there was neither path nor light. Soon she knew that she was lost.

" You can imagine how she felt. But you would not be so badly off; for you can speak and hear, which she could not. She ran hither and thither and only grew the more bewildered. At last she was very tired, hungry, and thirsty; but that was as nothing compared with the fear that she had of the night and the wild beasts that she knew would prowl about; and, besides, she thought of the anxiety of her father and mother.

" Worn out with fright and weeping, all at once

she found herself at a well. She knelt down eagerly and took a drink. When she looked about, she saw several well beaten paths; but she did not know which to take, since from her late experience she had found that not every path leads home. Then she remembered that whenever her mother was in trouble she would go to her room to pray; so she, too, knelt down and asked God to lead her out of the woods.

" Suddenly she hears strange sounds. They ring clearer and clearer in her ears. She does not know what is happening to her, what those sounds mean. She begins to tremble with fear, to cry, she wants to run away, when behold! a white sheep comes toward her from the wood, behind her a second, a third, a fourth, a fifth, till the whole flock stand about the spring. These are her father's sheep, for here comes the shepherd's large, white dog, and here is Barta, the shepherd, himself. She cried out Barta! and ran to meet him. The good shepherd was delighted to find the lost child, and greatly astonished to hear her speak. He took her in his arms and hastened to the farm-house, which was but a short way off. Lady Turynsky was there distracted with grief, for the sudden disappearance of her daughter had filled her with consternation. But her joy knew no bounds when Barta placed the little one in her arms all safe and sound and healed,— able to speak and hear. The happy parents, out of thankfulness to God, determined to build a chapel upon the spot where the miracle had been performed. The chapel you see yonder is the very same chapel, and the well near it is the well out of which she drank, and those woods are the same woods. But the little girl died long, long ago; Sir Turynsky and Lady Turynsky are dead, too; Barta the shepherd died, and Turyn castle is in ruins."

"What became of the dog and the sheep?" asked Willie.

"Why, the dog died; the old sheep dropped away one by one, the young grew and in their turn had lambs. Thus it is in the world, one goes another comes."

The children turned their eyes to the valley. They seemed to see knights riding about, a little girl running hither and thither in the woods, and behold! a beautiful lady on horseback, followed by attendants was coming toward them from the vale below. She had on a dark, tight-fitting jacket, her long, gray riding habit hung below her stirrups, and a long, green veil floated in the breeze from her black hat.

"Grandma, a knightess, a knightess is coming!" exclaimed the children.

"What an idea! there are no knightesses; it must be the Princess from the castle," replied Grandmother.

The children were greatly disappointed that it was not a " knightess."

"It is the Princess coming up to us!" again cried the children in a chorus.

"What are you talking about? How could a horse climb up here?" said Grandmother.

"Oh, but look! Orlando is climbing like a cat!" exclaimed John.

"Hush, I do not want to see it. Their Lordships have strange amusements," said Grandmother, as she held the children so they would not lean too far out of the window.

Presently the Princess was up the hill. She dismounted, threw her long skirt across her arm, and entered the arbor. Grandmother arose quickly and welcomed her.

" Is this Proshek's family? " she asked, studying the children's faces.

" Yes, your Grace," replied Grandmother.

"And are you their Grandmother? "

" Yes your Grace, I am their mother's mother."

" I am sure you must be happy in having such healthy grandchildren. I suppose you are good, obedient children? " continued the lady turning to the children, whose eyes were fixed upon her. At her question they looked down and whispered: " yes ma'am!"

" Hm, it will pass; " said Grandmother, "though sometimes — but we were no better."

The Princess smiled. Seeing a basket of strawberries on the bench, she asked where they had gathered them.

Grandmother at once spoke to Barunka: " Go, my child, offer the fruit to the princess. They are fresh, the children gathered them on our way here; they may taste good to your Grace. When I was young, I was very fond of strawberries, but I have not tasted them since the death of my child."

" And why? " asked the Princess taking the basket from Barunka.

" O, your Grace, that is a custom among us. When a mother loses a child, she eats neither strawberries nor cherries till St. John the Baptist. It is said that at that time the Virgin goes about heaven giving this fruit to the little children. If a mother has not been self-denying, and has eaten of this fruit, when the Virgin comes to the child of such an one she says: 'Poor child, there isn't much left for you; your mother ate your share.' For this reason mothers abstain from eating this fruit before St. John's, and if they can do it till St. John's they can do it after," added Grandmother.

The Princess held in her fingers a large strawberry, as red as her own beautiful lips; but on hearing this tale, she placed it back in the basket, saying: "I cannot eat now, and the children would have nothing themselves."

"O, your Grace, that makes no difference. Only eat, or take them home with you; we can gather some more," quickly said Barunka, pushing back the basket that the Princess was offering her.

"Thank you," replied the lady accepting the gift and smiling at the simple heartedness of the child. "To-morrow, however, you must come to the castle and get your basket; and be sure to bring your Grandma with you, do you understand?"

"We will!" exclaimed the children with as much assurance as they showed when they were invited to the mill by the miller's wife. Grandmother, indeed, wanted to raise some objections, but it was too late; the Princess bowed to her, smiled at the children, and was gone, disappearing among the trees like a beautiful vision.

"O Grandma, won't it be delightful to go to the castle! Papa says they have so many beautiful pictures there," said Barunka.

"And they have a parrot that speaks," cried John, clapping his hands.

Little Adelka, looking at herself said: " I shan't have to wear this dress, shall I?"

" Well, I declare, what a sight you are! What were you doing?" exclaimed Grandmother signing herself with the cross.

" I couldn't help it. John pushed me down into some strawberries," explained the little girl.

" You two are forever quarreling. What will the Princess think? Most likely she will say you are two little imps. But come, we must get started or we shall not reach the gamekeeper's to - day."

" I want you to understand, boys, that if you cut up as you usually do, I will never take you with me again."

The boys assured Grandmother that they would be very good.

" We shall see," she said, as they approached their destination. A few more steps brought them into a dense wood, through which gleamed the gamekeeper's white buildings. There was a large yard in front of the house, shaded by lindens and chestnuts. Beneath these there were several small tables and benches fastened to the ground. Several peacocks were seen strutting about on the green sward; Grandmother used to say that they had angel's plumage, a thief's step, and the devil's voice. A little way from the peacocks was seen a flock of speckled, blear - eyed guinea hens; white rabbits, pricking up their ears, ready to flee from the smallest danger; a handsome fawn, with a red band around its neck, lying at the door; and several dogs lounging about. Hardly had the children spoken to the dogs, when they gave a joyous bark and bounded out to meet them. The fawn, called by

Adelka, also came and with her blue eyes looked up lovingly at the child as if she would say· "Ah, it is you, who bring me those good morsels. Welcome here!" Adelka must have read this in her eyes, for she quickly put her hand in her pocket and brought out a piece of bread, which the fawn took and followed them to the house.

"What in the deuce is the matter here, you savage brutes!" cried a man's voice from within, and directly after, the gamekeeper, clad in a green jacket and a house cap, made his appearance.

"What welcome guests!" he exclaimed seeing Grandmother and the children. Come in, come in! Hector, Diana, Amina be quiet! One cannot hear his own voice," he said shaking his cane at the dogs.

The company entered the house, over the door of which was fastened a pair of deer's horns. In the hall hung several rifles, but very high so that the children could not reach them. Grandmother was always afraid of fire arms, and when the gamekeeper assured her that they were not loaded, she would still say: "Who can tell what may happen; the devil never sleeps!"

"Very true," replied the gamekeeper, "when God permits, a hoe may go off."

Grandmother was ready to forgive him anything, if only he did not swear; that, she could not stand. She put her hands on her ears, saying: "What is the good of such a foul mouth? one should sprinkle holy water when you leave."

The gamekeeper liked Grandmother, and so in her presence was very careful not to touch on the devil, who he said was always getting mixed up with his words.

"Where is your wife?" asked Grandmother as she entered the room and saw no one.

"Just make yourself at home till I call her; you know she is always busied about something."

The attention of the boys was attracted by a case in which gleamed hunters' knives and other arms. The girls played with the fawn that had followed them into the house. Grandmother, taking in at a glance the order and cleanliness of the room, remarked: "That's a fact, let a person come here on Friday or Sunday, everything is as clean as glass." Just then her eye fell upon the spinning that lay near the stove, tied up and marked ready for the weaver. As she was examining it very attentively, the door opened, and the mistress of the house entered the room.

She was still young, and in her neat house-dress and white cap cut a very handsome figure. Her welcome was hearty, and her honest face showed that it was sincere. "I was out sprinkling the linen; I am delighted with it; this year it will be as white as cambric," she remarked after excusing her absence.

"What industry!" replied Grandmother. "A piece out bleaching, and here a lot ready for the weaver. This will make cloth like parchment; if only he would work it up well, and not cheat you. By the way, are you satisfied with your weaver?"

"My dear Grandma, you know they all cheat."

"O you women, you women! I'd just like to know how the weaver could cheat you? You have everything reckoned out to the last thread!" laughed the gamekeeper. "But do sit down," he said to Grandmother who was still standing, admiring the spinning.

"Oh, never mind, I am not tired," she replied, as she seized little Nanny by the hand so she should not fall, for the little one was just learning to walk.

As soon as the mistress of the house stepped from the door, two tanned urchins were seen standing at the threshold; one fair-haired like the mother, the other dark like the father. They had followed their mother to the house, but when she entered into conversation with Grandmother, they did not know what to do; they felt bashful and remained standing outside.

"O you blue jays, is that the proper thing to do, to hide behind your mother's petticoats when your friends come to see you?" said the father. "Come forward and shake hands with our company."

They willingly obeyed. Grandmother gave them some apples, and said: "Next time you must not be bashful; it is not becoming for boys to hang about their mother's apron strings." The boys were silent, their eyes fixed upon the apples.

"Now, begone! show your friends the horned owl and give her that blue jay I shot to-day. Show them also the young pheasants and the puppies. But don't you race among the poultry like so many wild colts, or I'll —"

The last the children did not hear, for as soon as the father said 'Begone,' the whole crowd rushed like a hurricane through the door.

"What a whirl!" remarked the gamekeeper with a smile.

"Children will be children, — youthful blood!" added Grandmother.

"But if only those boys were not so wild! Believe me, Grandma, at times I am dying with terror. They climb up trees and over pitfalls, turn somersets, tear their trowsers, — it's dreadful to relate! I thank the Lord for this one good child; she is a treasure," said the mother.

"What can you expect, my good woman? The boys take after the father, the girls after the mother," replied Grandmother.

The mother laid Nanny in the father's arms that he might hold her awhile, — "Only till I get something to eat; I shall be back presently."

"A good woman that!" remarked the game-keeper as his wife stepped out of the door. "It would be a sin to offend her, — only if she were not so fussy about those boys; they won't break their necks. What is a boy good for, if he has no metal?"

"Excess is injurious in everything. Let boys have their own way, and they will walk upon their heads," remarked Grandmother; and yet that was exactly what she did with her own boys.

The gamekeeper's wife now entered loaded with provisions. The oaken table was covered with a white cloth, and upon it were placed majolica plates, and knives with deer-horn handles; then there appeared strawberries and cream, fritters and honey, bread and butter, and beer.

The hostess took Grandmother's distaff away, saying as she did so: "Never mind the spinning now, but come and help yourself! Cut your bread and spread it! The butter is fresh, — churned to-day; the beer is not watered. Those fritters are not so good, I baked them to-day haphazard; but when a thing is unexpected, it often tastes good. You don't eat strawberries? the children, however,

are very fond of them, especially with cream."
Thus she went on, urging Grandmother to eat, and
cutting slice after slice of bread, spreading it with
butter, and pouring honey over it.

Suddenly, as if she recollected something, Grandmother struck her forehead, saying: "O that old
head of mine! Just think, I never told you that we
met the Princess in the arbor."

"Please Grandmother, don't say anything till I
return. I must satisfy those children, so that they
will behave."

In the meantime, the children headed by Frank
and Bertie had rummaged through everything.
They were just standing before the house watching
Amina jump over a cane and fetch in her mouth
articles that were thrown to her, when the mother
came to the door to call them to luncheon. She
did not need to call them twice. "Now, sit down
under the trees and eat, but do not soil your
clothes," she said as she spread the food out before
them. The children sat down while the dogs
stood about wistfully looking into their faces.

As soon as the mother re-entered the house, she
begged Grandmother to proceed with the story
about the Princess. This she willingly did, relat-
ing word for word all that had been said and done
in the arbor.

"Don't I always say she has a good heart,"
remarked the gamekeeper's wife. " Whenever she
comes here, she asks about the children and kisses
Nanny on the forehead; and whoever is fond of
children cannot be so bad. But those servants
spread evil reports, as though she were,—who
knows how bad?"

"Do good to the devil, and he'll reward you with evil," said Grandmother.

"You are right," observed the gamekeeper. "That is what I say. We could not desire a better mistress, if it were not for those bailiffs about her, who by lying set her against us. That crew is of no earthly use, unless it be to rob the Lord of his time. When, dear Grandma, I observe these things, I think: 'O that a thousand streaks of lightning would go through you!' Isn't it enough to rouse one's wrath when such a clown, who doesn't know anything and is good for nothing but to stand behind a wagon like a wooden man and gape, gets as much as I, counts more than I, who, rain or shine, in mud and snow must wander about the woods, night and day, watching poachers and quarreling with them, and must care for all and be responsible for all. I do not complain, I am satisfied; but when such a blusterer comes here and turns up his nose, then, upon my soul, I would,— but what's the use of vexing one's self?" and the gamekeeper took a glass and drank down his indignation.

"Does that lady know all that is going on? Why doesn't some one have the courage to tell her, when he is wronged?" asked Grandmother.

"Zounds! who wants to put his finger into the fire? I often speak with her, and could tell her this and that; but I always think: 'Frank, hold your tongue, lest your own words turn against you.' Besides, she need not believe me; she will ask those above me, and then you have it! These will stand by each other, and I shall be left in the lurch. I spoke with her a few days ago, when she was

6

walking in the grove with that strange nobleman, who is visiting her. They had met Victorka, who frightened the Princess; they asked me about her.

"What did you tell them?" asked Grandmother.

"What should I say? I told them she was crazy, but that she harmed no one."

"What did they say then?"

"They sat down in the grass, the nobleman at the lady's feet, and ordered me to sit down and relate to them about Victorka and how she became crazy."

"And you gladly consented, did you not?" smiled his wife.

"My dear, who would not be at the service of a beautiful lady! Our Princess, 'tis true, is no longer young, but is still wondrously beautiful. Besides, what could I do? I was obliged to obey."

"O, you rogue! it is two years since I came here, and you expressly promised me that you would tell me the story about Victorka; and I do not know it yet. A beautiful lady I am not, and cannot give my orders, so I suppose I shall never know it. Is not that so?"

"O, Grandma, you are dearer to me than the most beautiful lady in the world, and if you wish to listen, I'll tell you the story, perhaps this very day."

"Your husband knows how to place a satin cushion," smiled Grandmother, "and if you do not object, I'll take him at his word. The aged are like children, and children you know are always ready for a story."

"I am not old, and yet I love to listen, too; only

begin, Father, begin; our time will pass away so much more pleasantly," said his wife.

" Mamma, please give us some more bread, we haven't a bit," said Bertie at the door.

" That is not possible! where could they have put all that bread?" wondered Grandmother.

" Half they ate, the other half they divided among the dogs, the fawn, and the squirrels; that is always the way. How they try my patience!" sighed the mother as she cut more bread. While she was distributing it and placing Nanny in the care of the nurse girl, the gamekeeper filled his pipe.

" My husband, — may his soul rest in peace, — also had this habit; before he began telling a story, his pipe had to be ready," said Grandmother, and a pleasant memory seemed to shine in her face.

" It's a bad habit, but it seems that the men have agreed upon it," said the gamekeeper's wife as she entered the room.

" Oh, now, do not pretend that you do not like it. Why, you yourself bring me my tobacco from town," replied the husband lighting his pipe.

" What can I do? To keep you good - natured one must satisfy every whim. You may begin," she said as she seated herself with her spinning next to Grandmother.

" I am ready, listen;" and watching the first cloud of smoke ascend to the ceiling, he leaned well against the back of the chair and began the story of Victorka.

CHAPTER V.

VICTORKA is the daughter of a peasant from Zernov. Her parents were buried long ago, but her brother and sister still live. Fifteen years ago she was a maiden, handsome as a strawberry, spry as a fawn, industrious as a bee; far and wide there was none equal to her, and no one could have wished for a better wife. Such a girl, with a dowry in prospect, doesn't remain under a cover. Her fame spread far and wide, and wooers passed each other at the door. Some pleased both father and mother, some were well-to-do peasants, so that, as they say, she would have come to a full crib; but she would not see it so, and only those found favor in her eyes who danced the best, and they only at the dance.

The father was not at all pleased that his daughter should dispose of her suitors in such an off - hand way, and at times he would remonstrate with her, telling her he himself would choose a husband for her and compel her to marry him. Then she would cry and beg her father not to drive her away from home; she assured him that she had time enough for marriage seeing she was but twenty, that she wanted to enjoy life, and that God only knew whether she would be happy after she was married. The father loved the girl dearly, and when she went on like this he pitied her, and seeing her pretty face thought: " It is true, there is

time enough, you will not be without wooers."
The people, however, thought differently; they
said Victorka was proud, that she was waiting for
some one to come after her in a carriage; they
prophesied that pride goes before a fall, that who
chooses the longest chooses the worst. They uttered these and similar sayings.

At that time the chasseurs were quartered in
the village, and one of them began to follow
Victorka. When she went to church, he went, too,
and always posted himself where he could look
straight at her. When she went cutting grass, he
was sure to be somewhere near her; in short, he
followed her like a shadow. People said he was
not in his right mind; when they spoke of him in
her presence she would say: "Why does that soldier follow me? He doesn't speak, he is like a
churl; I am afraid of him. I feel the cold chills
creeping over me whenever he is around, and those
eyes of his make my head swim."

Those eyes, those eyes! everybody said they
meant nothing good; some said that at night they
shone like live coals, and that those dark eyebrows
which overshadowed them like ravens' wings,
meeting in the middle, were a sure sign that he
possessed the power of " the evil eye." Some
pitied him, saying: " Dear Lord! is a person to be
blamed for such a fault, when he was born with it?
And, besides, such eyes injure only some people;
others need not be afraid of them." Nevertheless,
when he happened to look at one of the village
children, the mother hastened to wipe the child's
face with a white cloth; and when a child became
ill, the gossips at once said that the dark chasseur

had overlooked it. Finally the people became accustomed to his swarthy complexion, and some of the girls went so far as to say that he would be fairly good looking if only he were more agreeable. Their opinion of him amounted to this: "What's to be done with such a fellow? God only knows where he is from; perhaps he is not human; one feels like signing oneself when he is about, and saying: 'God with us and evil away!' He doesn't dance, nor speak, nor sing; let him alone." And they left him alone. But it was easy for them to say: "Let him alone," when he paid no attention to them; it was quite different with Victorka.

She feared to go out alone lest she should meet those wicked eyes. She enjoyed the dance no longer, for she knew that dark face was watching her from some corner of the room; she seldom went to the spinning bees, for if not inside, the dark chasseur was sure to be out by the window, and her voice choked in her throat and her thread broke. She suffered much. People noticed the change in her, but no one dreamed that the dark soldier could be the cause. They thought Victorka allowed him to follow her because she did not know how to get rid of him. Once she said to her mates: "Believe me girls, if now a suitor should come, I would marry him, were he rich or poor, handsome or hideous, if only he were from another village."

"What has got into your head? Have you trouble at home, that you are so dissatisfied as to want to leave us?"

"Think not thus of me! It's that soldier; while he is about, I cannot stand it here; you can't imagine how he torments me! Why, I cannot even say my prayers properly nor sleep in peace; for those eyes pursue me everywhere," said Victorka bursting into tears.

"Why don't you send him word not to follow you, that you can't endure him, that he is salt to your eyes?" said her companions.

"Why, haven't I done so? To be sure, I did not speak to him myself; how could I, when he comes like a shadow? But I sent word to him by one of his comrades."

"Well, and what did he say?" asked the girls.

"He said that no one had any right to tell him where he should or should not go; that besides, he had not as yet told me that he loved me; and that, therefore, I should not send him word that I wouldn't have him!"

"Of all things, such rudeness!" frowned the girls. "What does he think of himself? We ought to revenge ourselves upon him."

"Better let such an one alone; he could bewitch you," suggested the more prudent ones.

"Lack-a-daisy! what can he do to us? To do this he would be obliged to have something we had worn next to our bodies, and none of us would give him that, and we will accept nothing from him; then what need we fear? So, dear Victorka, don't you be afraid; we will go with you everywhere, and some day that churl will catch it from us," said the more courageous of her friends.

But Victorka looked about timidly and was not at all comforted by their words. She sighed: "Oh that God himself would free me from this cross!"

What Victorka had confided to her mates did

not remain a secret; it was told everywhere, till it went across the fields to the next village.

In a few days there appeared at Victorka's home a certain well dressed man from the neighboring village. Their conversation turned on this and that, until he owned up that his neighbor desired to have his son marry, that his son liked Victorka, and that he was sent as a match - maker, to find out whether or not they could come to arrange the betrothal.

"Wait a moment, I must ask Victorka. As far as I am concerned, I know Simon and his son Anton, and have nothing against it," said the father and went to call Victorka into the spare room for consultation.

As soon as Victorka heard the proposal she said: "Let them come."

The father thought it strange that she should decide so quickly, and asked her if she knew Anton, saying that she must not decide in haste and then change her mind and have them come to no purpose. But she remained firm, replying that she knew Anton Simon well, and that he was a very estimable young man.

"I am rejoiced at this," said the father, "besides, it's your own choice. In God's name let them come."

When the father had gone to tell the match-maker the result of the conference, the mother entered the room, and making the sign of the cross upon Victorka's head wished her joy.

"What pleases me the most is that you will not have either a mother - in - law or a sister - in - law in the house, that you will be the housekeeper your-self," said the mother.

" O dearest mother, I should marry him if I had to live with two mothers - in - law."

" That is so much the better, if you think so much of each other," said the mother.

" It isn't that, dear mother; I should have accepted any other young man as soon."

" For heaven's sake, what are you talking about! So many have come, and you refused them all."

" Then I was not followed by that soldier with those awful eyes," whispered Victorka.

" You have lost your senses! What of that soldier? What do you care for him? Let him go where he wishes, he cannot carry you away from your home."

" But, dearest mother, it is he, only he. My heart is heavy and full of sorrow; I am so uneasy and can find no peace anywhere," sobbed the girl.

" Why didn't you tell me long ago? I would have taken you to the blacksmith's wife; she knows how to cure such things. Never mind, to-morrow we shall go," she said, comforting her daughter.

The following day mother and daughter went to the old dame. It was said that she knew a great many things that other people did not know. Whenever anybody lost anything, when cows did not give the usual amount of milk, when any one was "overlooked," the blacksmith's wife always knew the remedy; she knew how to discover everything. Victorka confided to her all her trouble, telling her just how she felt.

" And you never spoke to him, not a single word?" inquired the dame.

" Not a word."

" Did he never give you, or send you by other

soldiers, something to eat, such as apples or sweet-meats?"

"Nothing at all. The other soldiers have little to do with him; they say he is so proud, and all his life such a recluse. They said this at our house."

"He is a real ghoul," said the blacksmith's wife with great assurance; "but don't you be afraid, Victorka, I shall help you; all is not lost yet. To-morrow I shall bring you something which you must carry with you everywhere. In the morning, when you leave your room, you must never omit to bless yourself with holy water and say: 'God be with us, and the evil one away!' When you go through the fields, you must not turn to the right or to the left, and should that soldier address you, never mind, though he speak as an angel. He can charm even with the voice. Better put your hands over your ears! Don't you forget this. If you are not better in a few days, we will try something else, but be sure to come again."

Victorka left in a happy frame of mind, hoping that she should again feel as light and cheerful as she used to be. The next day the blacksmith's wife brought her something tied up in a bit of red cloth, and herself sewed it around the girl's neck, giving strict orders at the same time that she must never take it off or show it to anybody. In the evening, when she was cutting grass, she caught a glimpse of somebody standing near the trees and felt the blood rush to her cheeks; but she plucked up courage and did not look around once, and having finished her work flew home as if she were pursued. The third day was Sunday. The mother was baking kolaches,* the father went to invite the schoolmaster and several others of the older neighbors to spend the afternoon, and the villagers putting their heads together said: "At Mikesh's, they will celebrate the betrothal!"

In the afternoon three men in Sunday clothes entered the yard; two had rosemary on their sleeves. The master of the house welcomed them at the door, and the servants standing near said: "May God grant you success."

"God grant it," replied the speaker, both for father and son.

The groom was the last to cross the threshold, and the women outside were heard to say: "A handsome youth, that Anton; he carries his head like a deer; and see, what a fine sprig of rosemary he has on his sleeve! Where did he buy it?" The men replied to this: "Yes, indeed! he may carry his head high when he carries off the fairest lass in the village, the best dancer, a good housekeeper, and wealthy, besides."

Thus reasoned many parents, and some were offended that Victorka had chosen one from across the fields. "Why wasn't this one or that one good enough for her? why this haste and these strange notions!" Thus they ran on, as is the custom on such occasions.

Before evening the marriage contract was finished. It was drawn out by the schoolmaster, the parents and witnesses putting down three crosses instead of their names, and Victorka gave her hand to Anton, promising that in three weeks she would be his wife. The next day, her friends came to

* A biscuit with some sauce rolled inside.

congratulate her, and whenever she appeared on the common, she was greeted with the words, "God grant you happiness, bride!" * But when the young people said: "What a pity that you are going away! Why do you leave us, Victorka?" then her eyes filled with tears.

For several days Victorka was happier, and when she had occasion to go out of the village was not oppressed with the fear that she had felt before. She wore the amulet from the blacksmith's wife, as she had done before she was a bride. She felt free from anxiety, and thanked God and the old dame for her delivery from danger. Her joy, however, was of short duration.

One evening she was sitting with Anton in the orchard. They were discussing plans for their future housekeeping, and were talking about the wedding. Suddenly Victorka stopped, her eyes were fixed upon the bush before her, and her hand trembled.

"What is the matter?" asked Anton much surprised.

"Look! between those branches before us,— don't you see anything?" she whispered.

Anton looked, but declared he saw nothing.

"It seemed to me that the dark soldier was watching us," she whispered so low as to be scarcely heard.

"Just wait, we'll make an end of that," cried Anton. He sprang up and searched all around, but in vain; he saw no one. "He will not escape so easily another time; if he persists in looking at

---

* In Bohemia a young woman is a bride from the day of betrothal to the day of marriage.

you even now, I'll make him rue it!" scolded Anton.

"Don't pick any quarrel with him, I beg of you, Anton. A soldier is a soldier. Father himself went to Red Hura, and he would have gladly paid something to the officer of that town for removing him from our village; but he said that he could not do it, even if he desired to; and, besides, it was no offense, when a man looked at a girl. Father learned from the soldiers, that that chasseur comes from a very wealthy family, that he enlisted of his own free will, and can leave when he chooses. If you begin a quarrel with him you will be sure to get the worst of it." Thus spoke Victorka, and Anton promised to let the soldier alone.

From that evening Victorka was again oppressed by moments of gloom and heaviness, and however confidently she pressed the amulet to her breast, whenever she felt those baleful eyes fixed upon her, her heart's loud beatings were not quieted thereby. She went to the blacksmith's wife for further advice.

"I don't know but that it is a punishment upon me from God; for what you have given me doesn't help me at all," said Victorka.

"Never mind, my child, never mind. I'll give it to him yet, even if he were Anti-christ himself. But first I must have two things from him. Before I secure those, you must avoid him as much as possible! Pray to your guardian angel and for those souls in purgatory for whom nobody else prays. If you redeem one, she will intercede for you."

"That is the worst, dear God-mother; my mind

is so disturbed that I cannot pray in peace," sobbed the poor girl.

"My child, why did you leave it so long, until the evil power overcame you? But with God's help we shall conquer that demon yet."

Victorka summoned all her courage; she prayed fervently, and when her thoughts began to wander she thought of Christ's crucifixion, of the Virgin Mary, so that the evil power should not overcome her. She guarded herself thus for two days; the third day, however, she went into the farthest corner of her father's fields to cut some clover; she told the workman to follow her soon, as she would hurry with the cutting. She ran like a fawn, and the people stopped their work to look at her and admired the grace of her movements. Thus she went, but home she was brought by the workman, on the green clover, pale, wounded. Her foot was bound in a fine, white handkerchief, and she had to be lifted from the cart and carried into the house.

"Holy Virgin! what has happened to you, my daughter?" lamented the mother.

"I stepped upon a thorn; it went deep into my foot and made me ill. Please take me into my room. I will lie down," begged Victorka.

They carried her in, laid her on her bed, and the father hastened to the blacksmith's wife. She came post haste, and with her a crowd of uninvited neighbors, as is generally the way. One advised burnet, the second, dragon's head, the third urged them to smoke it, the fourth, to conjure it; but the wise old dame was not put out by those differences of opinion. She bound up the swollen foot in a poultice of potato starch. Then she dismissed all

the visitors, saying that she herself would watch by
Victorka, and soon everything would be all right.

" Tell me, my child, how was it? You seem to
be greatly disturbed. And who was it that bound
up your foot in that fine, white handkerchief? I
hid it quickly so that those gossips should not
notice it," said the careful woman, placing Victorka's foot in a more comfortable position.

" Where did you put it? " quickly asked the
girl.

" You have it under your pillow."

Victorka reached for the handkerchief, examined
the bloody stains, the embroidered name, which she
did not know, and the color of her face changed
from white to crimson.

" My child, my child, I do not like your looks.
What am I to think of you? "

" Think that God has forsaken me, that nothing
can help me, that I am forever and ever lost."

" She has a fever and is raving," thought the
good woman, laying her hand on Victorka's cheeks;
but they were cold, and her hands were cold, too,
and only her eyes seemed to burn, as she fixed them
upon the handkerchief which she held with both
hands before her.

" Listen to me," began Victorka quietly, " but
do not say anything to any one. I will tell you
everything. Those two days I did not see him,—
of course you know whom I mean,— but to - day,
this morning it kept sounding in my ears: ' Go to
the clover field, go to the clover field,' as if some
one were whispering to me. I knew it was some
temptation, because he is often there sitting under
a tree on the hill; but somehow I had no rest until

I was on my way with the scythe and the bags. As I was going I thought I was my own worst enemy, but something kept whispering in my ears: ' Only go, go cut your clover, who knows whether he will be there? Why should you be afraid? Tomesh will follow you soon. Thus it drove me on till I came to the field. I looked toward the tree but nobody was there. ' If he is not there, the danger is past,' thought I, and took up the scythe to cut the clover. Then it occurred to me to try my luck. I wanted to find a four - leaved clover; for I thought: ' If I find one, I shall be happy with Anton.' I looked and looked, almost leaving my eyes on the clover, but I found none. Then I happened to look toward the hill, and whom did I see standing under a tree but that soldier! I turned away quickly; but at that instant I stepped upon some thorns that lay near the path, and one went into my foot. I did not cry out, but the pain was so intense that it grew dark before my eyes, and I think I must have fainted away. As in a dream, I felt that some one took me up in his arms and car-ried me away, and then in great pain I awoke. I was at the spring, and that soldier was kneeling at my side. He dipped his white handkerchief in the water and bound up my foot in it.

" ' My God!' thought I, ' what is going to hap-pen now? You cannot escape those eyes. It will be best if you do not look into them.' I suffered much from the pain, my head swam, but I did not utter a whisper, and kept my eyes closed. He laid his hand on my forehead and took hold of my hand. My blood froze with terror, but still I said not a word. Then he arose, sprinkled water in my face, and raised my head. What was I to do? I had to open my eyes. O my dear Godmother, those eyes of his shone upon me like God's dear sun! I covered my face with my hands, but when he began to speak, I could not withstand the charm of his voice. Oh, you were right when you said he could bewitch one with his voice; his words ring in my ears even yet. He said that he loved me, that I was his bliss, his heaven!"

" What wicked words! one can see that they are the snares of the Evil One! Unhappy girl, what were you thinking of that you believed him!" lamented the blacksmith's wife.

" Heavens! how could I doubt him, when he told me that he loved me?"

"Told you! what does that amount to? — all fraud and deception. He wants to deprive you of your reason."

" That is what I told him; but he protested on his soul's salvation that he loved me from the first time that he had seen me, and that he refrained from speaking with me and telling me so, because he did not want to bind me to his own unhappy fate, that followed him every where, never allowing him to enjoy any happiness. Oh, I do not remember what all he said, but it was enough to make one weep. I believed everything, I told him that I had been afraid of him, that out of fear I had become a bride, that I wore on my heart an amulet; and when he asked for it, I gave it to him," said Victorka.

" O my blessed Savior," lamented the woman, " she gives him the consecrated amulet, she gives him a thing warmed on her body! Now you are in his

7

power, now not even God can tear you from his claws, now he has bewitched you entirely!"

"He said that that witchcraft was love and that I should believe no other."

"Yes, yes, he said — love; I would tell him what love is, but all in vain now! What have you done? Why he is a ghoul, and he will draw your blood from your veins and then choke you, and you will not find rest even in your grave. And you might have been so happy!"

Those words frightened Victorka, but after a long pause she said: "All is lost; I shall go with him even if he lead me to perdition. Cover me; I am so cold!"

The blacksmith's wife covered her up with featherbeds, but Victorka was cold all the time and did not speak another word.

The blacksmith's wife thought a great deal of Victorka, and although her giving away the charm made her very angry, still the fate of the girl, whom she now regarded as lost, filled her with grief. All that Victorka had told her she kept to herself.

From that day Victorka lay like one dead. She did not speak, except some wandering words as if in her sleep; she did not ask for anything, she did not notice anybody. The blacksmith's wife did not leave her bedside, and exhausted all her store of knowledge to help her. But all was in vain. The parents grew more sorrowful day by day, and the lover went away each day with a heavier heart. The blacksmith's wife shook her head as she thought: "This is not of itself; how could it be, that none of those remedies that have helped so many others help her? That soldier has over-

powered her with some deadly charm, that is it!"
Such were her reflections night and day, and when
one night she happened to look out of the window
of the sick chamber and saw in the orchard the
muffled form of a man, whose eyes glowed like
burning coals,— she would have taken her oath
they did,— she was then sure that her suspicions
were correct.

But she was greatly rejoiced, when one day
Mikesh brought the news that the chasseurs had
received orders to leave.

"They could have all remained for aught I care,
all but that one; his departure gives me more satisfaction than if some one gave me a hundred in
gold. The devil himself brought him here. It
has been my impression for some time that since he
has been here our Victorka is not what she used to
be, and that, after all, he has used some black art
against her," said the father, and the mother and
the blacksmith's wife agreed with him. The latter,
however, hoped that after the removal of the evil
influence, all would be well again.

The soldiers marched away. That same night
Victorka was so much worse that they thought
they must send for the priest. Towards morning
she grew better, and continued improving until she
was able to sit up. The blacksmith's wife herself
accounted for this by the departure of the satanic
power, but still she was not displeased when people said: "That blacksmith's wife, she is a trump;
if it were not for her, Victorka never would have
walked again." And when she heard this again
and again, she at last believed that her skill had
saved the girl.

But all danger was not yet over. Victorka was around again, walked about the yard, but did not seem like herself. She spoke to no one, did not notice any one, and her expression seemed confused. The blacksmith's wife comforted the parents by saying that this, too, would in time be overcome; and she did not think it necessary that she should watch by her any longer. Victorka's sister Mary slept with her again as before.

The first night, when the girls were alone, Mary sat down on Victorka's bed and with a loving voice,— she is a very good soul,— asked her why she was so strange and what ailed her. Victorka looked at her but made no reply.

"You see, sister, I want to tell you something, but I am afraid lest you be angry."

Victorka shook her head saying: "Say what you wish, Mary."

"The evening before the soldiers left," began Mary; but hardly had she finished the last word, when Victorka seized her by the hand and quickly asked: "The soldiers went away, and where?"

"I do not know where they went."

"Thank God," said Victorka heaving a deep sigh and falling back upon her pillow.

"Now listen, Victorka, and do not be offended with me; I know you cannot endure that dark soldier, and that you will blame me for speaking to him."

"You spoke to him!" cried Victorka rising again.

"I could not help it, he begged me so to listen to him; but I did not look at him once. While you were so ill he used to come near the house; but

I always ran away, for I was afraid of him. One day he met me in the orchard and offered me some kind of herb. He asked me to prepare it for you and said that it would do you good; but I would not take it. I was afraid he wanted to give you a love potion. Then he begged me to tell you that he was going away, that he would never forget his promise, and that you should not forget yours, that you would meet him again. I promised him I would tell you and now I have fulfilled my promise. But do not be afraid, he will never come again, and you shall have no more trouble."

"Thank you, Mary, you are a good girl; but now you may go to sleep," said Victorka, as she caressed the round shoulders of her sister. Mary smoothed down her sister's pillows, said good night, and went to sleep.

The next morning, when she awoke, she found Victorka's bed empty. She thought her sister was about the house; but when she went into the living room, she was not there. She went out into the yard, but did not find her. The parents were surprised and sent to the blacksmith's to see if she had not gone to visit her god-mother, but she had not been there.

"What has become of her?" was the common question, while they searched every corner. The workman was sent to the house of Victorka's lover, to see if she had not gone there. When she was nowhere to be found, and when the lover came and knew nothing whatever of her, the blacksmith's wife owned up. "I think she ran away to follow that soldier!"

"That's a lie!" cried Anton.

"You must be mistaken!" said the parents; how could that be; she could not endure him!"

"Nevertheless, it is so," said she and related what Victorka had confided to her. Then Mary told the conversation she had had with her sister the evening before; and putting one thing to another, they were convinced that, impelled by some secret infernal power which she could not withstand, Victorka had followed the soldier.

"We must not blame her, she could not help it, only she ought to have come to me while it was yet time. Now it is too late. He has bewitched her, and as long as he wishes she must follow him. And suppose you find her and bring her home, she must seek him again," said the old dame with much emphasis.

"I shall go to seek her, let it be how it will. Perhaps she will listen to me, for she was always a good girl," said the father.

"I will go with you, father!" exclaimed Anton, who had listened to all in breathless silence.

"You shall remain at home," replied the father. "When a person is angry, he is not apt to consult his reason, and you might do something for which you would be put in a cool place or get a white coat. * Then too, you have suffered enough already; why should you seek further sorrow. She can no longer become your wife, put that out of your mind entirely. If you wish to wait a year for Mary, you may have her, she is a good girl. I should like to have you for my son, but I do not urge you, act according to your own judgment." Hearing these words all the family wept. The father tried

* Be put in prison or be taken into the army.

to comfort them. "Do not weep, that will do no good; if I do not bring her back, we must leave her with God."

The father took a few dollars for his journey, told the household what must be done in his absence, and started on his journey. Along the way he asked many persons if they had seen his daughter, describing her from head to foot, but nobody had seen her. At Joseph-hof, they told him that the chasseurs went to Hradetz, and at Hradetz he learned that that dark soldier had been put into another division, and that he wanted to be discharged. What had finally become of him they could not tell, but they knew that it was the very same soldier that had been quartered at Zernov. He found no traces of Victorka. He was advised to apply at the police office, but he would hear nothing of this.

"I'll have nothing to do with the police. I don't want her to be brought home like a vagrant, so that people will point the finger at her. She shall not be thus disgraced. Let her be wherever she will, she is in God's hands, without whose will not a hair can fall from her head. If she is to return, she will return; if not, then God's will be done; she shall not be dragged before the public."

This was the father's decision. He begged the gamekeeper at Hradetz, if he should see Victorka or hear anything of her, to tell her that her father sought her, and, if she wished to return, to provide her with a suitable escort. The gamekeeper promised all; for many a good day had he enjoyed at the home of Mikesh. Then the father returned home, his mind at peace, knowing that he had done all that was in his power.

All mourned for Victorka. They paid for prayers and masses that she might return. After waiting a half a year, three quarters of a year, and hearing no news of her, they gave her up as lost.

One day the shepherds brought news to the village that they had seen a woman with black hair in the woods, about as tall as Victorka. Mikesh's whole household went out and searched through the woods, but not a trace was found of any such person.

At that time I was in the first year of my apprenticeship to my predecessor, my late father-in-law. Of course we heard of this, too, and when I went into the forest the next day, he told me to look around and see if I could not discover such a person. That very day, I saw in the woods just above Mikesh's fields, under two firs that had their branches intermingled, a woman sitting. Her hair hung in a tangled mass over her shoulders, and although I had known Victorka, I never should have recognized her in that neglected, wild looking creature. But it was she. Her clothes were of city style, and although much tattered still showed marks of elegance. I noticed, too, that she was soon to become a mother. I got away very quietly and hastened to tell the news to my master. He, in turn, went to tell it at Zernov. The parents wept bitterly and would have preferred to see her in her grave. But what could be done? We agreed to watch where she went and slept, that we might quiet her if possible. One evening she came clear to her father's orchard, sat down, held her knees in both arms with her chin resting upon them, and fixed her eyes upon one spot. Her mother wanted to approach her, but she rose quickly, jumped over the fence, and disappeared in the woods. My master said that they should place some food and clothes for her in the woods, and that perhaps she would notice it. Her parents at once brought what was necessary, and I myself placed it in a convenient spot. The next day I went to see. Of the food the bread only was missing, and of the clothes, the petticoats and the underwear. The rest remained untouched, and on the third day I took it away, lest some one for whom it was not intended should take it. For a long time we could not discover where she slept, until I found out that it was in a cave under three fir trees, — sometime they must have cut stone there. The entrance is covered up with growing shrubbery, so that one not well acquainted with it would find it with difficulty. Once I entered the cave; one or two persons could find room in it. Victorka had nothing there except some dry leaves and moss. That was her bed. Her friends and relatives, and especially her father and Mary, who was then Anton's promised bride, watched for her in many places; they wanted to speak with her and to take her home, but she shunned all intercourse with people and was rarely seen in the day time. When at last she came to the house and sat down, Mary stepped quietly to her and with her coaxing voice said: "Come, Victorka, come with me once more to our room; it is so long since you have slept with me, and I am so lonely. Come and sleep with me!"

Victorka looked at her and allowed herself to be

taken by the hand and led into the hall; all at once she sprang away and was gone. For many days she was not seen near the homestead.

One night I was standing waiting for game not far from The Old Bleachery; the moon shone so that it was as light as day. All at once I saw Victorka coming out of the woods. When she walks, she always has her hands folded upon her breast and her head bent forward, and she steps so lightly, that she scarcely seems to touch the ground. At this time she went in this way directly to the dam. I used to see her quite often near the water or on the side of the hill under that large oak, and so I did not pay any special attention to her then. But when I observed more closely I saw that she was throwing something into the water, and I heard her laugh so wildly that my hair stood up in terror. My dog began to howl. Victorka then sat down on a stump and sang; I did not understand a word, but the tune was that of the lullaby which mothers sing to their children:

> Sleep, my baby, sleep,
> Close thy eyelids, sweet,
> God himself will slumber with thee,
> And his angels rock and guard thee,
> Sleep, my baby, sleep!

That song sounded so mournful in the still night that I could hardly remain at my post. For two hours she sat there and sang. Since that time she is at the bank every evening singing that lullaby. In the morning I told my master, and he guessed at once what she most probably threw into the water,— and it was true. When we saw her again, her form was changed. Her mother and the others

shuddered; but what could be done? The unknow-
ing cannot sin! Gradually she learned to come to
our door, usually when driven by hunger, but she
would do then as she does now: She came, posted
herself at the door, and remained standing. My
wife, who was then a girl, quickly gave her something to eat. She took it without a word, and flew
away to the woods. Whenever I go on my rounds,
I give her bread, which she takes; but if I attempt
to speak to her, she runs away without accepting
anything. She is very fond of flowers; if she does
not carry some in her hand, she has them in her
belt, but when she sees a child, she gives them
away. Who can tell whether she knows what she
does. I should like to know what is going on in
that deranged head of hers, but who can explain it,
she least of all!

When Mary and Anton were married, and
while they were at the church at Red Hura, Victorka came to the farm. God knows whether it
was a mere accident, or whether she heard of her
sister's wedding. She had her apron full of
flowers; as soon as she came to the door, she scattered them over the yard. Her mother began to
call her, and brought her out some kolaches and
whatever other dainties she had, but she turned and
ran away.

Her father was broken down with grief; he
loved her. The third year he died. I happened
to be in the village at the time. Both Anton and
his wife asked me with tears whether I had seen
Victorka. They wanted to bring her to the house
and did not know how. The father could not die
and they all believed she held his soul. I returned

to the woods, thinking that if I saw her, I would tell her, whether she understood or not. She sat under the fir trees; I went past her as though by accident, and quietly, so as not to frighten her, said: " Victorka, your father is dying. You might go home."

She sat still as though she had not heard me. I thought: " It is of no use," and went back to the village to tell them. While I was still speaking with Mary at the door, the workman cried: " Victorka is really coming into the orchard! "

" Anton, call all the friends out, and hide yourself, that we may not frighten her," said Mary and went into the orchard.

Presently she led Victorka into the room. She was playing with a primrose and did not once raise her beautiful, but confused black eyes. Mary led her as if she were blind. All was silent in the room. On one side of the bed the mother knelt, at the foot the only son, the father had his hands folded on his breast, his eyes were turned to heaven; he was in the agony of death. Mary led Victorka clear to his bedside. The dying man turned his eyes upon her and a blissful smile passed over his features. He tried to raise his hand but could not. Victorka probably thought that he wanted something, so she placed the primrose in his hand. Once more the dying man looked at her, heaved a deep sigh,— and was dead. Victorka's presence had helped him to cross the dark river. The mother began to weep, and as soon as Victorka heard so many voices she looked wildly about her, turned to the door, and fled.

I do not know whether she ever again entered

her home. During these fifteen years, that I have been living here, I have heard her speak but once. To my dying day I shall not forget it. I was going down to the bridge; on the road were the workmen from the castle hauling some wood, and in the meadow I saw " Golden Hair." That was the secretary from the castle; the girls nicknamed him so, because they could not remember his German name, and because he had very beautiful golden hair, which he wore quite long. He was walking along in the meadow, and because it was warm he took off his cap and went bareheaded.

All at once, as if she had fallen from the sky, Victorka rushed out, seized him by the hair, shook and tore him as if he were a man made of gingerbread. The German screamed with all his might, I flew down the hill, but Victorka raged and bit him in his hands screaming: " Now I have you in my power, you snake, you devil! Now I'll tear you to pieces! What did you do with my lover? You devil, give me back my lover!" She became so enraged that her voice became broken, and we could not understand her. The German also did not understand her, he was dumbfounded. Had it not been for the workmen, we could have done nothing with her. Seeing the struggle they ran to the scene, and with their assistance the secretary was finally extricated from her hands. When, however, we tried to hold her, she gave a sudden jerk, and before we were aware was out of our hands and ran to the woods, where she stood throwing stones at us and cursing so that the skies trembled. After that I did not see her for several days. The German became ill from his fright, and was so afraid of Victorka that he left his place. The girls laughed at him, but what of it! he who runs away wins, and his absence will not keep the grain from growing. We have not missed him.

"There now, Grandma," concluded the game-keeper, "you have Victorka's whole history, partly as I heard it from the late blacksmith's wife, and partly from her sister Mary. What happened besides, who knows? but she must have had a hard time, and he who carries her ruin upon his conscience has a heavy load!"

Grandma wiped her tear-stained cheeks, and said with a pleasant smile: "I am a thousand times obliged. One must confess that you can relate a story as well as a writer; one could listen and listen and forget that the sun is behind the mountain." Grandmother pointed to the long shadow in the room and began to put up her work.

"Wait a few moments, till I feed the poultry, and I will go with you down the hill," begged the hostess, and Grandmother gladly waited.

And I'll escort you down to the bridge, for I must go to the woods yet," said the gamekeeper, rising from the table.

The housekeeper hurried outside and presently there was heard in the yard a loud calling: "Chick, chick, chick!" and the poultry were seen flying from all directions. First came a flock of sparrows as though the call were meant for them. The house-wife remarked: "Well, well, you are always the first;" but they acted as though they did not hear her.

Grandmother stood by the door, keeping the children near her lest they should frighten away

the poultry which she watched with the greatest
delight. And what poultry! White and gray
geese with goslings, ducks with ducklings, black
Turkish ducks, beautiful chickens of home raising,
and long legged Tyrol chickens, top-knotted and
with ruffled collars, peacocks, doves, Guinea hens,
turkeys with their gobbler, who strutted about and
swelled as though he were the lord of all. The
whole flock rushed into one heap, each striving to
get the largest possible share of the supper. They
stepped upon one another's heels, jumped over one
another, crawled under and crept through wherever
a space could be found; and the sparrows, those
vagabonds, when they had their own crops well
filled, walked over the backs of the foolish ducks
and geese. Not far off sat the rabbits, and a tame
squirrel, with its tail over its head like a helmet,
looked down upon the children from a chestnut tree.
Upon the fence sat the cat, having a longing eye
fixed upon the sparrows. The fawn allowed Barunka to scratch its head and the dogs sat quietly
near the children, for the housewife held a switch
in her hand. Still when the black cock ran after
the gosling that had taken his food from his very
mouth and the gosling ran near Hector's nose, the
dog could not refrain from grabbing at it.

" See that old loon! " cried the housewife, as
her switch whizzed about the dog's ears.

Hector was ashamed that he should be thus reproved before his younger companions, and with
his head down he crawled into the hall. Grandmother remarked: " Of course the son cannot be
better than the father." Hector was the son of
Sultan, who killed those beautiful ducklings.

The feeding was over; the poultry went to their roosts. Frank and Bertie gave the children some peacock feathers, the housewife gave Grandmother some Tyrol chickens' eggs for hatching, and taking Nannie in her arms she was ready to accompany them a part of the way. The gamekeeper, throwing his rifle over his shoulder and calling Hector, followed them.

At the foot of the hill, the gamekeeper's wife bade them good night and returned home with the children; at the bridge the gamekeeper shook hands with them and turned to the woods to lie in wait for game. John watched him till he disappeared in the woods, and then said to Barunka: "When I am a little older, I will go with Mr. Beyer; and then I, too, can go out and lie in wait for game."

"Yes, but they would be obliged to send some one with you, for you are afraid of forest women and fiery men," laughed Barunka.

"O, what do you know about it?" frowned John, "when I am older, I shall not be afraid."

Passing the dam, Grandmother noticed the moss-covered stump, and thinking of Victorka, sighed deeply: "Unhappy girl."

CHAPTER VI.

THE following day, before noon, the children headed by Grandmother sallied out of the house.

"Now, remember to behave well," said the mother at the door; "do not touch anything in the castle, and do not forget, when you get there, politely to kiss the hand of the Princess!"

"I shall see that everything is done properly," replied Grandmother.

The children looked like newly opened blossoms, and Grandmother, too, had on her best: a clove colored linsey-woolsey petticoat, an apron white as snow, a damask sky-blue jacket, a cap with the dove-knot, and the garnet necklace with the dollar. Across her arm she carried her shawl. "Why do you take that shawl, it will not rain?" said her daughter.

"It seems as if I have no hands when I have nothing to carry," replied Grandmother.

They made a turn around the orchard and found themselves in the narrow path.

"Now go carefully, one behind another in the path, so as not to soil your clothes in the wet grass. You Barunka, go ahead; I will lead Adelka, for she doesen't know how to keep in the path," said Grandmother as she took Adelka's hand, who was looking at herself with great satisfaction. In the orchard Blackie was running about,— that was Adelka's hen, the one Grandmother brought from the mountain village; it was so tame that it would eat out of the children's hands, and every time it laid an egg it came to Adelka, who gave it a piece of roll that she had saved from her breakfast.

"Go to Mamma, Blackie, I left the roll for you there; I am going to see the Princess," said Adelka to the hen, but the hen ran to her as though she did not understand, and tried to pick at her dress.

"You foolish hen, don't you see my white dress? Vsh-sh-sh!" cried the child, but the hen refused to go, until Grandmother struck it with her shawl.

They went a little further; when lo! a new danger threatens their white clothes. The dogs are running upon the hillside; they wade the stream, shake themselves a little, and with a bound are at Grandmother's side.

"A plague on you! who called you? away at once!" scolded Grandmother, shaking her fist at them. The dogs hearing her angry voice and seeing the upraised arm, stood still a moment wondering what it could mean. The children scolded, too, and John took up a stone to throw at them; but instead of hitting them it fell into the stream. The dogs accustomed to fetch things thrown into the water, and thinking the children meant to play with them, bounded into the water and in an instant were back again near the terrified children; they screamed and hid behind Grandmother, who herself was at her wit's end to know what to do.

"I'll run home and call Betsey," suggested Barunka.

"No; it is not well to turn back, it often brings bad luck," objected Grandmother.

Fortunately the miller happened to come along, and seeing how things stood drove the dogs away.

" Whither bound, a wedding or a festival?" he asked.

" There is no wedding, sir; we are going to the castle," replied Grandmother.

" To the castle! Well that's something? What will you do there?" wondered the miller.

"The princess invited us," explained the children, and Grandmother added how she had met that lady in the arbor.

" Well, well!" said the miller, taking a pinch of snuff; " when you return, Adelka must tell me what she saw there; and, John, if the Princess should ask you where the finch goes when she follows her nose, you won't know, will you?"

" She won't ask me," replied John, running away to escape further questioning. The miller smiled mischievously, said good bye, and turned toward the dam.

When they reached the inn, they saw Kuderna's children playing with paper mills. Celia held the baby.

" What are you doing here?" asked Barunka.

" Nothing," they replied, curiously eyeing the children's pretty clothes.

" We are going to the castle," began John in a boasting manner.

"Hm, what of it!" replied Lawrence with a toss of the head.

" And we'll see the parrot!" chimed in Willie.

" When I grow up, I shall see parrots and many other things; father says I am to travel and see the world," said the bold Lawrence; but Wenzel and Celia said, " If we could go too!"

" Never mind, I'll bring you something and tell

you all about it," said John, trying to comfort them.

Finally they reached the park without any more interruption, and were joined by their father who was waiting for them.

The park belonged to the castle but was free to the public. It was near The Old Bleachery, but Grandmother seldom went there, especially when the nobility were at home. She admired the skill with which everything was arranged, the beautiful flowers, the rare trees, the fountains with their golden fishes; still she preferred to take the children to the meadow or to the woods. There, on the soft green carpet, they could roll about as they pleased, smell every flower, or pick enough of them to make bouquets or garlands. Oranges and lemons did not grow in the fields, but here and there stood a cherry tree or a wild pear tree loaded with fruit, and any one could shake down as much as he pleased. Again, in the woods there were plenty of strawberries, huckleberries, mushrooms, and hazel nuts. There were no fountains in the woods, but they used to stand at the dam and watch the water rush down, bound back, and breaking into millions of drops fall down again, turn over in the foaming kettle, and then flow down the stream. There were no golden fishes above the dam, but whenever Grandmother went by she took some crumbs from her pocket, put them into Adelka's apron, and when she threw them into the water, shoals of fishes appeared at the surface. The silvery white chubs ventured nearest the surface to chase after the crumbs; among them darted about the straight-backed perches, and a little way off glanced here and there the slender barbels with their long whiskers. One could also see the broad carps and flat-headed eel-pouts.

In the meadow, Grandmother met many people, who greeted her with "Praised be Jesus Christ!" or "God grant you a good day?" Then they stopped and asked: "Whither bound, Grandma?" "How do you do?" "How are your folks?" and she always heard some news.

But at the castle she was quite bewildered. Here ran a gallooned waiter, there a chamber maid in silk; here a lord and there a lord; and each held his head higher than it grew and strutted about like the peacocks that alone had the privilege of walking about on the sward. Whenever any one did greet Grandmother, he mumbled carelessly, "Guten Morgen," or "Bon Jour," and she blushed, not knowing whether she should reply "For ever," or "God grant it?" She used to say: "In that castle, it is a perfect Babylon."

Before the castle sat two gallooned servants, one on each side of the door; the one to the left had his hands folded in his lap and was staring into space; the one to the right had his clasped over his breast and was gaping into the sky. When the party reached the door, they greeted Mr. Proshek in German, each with a different accent.

The floor of the entrance hall was of white marble, and a brilliant table artistically wrought stood in the middle. Around the walls were plaster of Paris casts standing on green marble pedestals, and representing various mythological characters.

At one of the doors sat the chamberlain in a

swallow-tailed coat; he was asleep. Mr. Proshek led Grandmother and the children into the hall, and the chamberlain, hearing some noise, awoke and seeing who it was, asked Mr. Proshek what business brought him to the castle.

"Her Grace, the Princess, desired that my mother should visit her to-day with the children. I beg you, Mr. Leopold, to announce them," said Mr. Proshek.

Mr. Leopold elevated his eyebrows, shrugged his shoulders, and replied, "I do not know whether the Princess will receive any company to-day; she is in her cabinet, working; however, I can announce them." He arose and very deliberately entered the door by which he had been watching. Presently he returned and with a gracious smile motioned the visitors to enter. Mr. Proshek went back and the company entered the elegant parlor. The children held their breath, while their feet slipped upon the floor, smooth as glass. Grandmother was as in a vision; she was afraid to step upon the beautiful rugs. "It is a thousand pities!" she said to herself. But what could be done? They lay everywhere and the chamberlain walked upon them. He led them through the concert hall and library to the cabinet; then he returned to his post grumbling: "Their Lordships have odd whims that one should be at the service of a common old woman and children!"

The cabinet of the Princess was decorated with green hangings inwrought with gold, curtains of the same stuff were at the door and over one window, which was as large as a door. Many pictures of various sizes hung upon the walls, but

all were portraits. Opposite the window was the
fireplace, made of gray marble variegated with
black and green; upon the mantel stood two vases of
Japanese porcelain, holding beautiful flowers whose
perfume filled the whole cabinet. On both sides
were shelves of costly wood, skillfully wrought.
Upon these were laid out various articles, valued
partly for their artistic worth and partly for their
costliness; also natural objects, such as shells,
corals, stones, and the like. Some of these were
souvenirs from journeys, some keepsakes from
friends. In the corner of the room near the
window stood a Carrara marble statute of Apollo,
and in the opposite corner, a writing desk. At this
desk, in an arm chair covered with dark green
plush, sat the Princess, dressed in a white morning-
gown. As Grandmother and the children entered
she laid aside her pen to welcome them.

"Praised be Jesus Christ!" said Grandmother,
bowing respectfully.

"Forever!" replied the Princess, and welcomed
her guests.

The children were so bewildered that they did
not know what to do, until Grandmother winked
at them, when they went to kiss the hand of the
Princess. She kissed them on the forehead and
motioning to a stool covered with plush and
ornamented with golden tassels, she invited Grandmother to sit down.

"I thank your Grace, but I am not tired," was
the reply. The fact was she was afraid to sit down
lest the stool should break down or roll away with
her. Still, when the Princess asked her again, she
spread her white shawl over the stool and sat

down saying: " So we should not carry away your Grace's sleep."* The children stood still and trembling with awe, but their eyes wandered from one object to another; the Princess observing this asked, " Do you like it here? "

" Yes, ma'am," they replied in chorus.

" No wonder," added Grandmother. " They would find enough here to amuse them and they would need no coaxing to remain."

" And you? Would you not like it here, too? " asked the Princess.

" It's like heaven, still I should not want to live here," replied Grandmother.

" Why not? " asked the Princess greatly surprised.

" What should I do here? You have no house-keeping. I could not spread out my feathers here for stripping, nor take my spinning out; what could I do? "

" And would you not like to live without care and labor, and take some comfort in your old age?"

" Indeed, it will be soon enough that the sun shall rise and set over my head, and I shall sleep free from care. But as long as I live and God grants me health, it is fitting that I labor. An idler costs too much when he costs nothing. Besides, no one is wholly free from care, one has this cross, another that, but all do not sink beneath its weight."

Just then a small hand turned aside the curtain at the door; and there appeared the lovely face of a

---

*It is a common belief that if a person does not sit down when coming into a strange house, its inmates will not sleep well.

young girl, whose head was adorned with long
blonde braids.

" May I come in?" she asked.

" Certainly, you will find pleasant company,"
replied the Princess.

Into the cabinet stepped Countess Hortense, the
ward of the Princess, as was said. Her figure was
slender and undeveloped; she wore a simple white
dress, her round straw hat hung over her arm, and
in her hand she held a bunch of roses. " Oh what
charming little children!" she exclaimed. " Surely
they are Proshek's children, who sent me those de-
licious strawberries yesterday?"

The Princess nodded. The Countess bent down
to give each child a rose; then she gave one to
Grandmother, one to the Princess, and the last she
placed behind her belt.

" This bud is as fresh as yourself, gracious
Countess," remarked Grandmother smelling the
rose, "may God protect and keep her for you," she
added turning to the Princess.

" That is my earnest prayer," replied the
Princess as she kissed the forehead of her ward.

" May I take the children away for a while?"
asked the Countess looking both at the Princess
and Grandmother. The former nodded, but
Grandmother said they would be a great trouble,
for those boys were like hounds and John was a
regular scapegrace.

But Hortense smiled and offering both her hands
asked: " Do you want to go with me?"

" Yes ma'am, yes ma'am!" cried the children in
a chorus, taking hold of her hands. She bowed
both to the Princess and her company and disap-

peared. The Princess then took a silver bell and
rang it; in an instant the chamberlain appeared at
the door. The Princess ordered him to see that
breakfast was served in the small dining room, and
gave him a package of papers to care for. He
bowed and left the room.

While the Princess was speaking with the
chamberlain, Grandmother was looking at the portraits upon the walls of the cabinet.

"O dear Lord!" she exclaimed when Leopold
was gone, "what strange costumes and faces!
This lady is dressed just as the late Mrs. Halashkov
used to be dressed, — may her soul rest in peace!
She used to wear high heeled shoes, a high bonnet,
her petticoats puffed out, and her waist laced so
tight that she looked as if she had been cut in two
by a whip lash. Her husband was a city alderman
in Dobruska, and when we went there on a pilgrimage, we saw her at church. Our boys called
her a poppy doll, because in those petticoats and
that powdered head she looked like a poppy blossom with the petals turned backwards. They said
it was a French style of dress."

"That lady is my grandmother," said the
Princess.

"Indeed? She is a fine lady," replied Grandmother.

"The picture to the right is my grandfather,
and the left one is my father," continued the Princess.

"Very nice people! Your Grace does not deny
her father; and may I ask, where is your mother?"

"There is my mother and sister," said the
Princess pointing to two portraits above her writing desk.

" A lovely lady, it gives one pleasure to look at her; but your sister does not resemble either her father or her mother; it is sometimes the case that a child takes after some distant relative. The face of this young man seems familiar to me; I cannot recollect where I saw it."

" That is the Russian Emperor, Alexander, you did not know him."

" Indeed I knew him! why, I stood about twenty steps from him. He was a handsome man, here he is somewhat younger, but still I recognized him. He and the Emperor Joseph were excellent men."

The Princess motioned to the opposite wall, where hung a picture,— a life size figure of a man.

" The Emperor Joseph!" exclaimed Grandmother clasping her hands. " A perfect likeness! How you have them all together! I did not dream that I should see the Emperor Joseph to-day. God grant his soul eternal glory; he was a good man, especially to the poor. This dollar he gave me with his own hand," said Grandmother as she drew the silver dollar from her bosom.

The Princess was pleased with Grandmother's simple-heartedness and timely remarks; so she asked her to relate how the Emperor came to give her the dollar. Grandmother needed no coaxing and at once began to tell the story of her dollar. The Princess laughed heartily. When Grandmother took another look about the cabinet, she espied the portrait of King Frederic.

" Why, this is the King of Prussia!" she exclaimed. " I knew that ruler well, too. My late husband George served in the Prussian army, and I spent fifteen years in Silesia. Once he had George called out of the ranks to him, and made him presents. He liked tall men, and my George was the tallest man in the regiment and well grown, like a maiden. Little did I think that I should look down into his grave! a man like a rock, and he is gone long ago and I am still here." She sighed and wiped the tears from her wrinkled cheeks.

"Did your husband fall in battle?" asked the Princess.

"Not exactly, but he died from the effects of a wound received in battle. When that rebellion broke out in Poland, and the Prussian King with the Russians invaded the country, our regiment was with them. I followed the army with my children; we had two then, the third was born in the field. That is Johanna, who is now in Vienna; and I think that she is so courageous a girl, because from her birth she had to become accustomed to all sorts of hardships like a soldier. That was an unfortunate battle. After the first skirmish my husband was brought to me into the tent. A cannon ball had taken off his leg. They cut it off. I took all the care of him that was possible. As soon as he was a little better, he was sent back to Neisse. I was rejoiced. I hoped that when he got well they would not want him as a cripple, and that we could return to Bohemia. But my hopes were disappointed. He began to fail, and nothing could be done. I knew that he must die. What little money I had I gave for medicines and yet he was not helped. It seemed to me that I must lose my reason or that my heart must break from grief. But a person can endure much. I was left with three orphans, not a penny of money, and but little clothing. In that same regiment there was a certain Lehotsky, who was my husband's best friend. He took me up, and when I told him I could weave blankets, he got me a loom and set me up in the trade. May God reward him! What I had learned in my youth as a pastime now did me good service. My work sold well, so that I soon paid off my debt to Lehotsky, and supported myself and the children comfortably. Although there were very good people in that town, I was very lonesome, and from the time my husband died I felt as forsaken as a pear tree in a grain field.* I often thought I should be better off at home, and one day I broached the subject to Lehotsky. He discouraged the thought and assured me that I should certainly get a pension and that the King would care for my children. I was thankful, but finally decided to return home. The German language was a great obstacle to me. While we were at Glatz, I was better off, for there Bohemian was spoken more than German; but at Neisse, it was just the opposite, and I could not learn that language. Hardly had we made ourselves comfortable when the flood came. Water is a fearful element when it becomes angry; one can not escape it even on horseback.

" It came so suddenly that people barely escaped with their lives. I quickly picked up what I could, tied the bundle upon my back, took the youngest child in my arms, held the elder two by the hands, and so we fled, wading to our ankles in the water. Lehotsky came to our assistance, led us to the

* In Bohemia, one often sees a solitary pear tree in the field; so that the phrase "as lonely as a pear tree in a field" has become a common saying.

higher town, where good people received us kindly and gave us shelter.

"The report soon spread through the town that I had lost almost everything, and these good people at once came to my aid. The commander of the regiment sent for me, and told me that I should get several dollars a year and steady work; that the boy would be taken into a military school, and I could place the girls in the Royal Institute for Women. This did not comfort me at all, and I begged them, if they wished to show me some kindness, to give me a little money so that I could return to Bohemia. I said I would not part with my children, that I should bring them up in my faith and language. This they would by no means permit, and told me that if I did not remain there, I should get nothing. 'If nothing, then nothing,' thought I, 'God will not leave us to perish from hunger,' and so I thanked the King for all, and left."

"I think your children would have been well provided for," observed the Princess.

"Very likely, your Grace; but they would have become estranged. Who would have taught them to love their home and their mother tongue? Nobody. They would have learned a strange language, strange customs, and finally would have forgotten their own kin. How could I then justify myself before God? No, no, who is born of Bohemian blood, let him learn to speak the Bohemian tongue! I asked for permission to leave, picked up the little clothing I had left, took my children and bade farewell to the town where I had seen so many bitter, as well as happy days. The housekeeper loaded my children with as much food as they could carry and gave me several dollars for the journey. May God repay their children what good those people did to me! Poor Lehotsky went with us about six miles, carrying Johanna. He was sorry we were going away, for our house was always like a home to him. At parting we both wept. While he remained at Neisse, he went regularly to George's grave to pray a Pater-noster; they loved each other as brothers. He lost his life in the French war. God grant his soul eternal rest!"

"And how did you get to Bohemia with those children?" asked the Princess.

"We suffered much on the journey, gracious lady. Not knowing the way, we wasted much time wandering about to no purpose. Our feet were covered with bloody blisters, and often we cried from hunger, weariness and pain, when we could find no habitation. We got safe to Kladrau Hills, and there I felt quite at home. I came from Olesnic near the borders of Silesia, but I suppose your Grace doesn't know where that is. When I was near home, another burden began to weigh upon my heart. I wondered whether my parents were still living, and how they would receive me. When I left home they had given me a good outfit, and now I was returning with empty hands and bringing them three orphans. 'What will they say to me?' That question kept sounding in my ears. I feared, too, that some sad change might have taken place in the two years during which I had not heard from them."

"And did you never write to them, at least your husband, if not you?" wondered the Princess.

"The custom of sending letters is not common

among us. We think of each other, pray for each
other, and as we have opportunity, we send word
by some friend how each one is doing. A person
doesn't know where such a letter may go, and into
whose hands it may fall. My father used to write
letters to soldiers who went from our village and
were somewhere far beyond the boundaries, so that
their parents might find out whether they were
alive or not, or when they wanted to send them a
little money. But when they returned, they said
they never got anything, and so it is, your Grace;
when a letter comes from a person of the lower
classes, it is very apt to remain here or there."

"You are mistaken, my good woman," quickly
said the Princess, "every letter, let it come from
whom it will, must come into the hands of the
person to whom it is addressed. No one can keep
it or open it, there is a severe penalty for this."

"It is a proper thing, and I gladly believe it;
but after all, we prefer to confide in some good
friend. Upon such a bit of paper one cannot put
everything, and the reader would like to know this
and that, and there is nobody there to ask; but
when one of those good pilgrims or peddlers comes
along, he tells everything word for word. I, too,
should have heard more about my folks, but on
account of those disturbances, there was very little
travel.

"It was dark when we arrived in the village. It
was summer and I knew that at that hour they
would be at supper. We left the road and went
through the orchard so as not to be observed. The
dogs came out from our house and barked at us; I
called them but they only barked the louder. The

tears filled my eyes, my heart felt heavy,— for the moment I forgot that it was fifteen years since I had left home and that they were not the same dogs that we had then. In the orchard, I noticed many young trees, the fence was repaired, the barn had a new roof, but the pear tree under which George and I used to sit, had been touched by God's messenger (lightning) and its top was gone. At the cottage near by there was no change; it had been taken by father from the late Widow Novotny for an annuity. She was the woman that made those woolen blankets, and my husband was her son.

" There was a little garden near the cottage, for she always liked to have a bed of parsley, onions, some little corner of sweet balsams, sage, and such herbs as are needed in the household. George made her a fence of wicker work around the garden. That same fence was there still, but the ground had been neglected and allowed to run to grass; only a few onions were still seen. An old dog, half-blind, crawled out of his kennel. 'Old fellow, do you know me?' I said to him, and the brute began to rub himself about my feet. To be recognized and welcomed by this dumb animal touched me so that I burst into tears.

" The children, poor things! looked at me wondering why I wept. I had not told them that we were going to their grandmother's; for I thought that if my parents should be displeased with me, the children must not know it. Caspar, the oldest, asked: 'Why do you cry, mother? shan't we get a night's lodging here? Sit down and rest. We can wait; then I shall carry the bundle for you. We are not hungry.' Both Johanna and Theresa agreed with him, but I knew they were hungry, for we had gone several hours on our journey without coming upon any habitation.

"'No, my children, that is not why I am weeping,' I replied. 'We have reached our journey's end; here in this house your father was born, your mother in that one yonder. This is the home of your grandparents. Let us thank God for bringing us home safe, and pray that we may receive a fatherly welcome.' The prayer finished, we went to the cottage, for I remembered that my parents lived there, having given the homestead to my brother for an annuity. Upon the outside of the door was still pasted the picture that George had brought his mother from the Vamberitz shrine, — the Virgin with the fourteen helpers.* A burden fell from my heart as soon as I saw it. I thought: 'They blessed me when I left, and welcome me as I return;' and much comforted I entered the house with confidence.

"Father, mother, and old Betsey sat at the table eating soup out of one dish,— it was milk soup thickened with flour and egg. I remember it as if it were yesterday. 'Praised be Jesus Christ!' I said. 'For ever' was the reply. 'May I beg for a night's lodging for myself and these children? We come from far, we are tired and hungry,' I said, my voice trembling with emotion. They did not recognize me; it was somewhat dark in the room 'Lay down your baggage, and sit down by the table!' said father and laid aside his spoon. 'Betsey,' said mother, 'go cook some more soup. In the meantime, sit down, mother, take some bread

* Saints.

and give the children. Then we will take you to
sleep up in the garret. Where do you come
from?'

"'Clear from Silesia, from Niesse,' I replied.
'Indeed! That's where our Madaline is,' cried
father. 'I beg you, my good woman, didn't you
hear anything of her?' asked mother approaching
me closely, 'Madaline Novotny, her husband is a
soldier. She is our daughter, and we haven't heard
for two years what she is doing and how she is.
I've had bad dreams lately; not long ago I dreamed
that I lost a tooth; so I have that girl and her children on my mind constantly, and I wonder whether
something has not happened to George, since they
have those battles all the time. God only knows
why those men cannot let each other alone!'

"I wept, but the children hearing their grandmother speaking thus, pulled at my skirt and asked:
'Mamma, are these our grandmother and grandfather?' As soon as they said this mother recognized me and fell upon my neck, and father took
the children into his arms; and then we told each
other every thing that had happened. Betsey ran
to fetch brother and sister, sister-in-law and
brother-in-law, and before long the whole village
was together, and not only my relatives and old
friends, but everybody else welcomed me as though
I had been a sister to them all. 'You did well to
return home with those children,' said father; 'true,
the earth is the Lord's, but one's own country is
always dearest, as ours is to us, and thus it should be.
As long as God gives us bread, neither you nor your
children shall suffer, even if you cannot work.
That which befell you is indeed a heavy blow, but

lay it aside! Think: "Whom God loveth he chastiseth." '

"Thus I was again among them, and was as their own. My brother offered to let me have a room in his house, but I preferred to remain with my parents in the cottage where my husband had lived. The children soon were entirely at home, and my parents loved them dearly. I sent them regularly to school. When I was young, girls did not learn to write; it was thought enough if they could read a little, and that only the town girls. And yet it is a great pity and a sin when a person has the gift of the Holy Ghost and does not improve it. When, however, there is no opportunity, what is one to do? My husband was a man who knew the world, he knew how to write, too; in short, he was fit for a wagon or a carriage. And that is well; every-body might be so!

"I wove blankets as before and earned many a handsome groschen. Those were hard times — war, disease, and famine everywhere. A bushel of rye cost a hundred guilders in bank notes! that is something to say. But God loved us, and so in one way and another we managed to pull through. The distress was so great that people went about with money in their hands unable to buy My father was a man whose like is seldom found; he helped every-body where and how he could. When the neighbors were driven to the last extremity, they usually turned to him. Sometimes the poorer peasants came to him saying: 'Let us have a bushel of rye; we haven't a crust of bread in the house!' He would say: 'As long as I have, I give; when I have no more, others will do it,' and at once mother was sent to fill the bag. Money, however, he would not take, no, indeed! 'Why, we are neighbors, and if we do not help each other, who will help us? When God blesses your harvest, return the grain and we shall be even.' Thus it was that father had thousands of 'God repay you's!' And mother was the same. Why, she would have gone to the cross roads to look for a beggar, if none happened to come along. And why should we not help people! We had enough to eat, enough to wear; why should we not share the remainder with others? This is no merit, but merely a Christian duty. But when a person denies himself to help others, that is a real virtue. Indeed, it came to that pass that we ate only once a day, that others might have something, too. And we stood it until the sun shone again. Peace returned to the land, and times grew better and better.

" When Casper finished his schooling he wanted to learn weaving, and I did not object. A trade is a master. When his apprenticeship was finished, he went into the world. My husband used to say that a tradesman rolled out on the oven * wasn't worth a kreutzer.

" After several years he returned, settled at Dobrusitz, and is doing well. The girls I trained carefully to do housework. About this time, my cousin from Vienna came into the village; she took a liking to Theresa and said she would take her to Vienna and care for her. It was very hard for me to part from her, but I thought it would not be right for me to stand in the way of her good fortune. Dorothy is a good woman; they are well-

* Who never goes away from home.

to-do and have no children. She cared for Theresa as for her own child, and when she married gave her a good outfit. At first I was somewhat vexed that she chose a German, but now I do not mind it. John is a good and worthy man, and we manage to understand each other. And the children — they are mine. Johanna went to Dorothy in Theresa's place, and she, too, is well pleased with her home. This new generation is quite different from the last. I never wanted to go away from home, especially among strangers.

" After a few years my parents died only six weeks apart. They left the world quietly as a candle is blown out. God did not leave them to suffer, and they did not mourn for each other long; they had lived together for sixty years. Soft they made their bed, and softly they rest. God grant them eternal glory! "

" Were you not lonesome when all your children left you? " asked the Princess.

" Well, your Grace, blood is not water. At times I shed many tears, but I would not sully the children's happiness by complaining. Besides, I was not alone. Children continue to be born, and one can always find something to occupy one's mind. When I saw the neighbor's children growing up from childhood to maturity, it seemed as if they were my own. If we but have hearts that feel for others, we shall find that others love us, too. My children urged me to go to Vienna. I knew I should find good people there and that I would be well provided for; but it is a great distance, and travel is hard for one so old. Then suppose God should think of me; after all, I want my bones to rest among my old friends and relatives. But, your Grace, pardon my simplicity; I am talking as if I were at a spinning bee," said Grandmother rising from her seat.

" Not at all, my dear woman, your story is very interesting to me, and you cannot think how grate-- ful I am to you," said the Princess, laying her hand on Grandmother's shoulder. " Now come with me to breakfast. By this time, I suppose the children are hungry." So saying she led Grandmother out of the cabinet into the dining room, where coffee, chocolate, and various delicacies were awaiting them. The chamberlain stood there waiting to re- ceive orders; the Princess sent him to bring the Countess and the children.

In a few moments they came rushing in, exclaim- ing: " O Grandma! see what the Countess Hortense gave us!" Each tried to be the first to show the pretty gift he had received.

" How beautiful! In all my life I never saw anything like it; I hope you did not forget to thank her?"

The children nodded.

" I wonder what Manchinka will say when she sees this? and Cilka. and Vaclav?" said Grand- mother.

" Who are Manchinka and Cilka, and Vaclav?" asked the Princess.

" I can tell you that, dear Princess; the children told me," said the Countess. " Manchinka is the miller's daughter, and Cilka and Vaclav are the children of a certain organ grinder, and he has four besides. Barunka says they eat cats, squirrels, and crows, and all the people shun them."

"Why, because they are poor, or because they eat cats and squirrels?" asked the Princess.

"On account of the latter," replied Grandmother.

"Well squirrel is not bad food, I have tasted it myself," said the Princess.

"But, your Grace, there is a great difference between eating something as a delicacy and eating it out of necessity. The organ grinder himself is provided with a good stomach, the children as a matter of course need a great deal, and all must come out of that music. It is but natural,— they have little for the outside, little for the inside, and the house is as bare as the palm of the hand."

While this conversation was going on, the Princess took her seat at the table, Hortense placed the children on each side of herself, and Grandmother was obliged to sit down, too. The Countess wanted to pour her out some coffee or chocolate, but she said she did not drink coffee nor that other beverage.

"Then what do you have for breakfast?" asked the Princess.

"From my childhood, I have been accustomed to eat soup, mostly sour; in the mountains we like that the best. Sour soup and potatoes for breakfast, potatoes and sour soup for dinner, supper the same; Sundays we usually had, in addition to the soup and potatoes, a slice of oaten bread. This is the regular fare of people living in the Riesengebirge, and they are thankful when they have enough of it; for in hard times they are glad to get a little bran. Further in the interior, people have peas, whiter flour, cabbage, and sometimes a little meat; they live well! But the poor must not accustom themselves to dainties, else they would soon be at the end of their means. Besides, such things are not nourishing."

" There you are mistaken. Such victuals are very nourishing, and if those people could have a little meat each day and some good drink, they would gain more strength than all those other things put together could give them," replied the Princess.

" Well, well, one learns something new every day. I always imagined that the wealthy classes were so thin and pale because they lived on delicacies that were not nourishing."

The Princess smiled, but said nothing. She handed Grandmother a small glass of sweet wine saying as she did so: "Drink, good woman, drink, this will warm you and do you good."

Grandmother raised the glass, saying: " To your Grace's health!" and drank a little; she also took some pastry so her hostess should not be offended.

" What is that the Princess is eating out of those shells? " asked John in a whisper of Hortense.

" They are little creatures from the sea and are called oysters," was the reply.

" I don't think Cilka would eat them," added John.

" Various things are good for food, and there are various tastes," explained the Countess.

While they were thus talking, Barunka slipped something into Grandmother's pocket, whispering: " Hide it for me, Grandma; it's money. Miss Hortense gave it to me for Kuderna's children. I might lose it, you see."

The Princess overheard what Barunka said and her eye rested upon the Countess with inexpressible pleasure. Grandmother, too, was so pleased that she could not remain silent; so turning to the young lady, she said: " May God bless you, dear Countess!" Hortense blushed, and turning shook her finger at Barunka, whose face in turn became crimson.

" Won't they be delighted! Now they can clothe themselves."

" We will add something to it, so they can help themselves in other things, too," added the Princess.

" It would be an act of charity, if you could help these people, but not with alms," said Grandmother.

" How then? "

" As long as Kuderna behaves well, he should have steady work; I think that would be all the time, for he is both honest and willing. God reward you for all. But alms, your Grace, help such people only for a time. They buy various things, often what is unnecessary; and when those are eaten and worn out, they are as badly off as ever and dare not come to ask for more. But if Kuderna had some steady employment, he would be helped, and your Grace would be profited, if she gained a good laborer and a faithful servant. Besides, it would be doing an act of charity."

" You are right; but what employment could I give him,— a musician? "

" O your Grace, that is not difficult. He would be delighted to be a watchman either of your fields or forests. Besides, he could carry his organ with him, as he usually does, to cheer himself up. Oh, they are a merry crew!" added Grandmother.

" I shall see what can be done for him," said the Princess.

" O my dear, good Princess!" exclaimed Hor-

tense, as she arose to kiss the hand of the bene-
factress.

"Only the good are accompanied by angels,"
said Grandmother glancing at the lady and her ward.

The Princess was silent a moment, then said
deeply moved: "I shall never cease to thank God
for giving her to me." Then turning to Grandmother she said: "I should be pleased to have a
friend who would always tell me the truth in a
direct and sincere manner."

"O your Grace, should you desire it, such a
friend can readily be found; but it is not easy to
keep him."

"You think I would not value him?"

"Why should I think so? but that is the way it
usually is. Sometimes such frank conversation is
agreeable and then again it is not; and then that is
the end of friendship."

"You are right. But from this day you have
the privilege of saying to me, whatever you wish;
and should you have a petition, rest assured I shall
grant it, if only it be in my power." Saying this
the Princess rose from the table; the rest did the
same. Grandmother bent down to kiss the hand of
her hostess, but the latter would not allow it and
kissed Grandmother's cheek instead. The children
picked up their gifts, and with much reluctance
prepared to go home.

"Come to see us, too, Miss Hortense," said
Grandmother as she took Adelka from her arms.

"Yes, come," echoed the children. "We will
gather strawberries for you."

"I thank your Grace for all,— God be with
you," said Grandmother taking her leave.

"Depart with God!" said the Princess bowing. The Countess accompanied them to the door.

The chamberlain, coming to clear the table, elevated his eyebrows as if he would say: " A strange whim! Such a lady amuse herself with an old granny!"

The Princess, however, stood by the window watching the departing ones as long as the children's white frocks and Grandmother's dove-knot could be seen through the green foilage. Returning to her cabinet she whispered: "Happy woman!"

CHAPTER VII.

THE meadow belonging to the castle is covered with flowers; in the middle of the meadow is a knoll covered with a dense growth of wild thyme. In the wild thyme Adelka is sitting as in a bed; she is watching a lady-bug, which runs hither and thither over her lap, from her lap upon her leg, and from her leg upon her green boot. "Don't run away, little one; stay here, I won't harm you," says the child, picking up the bug and placing it back upon her lap.

Not far from Adelka, John and Willie are sitting by an ant hill watching the busy little creatures at their work. "Look, Willie! how they hurry about. And see! this one lost an egg, and this second one picked it up and is carrying it away into the hill."

"Wait, I have a piece of bread in my pocket; I will give them a crumb, to see what they'll do?" He took the bread from his pocket and placed it in their way. "Look! look! how they rush to it, and wonder where it came from. And see! they are pushing it further and further. Do you see the others coming from all directions? but how do the others know there is something here?"

Just then they were interrupted by a pleasant voice, which asked: "What are you doing here?"

It was the Countess Hortense riding upon a white pony; she had come close to them without being observed.

"I have a lady-bug," said Adelka, showing her closed hand to the Countess, who had dismounted and approached her.

"Let me see it?"

Adelka opened her hand, but it was empty. "Oh, my! it ran away," said the child frowning.

"Wait, it isn't gone yet," said the Countess; and she carefully picked up the lady-bug from the little girl's bare shoulder. "What will you do with it?"

"I will let it fly away. Now watch, how it will go!" Adelka placed the lady-bug upon her palm, raised her hand, and said: "Pinko linko, pinko linko, fly away into God's window."

"Go, go, not so slow!" added Willie, giving Adelka a slight stroke upon the hand.

At that instant the lady-bug raised its red-spotted cloak, spread out the delicate wings that had been folded under it, and flew away into the sky.

"Why did you push it?" scolded Adelka.

"So it should go the sooner," laughed the boy, and turning to Hortense, he took her by the hand saying: "Come, Miss Hortense, come to see the ants. I gave them a bit of bread, and there are swarms of them around it!"

The Countess put her hand into the pocket of her black plush jacket, and brought out a piece of sugar; handing it to Willie she said: "Place this in the grass and you will see how, in an instant, they will surround it. They like sweet things."

Willie obeyed, and when he saw how in a very short time the ants, running from all sides, surrounded the sugar, carrying away the tiniest bits, he was greatly surprised and asked the Countess: "Tell me, Miss Hortense, how do these ants know there is something good here, and what are they doing with those eggs that they carry in and out of the hill all the time?"

"The eggs are their children, and those that carry them are the guardians and nurses. When the day is warm they carry them out of their dark chambers into the sunshine, so that they may be warmed up and grow better."

"And where are their mammas?" asked Adelka.

"They are in the house, laying eggs, so that the ants shall not die out. The fathers walk about them, talk with them, and cheer them up, to keep them from being lonesome; and the other ants, that you see running about, are the workers."

"And what do they do?" asked John.

"They gather food, build and repair the house, take care of the pupas,—the growing children,—and keep the house clean; when one of their number dies, they carry him away; they stand guard, that no enemy may come upon them unawares, and fight to protect the colony. All this is done by the workers."

"How do they understand each other when they cannot speak?"

"Although they have not such a language as people use, still they understand each other. Did you not observe how the first one that found the sugar at once went and told the others, and how they came running from all directions? See how when they meet they touch one another with their feelers, as if they said a few words in passing; and groups of them are standing in various places as if they were discussing something."

"In those hills, have they parlors and kitchens?" asked Adelka.

" They do not need kitchens, for they do not cook; but they have chambers for the children and the mothers, halls for the workers, and their houses have several stories, with passages from one story to another in the inside of the hill."

" How do they know how to build it so it will not break down?" asked Willie.

" Indeed, they build well, and when no stronger power breaks down their house it lasts as long as they need it. They make the walls and rafters out of tiny chips, straws, dry leaves, grass and earth. They dampen the earth in their mouths, knead it, and use it as masons do bricks. They like best to build when the mist is falling, for then the ground is just damp enough for their use."

" Who taught these creatures all this?" again asked the little boy.

" God gives these creatures something that we call instinct, by which they know what to do without being taught. Some show so much skill and wisdom in the management of their households and providing for their wants, that it seems like human reason. When you go to school and learn how to use books, you will learn all such things as I have learned them," added the Countess.

While they were thus talking, Grandmother and Barunka came, bringing their aprons full of flowers and their arms full of herbs that they had gathered in the meadow. The children began to tell what they had learned about the ants, and the Countess asked what they were going to do with all those herbs.

" This, dear Countess, is some caraway and some agrimony. The caraway is dried, the seeds used in cooking and in bread, and the straw for the children's bath; the agrimony is very useful as a gargle for sore throat. The neighbors know I always have on hand some of these medicinal herbs, so they send to me when they need them. It is well to have something of this kind in the house, for if one does not need it oneself, it may be of use to others."

" Is there no apothecary in the village?" asked the Countess.

" Not in the village, but in the town, an hour's journey from the village. But suppose it were in the village! A Latin kitchen is an expensive kitchen, and why should we pay dearly for what we can make ourselves?"

" I suppose the physician gives you a recipe how you are to prepare the medicine?"

" No, indeed! What would a person come to, if he called in a physician for every little illness! He lives an hour's journey from here, and it would be about half a day before he would come after he was called; in the meantime the patient might die, if there were no domestic remedies. And when he comes, what a fuss! Several kinds of medicines, plasters, leeches, and what not? The family become almost distracted, and the patient is sure to become worse from fright. I do not believe in doctors; my herbs have always proved sufficient for me and the children. Still, when others are ill, I say, ' send for the doctor.' But when God visits one with heavy illness, the doctors themselves know not what to do, but leave nature to take her course. And after all, God is the best physician; if one is to live, he will get well without the aid of the doctors, and if he is to die, the whole apothecry shop cannot save him."

" Are all those in your apron medicinal herb'?" asked the Countess."

"Oh, no, Miss Hortense," replied Barunka quickly; "these in our aprons are flowers for garlnds. Tomorrow is Corpus Christi, and Manchinka and I are to march in the procession and carry garlards."

" And I, too, I am going with Hela," added Adelka.

" And we are to be little peasants! " exclaimed the boys.

" Who is Hela?" asked the Countess.

" Hela is from town; she is the daughter of my godmother, who lives in that big house that has the lion on it."

" You should say from the hotel," explained Grandmother.

" Miss Hortense, will you go to the procession, too? " asked Barunka.

" Certainly," replied the young lady, as she seated herself in the grass and began to help sort the flowers.

" Did you ever carry garlands on Corpus Christi?" further asked Barunka.

" No; but while I lived in Florence I once carried a garland upon a festival of the Madonna."

" Who is the Madonna?"

" Madonna is what they call the Virgin in Italy."

" Miss Hortense then comes from Italy? Is it where our soldiers are now quartered?" asked Grandmother.

" Yes; but not in Florence, the city I come

from. That is the place where they make those beautiful hats from rice straw. There rice and corn grow, and sweet chestnuts and olives are found in the woods. One can see groves of cypress and laurel, beautiful flowers, and a blue, unclouded sky."

"Oh, I know!" exclaimed Barunka, "that is the city you have painted in your room, is it not, Miss Hortense? In the middle is a wide river, and above the river, on a high hill, is built the city. O Grandma, such beautiful houses and churches! On one side are so many small houses and gardens; by one of those houses a little girl is playing; by her side sits an old lady,— they are Miss Hortense and her nurse; isn't it so? You told us that while we were at the castle," asked Barunka turning to the Countess.

The Countess did not reply at once; she was buried in deep thought and her hands lay motionless upon her lap. At last she said with a deep sigh: "Oh bella patria! Oh cara amica!" and her eyes filled with tears.

"What did you say, Miss Hortense?" asked the inquisitive Adelka, lovingly leaning to the young lady.

Hortense bent her head upon the head of the child, and did not try to restrain the tears that fell down her cheeks into her lap.

"Miss Hortense thinks of her home and her relatives, said Grandmother; you children do not know what it is to leave the home of your childhood. However one may· prosper elsewhere one can never forget it. You, too, will sometime learn to understand this. Has your Ladyship any relatives in Florence?"

"None; I have no relatives that I know of in the whole world," replied the Countess sadly. "Giovanna, my good nurse, still lives in Italy, and at times I feel very lonely and long to see her and my old home. But the Princess, my second mother, has promised to take me there soon."

"How did the Princess come to know you, when you lived so far away?"

"She and my mother were good friends, having known each other for many years. My father was wounded at the battle of Leipsic, and returned to his villa in Florence, where in a few years he died from the effects of his injury. This I learned from Giovanna. My mother grieved so much that she, too, died and left me, a poor little orphan, all alone in the world. When the Princess heard of it, she came to Florence and would have taken me with her, but for my nurse who loved me dearly. So she left me with her and placed the villa and all within it in her charge. My nurse brought me up, being both a mother and teacher to me.

"When I was grown up the Princess took me to herself. Oh, I love her dearly, as I should have loved my own mother."

"Yes, and the Princess loves you as her own child, too," said Grandmother; "I saw it when I was at the castle, and it made me think very highly of her. This reminds me of the Kudernas. When Barunka gave them that money from you, they almost jumped to the ceiling with joy; but when the father heard that he was selected to be watchman of your fields, his amazement and delight were too great to be expressed. As long as they

live they will not forget to pray for you and for
her Grace, the Princess."

"For all that, they have no one to thank but
you, Grandma, and your good word," said the
Countess.

"Yes, but what would it have profited if that
good word had not fallen upon good ground? no
blessing could have come from it," replied Grandmother.

The bouquets arranged, Grandmother and the
children were ready to start for home.

"I'll go with you to the cross-road," said the
Countess, taking her pony by the bridle. "If you
wish, boys, you may have a short ride."

The boys gave a shout of delight, and in an
instant John was upon the saddle.

"O, that's a madcap!" said Grandmother seeing
how boldly he acted. Willie, too, acted as though
he were not afraid, but when the Countess helped
him to mount, he turned red clear to his ears, and
only when John laughed at him did he become
more courageous. Little Adelka, too, was seated
upon the pony, but the Countess walked by her
side and held her. The children were delighted,
but the boys laughed at her, said she sat up there
like a midget, like a little monkey, and made fun
of her until Grandmother ordered them to be
still.

At the cross-roads the Countess herself mounted
her white pony, dropped her blue skirt down over
the stirrups, fastened her black hat, and once more
bowing to Grandmother and the children rode
away. As soon as her pony heard the order
"Avanti!" he flew with her through the rows of

trees like a sparrow.   Grandmother and the children slowly wended their way to The Old Bleachery.

The next day was beautiful, the sky was as
clear as if it had been swept.   Before the house
stood a carriage; in the carriage were John and
Willie in white trousers and red jackets, and holding garlands in their hands.   Mr. Proshek stood
admiring the fine horses, patting their shining hips,
or playing with their luxuriant manes, and with a
practiced eye studying their harness.   From time
to time he stepped toward the house, calling into
the window: " Are you not ready yet?   Do hurry
up!"

" In a minute, father, in a minute!" voices from
the inside reply; but that "minute" proves to be a
long while.   Finally Grandmother sallies out with
the little girls, among whom is Manchinka.   They
are followed by Mrs. Proshek, Betsey, and Vorsa.
" Take good care of everything and don't neglect
the poultry," said Grandmother as she was starting.

Sultan wanted to play with Adelka; he smelled
her garland, but she raised it above her head, while
Grandmother drove him away, saying: " You foolish fellow, don't you see Adelka cannot play with
you to-day?"

" They look like angels," said Betsey to Vorsa,
as the girls were getting into the carriage.

Mr. Proshek mounted to the box beside the
coachman, gathered up the reins, and made a
peculiar smacking noise with his lips; upon which
the horses raised their heads proudly, and the carriage rattled off to the mill as if carried by the
wind.   The dogs started to follow, but when the
master shook his whip at them, they turned back to

the house, stretched themselves in the sun at the door, and soon began to snore.

How beautiful it is in the city! The houses are decorated with greens, the streets are covered with rushes, and the oval-shaped common is like a grove. Along the sides of the common altars are set up, each more beautiful than the last. In the middle, where stands the statue of St. John under the green lindens, is a mortar, around which are gathered a group of boys and young men.

"They are going to shoot from that," said Mr. Proshek to the children.

"Oh, I shall be afraid!" exclaimed Adelka.

"Why should you be afraid, it won't make any more noise than when a pot falls from the shelf," said Manchinka to reassure the little girl.

Such sounds Adelka was accustomed to hear at home, so she was satisfied.

The carriage stopped at a large house, upon which hung a shield with a white lion and a large bunch of grapes.

The party were met at the door by Mr. Stanicky, who, raising his plush cap decorated with a long tassel, welcomed them warmly. Mrs. Stanicky, in her silver embroidered cap and short silk basque, smiled graciously upon the comers, and when little Hela tried to hide behind her, she took her by the hand, and seizing Adelka with the other placed them side by side, saying: "Come, show yourself, that we may see how you will look together!"

"Like twins," decided Grandmother. The little girls cast sidelong glances at each other, but again bashfully hung their heads.

Mr. Stanicky gave his arm to Mr. Proshek, and

entering the house urged the rest to follow. " Before the procession begins we can have a chat over a glass of wine," he said cheerily.

Mrs. Proshek went, but Grandmother remained outside with the children. She said: " You have time enough, since you go with the nobility, but if I wait, the church will be so crowded that I never can get in. I shall stay here with the children." She remained standing by the door.

In a few moments two little boys with red jackets were seen turning the corner, then two more, and John cried out: " They are coming!"

" Adelka, and you, Hela, when you march in the procession, look well before you, so you do not stumble over something and fall, and you, Barunka, keep an eye on them. You, boys, behave well, lest an accident happen with the lights! When you are in the church at the altar, pray earnestly so that God will be pleased with you and bless you!"

While Grandmother was thus admonishing the children the schoolmaster came up with his pupils.

" Good morning, sir; I bring you an addition to your party. I hope you will have patience with these little ones."

" They are welcome, Grandma," replied the old schoolmaster smiling; " you see I have them here hit and miss, some large, some small," and while speaking he found places for the children in the procession.

When they reached the church, the children took their places near the altar, but Grandmother remained near the door with some neighbors. The last bell rang and the people hurried into the church from all directions. The sexton gave the boys that represented farmers lighted candles to hold, the small bell rang, the priest stepped to the altar, the mass began. The little girls folded their hands, fixed their eyes upon the altar and for a while prayed devotedly; but finally they grew tired, their eyes wandered about in all directions, and soon they discovered the pleasant face of the Countess who was seated above in the oratorium. But behind her sat Mr. and Mrs. Proshek, and he gave them a severe look to make them turn again to the altar. Adelka, however, did not understand it, and so looked up and smiled until Barunka pulled her dress, whispering: "keep your eyes upon the altar."

The benediction was over. The priest took the holy eucharist into his hands, and the people began to sing: "Lamb of God, Christ, have mercy upon us!" their voices mingling in a grand chorus with the chimes of the bells.

The children headed the procession, the little peasants with burning candles, and the girls with garlands and bouquets of flowers, which they scattered about as they went. Behind them came the priests, the elders of the city, the dignitaries of the whole realm; then the common citizens of the town; and lastly the country folk, among whom was Grandmother. Flags of various kinds flew over their heads, the perfume of incense mingled with the perfume of flowers, and the occasion was made more impressive by the ringing of the bells. Those who could not join the procession stood at the doors and windows to see it. And what a feast for the eyes! What costumes, what elegance! Here gaily dressed children, there the rich robes of the clergy; here a gentleman with a blue cloak, there a frugal peasant with one at least fifty years old; here a stalwart youth with an embroidered jacket, there the father with a cloak touching his heels; ladies, simply but elegantly dressed, standing beside those covered with jewels and tawdry finery.

There stood women of the town in caps of lace or of silver and gold embroidery; the farmers' wives in stiffly starched cambric caps or in white head shawls; girls with red kerchiefs or bare heads, their hair held back by beautiful fillets.

As every one knew by the sign that Mr. Stanicky's house was a hotel, so the dress of the people was an index to their minds and often to their occupations? The capitalist could readily be recognized from the tradesman or from the public officers; the farmer, from the day laborer; and from the dress one could see who still adhered to the " good old ways," or, as Grandmother said, followed the world and its new fangled notions.

Grandmother tried to be as near as possible to the children, so that if anything happened, she would be on hand. All, however, went off well, only Adelka jumped and put her hands to her ears whenever a shot was fired.

After the celebration, they went to the hotel where the carriage was waiting. Christina came with them from the church and Grandmother asked her to ride with them, since Mr. and Mrs. Proshek were to stay to dinner.

" I should like to ride with you, but I want to go with the girls," replied Christina, as she cast a glance upon a group of young men who were standing in the churchyard, waiting to accompany the girls home.

There was one among them with a handsome face and an honest look and a form tall and straight as a poplar tree. His eyes seemed to be searching for some one in the crowd, and when they accidentally met those of Christina, both he and the girl turned crimson.

Grandmother and the children went home with Hela, and Mrs. Stanicky made them stay to take some refreshments. Grandmother took a glass of wine out to Christina, who would not enter the barroom, because there were so many men there; but before she could give it to her, the tall youth entered the bar-room, ordered a glass of wine, and stood with it by Christina.

As it was considered proper for a girl to be very bashful on such occasions, she refused to take it, until tired of coaxing he said in an injured tone: " So you won't take this from me ? " At this point she took the tiny goblet and drank to his health. Then both took a sip from Grandmother's glass, as she said : " You came just in the nick of time, Jacob, I was thinking which one of those young men I could ask to go with us. I am afraid to ride with those wild horses, when Mr. Proshek or some one else that is trustworthy is not along; for Wenzel is so careless. Can you come ? "

" Most willingly," replied Jacob as he turned to the bar to pay for the wine.

The children bade Hela good-bye, took leave of their parents and Mr. and Mrs. Stanicky, and got into the carriage; Christina got in with them, Milo sprang upon the box next to the coachman, and off they drove.

" See what airs Jacob Milo puts on!" said

the young men on the walk as the carriage rolled by.

" Yes, indeed, haven't I cause! " he replied as he cast a glance into the carriage.   One of the young men who had thus spoken and who was his best friend waved his cap and hummed,

> " Love, God's own love,
>   Where is it found?
> On the trees it grows not
>   Nor yet on the ground."

The last was not heard on account of the rumbling of the carriage.

" I wonder if you prayed, boys? " asked Grandmother.

" I prayed, but I don't believe Willie did," said John.

" Don't you believe him, Grandma, I said the Lord's prayer over and over again, but John pushed me and wouldn't let me alone in the procession," said Willie.

" Johnny, Jonnny, you Godless child! This year I must complain of you to St. Nicholas," said Grandmother very severely.

" And you won't get anything, wait!" said Adelka.

" What kind of presents do *you* get, Christina? " asked Barunka.

" None; it is not the custom among us to give presents.   Once, however, I got a wish from a certain tutor who gave lessons at the steward's in the castle.   I have it here in my prayer book." As she said this she took out a piece of folded paper, upon which was a wish in verse; around the verse was painted a wreath of roses with forget-me-nots pricked in the paper. "I kept it on account of the wreath; for I don't understand the wish at all."

"Isn't it Bohemian?" asked Grandmother.

"It is Bohemian, but so learned; hear how it begins: 'Hear me, dearest lady ward!' Now, I don't know what he means, and he goes on in this way through the whole wish. I am not a ward, for thank God, I still have my mother; I believe that man's books turned his head so that he himself did not understand what he wrote."

"You must not think so, dear girl. That was a man of great wisdom, well versed in learning; such an one's reason cannot come down to ours. While I lived at Kladrau, near us dwelt just such a literary master; his housekeeper,— they say all such men abjure marriage,— used to come to our house quite often and tell us what a grumbling fellow he was. The whole day long he was buried in his books like a mole; if Susannah had not said: 'Master, dinner's ready,' he would not have thought of eating. Susannah had to remind him of everything; but for her the moths would have eaten him up. Every day he spent an hour out walking, but all alone, for he did not like company. As soon as he went out I used to run over to see Susannah; she was fond of sweet mixed drinks, and although I never liked that burning stuff, I had to drink a small goblet with her. She used to say: 'My master must not see it, for he drinks only water, unless he puts in a few drops of wine. He says to me: "Susannah, water of all drinks is the most healthful; always drink water, and you will be well and happy."' And I

think: " All right; but sweet whiskey agrees better
with me." He would want me to live like a bird.
Eating and drinking are nothing to him, except to
keep a person alive. His food is his books; no
such fare for me, thank you.'

" Thus Susannah would go on. Once she took
me into his parlor. In all my life I never saw so
many books; they were piled up like firewood.
'Just see, Madaline, my master has all that in his
head; I often wonder it has not made him
crazy. It's like this, if it were not for me, he
would die of hunger like a child. I must see to
everything, for he doesn't understand anything
except his books. One needs great patience to get
along with him. But, at times, even my patience
is exhausted, and when I speak out he goes as if a
dog had bitten him, and doesn't say a word, till at
last I feel sorry for him. At times, however, a
good scolding is necessary. Madaline, you won't
believe it, but his room was as full of dust as the
middle of the common, and the cobwebs were as
thick as in an old belfry; and do you suppose I
could come in with the duster? No, indeed! I
thought to myself: " I'll out-wit you yet." It was all
the same to him, but my reputation was at stake; it
was a disgrace to me, when people came and found
him living in such disorder. I begged one of his
friends, whom he especially liked, to keep him a
long time when next he came to see him, and
while he was gone I gave his room a good cleaning
and dusting. And would you believe it, Madaline?
that man did not know it had been cleaned until the
third day, when he remarked that somehow there
seemed to be more light in the room. More light

indeed! As if there shouldn't be more light! Thus one must know how to manage these book-worms.

"Whenever we met she had some new complaint against her master, but for the whole world she would not have left him. Once he caused her a great deal of anxiety. While he was out walking he met a friend who was on his way to the Riesengebirge mountains. He asked her master to accompany him, saying that they would return soon, and he started just as he was. Susannah waited and waited, but the master didn't come; the night approached, he was nowhere to be seen. She came to our house frightened, crying, and we had all we could do to quiet her. The next morning she found out how he went away; then she scolded and carried on at a terrible rate. He came back about the sixth day, and she had been getting dinner and supper for him all that time. When he returned she came over to our house saying: 'When I began to scold him he only said: "Well, well, don't make such a fuss! I went out for a walk and thought I'd stop to see the Snow Cap, so I could not return immediately."'

"Once she brought us several books, saying that her master had written them, and asked us to read them. My husband was a good reader, so he read, but did not understand them at all; he also knew how to make verses, but we did not understand those either,— it was all too learned. Susannah, however, said: 'Well, that pays, to rack his brains over what nobody can understand!' But the people of the town spoke very highly of him some declaring that his wisdom was beyond comprehension."

"I am like that Susannah," said Christina, I care nothing for his learning, when I do not understand it. When I hear a pretty song or one of your stories, Grandma, I enjoy it more than the most learned discussion. But have you heard that new song that Barla made at Red Hura?"

"My dear girl, those worldly songs do not interest me any more. I pay little attention to them. Those days when I would have gone a long distance for a new song are past; now I sing only my hymns," replied Grandmother.

"What kind of a song is it?" asked Manchinka.

"If you like I'll teach you to sing it; it begins:

> "What does that birdie say
> On the oak, who sings all day?"

"Christinka, you must sing it over for me, when I come to your house to-day," said Milo, turning to the company in the carriage.

"With the greatest pleasure," she replied, and continued: "We were raking hay on our master's fields. Barla came then, too, and while we were resting on the hillside, Anna Ticanek said: 'Barla make us a song!' Barla thought a while, smiled, and began to sing:

> 'What does that birdie say
> On the oak, who sings all day?
> Little birdie sings so gay,
> "Maids in love are pale alway."'

Anna, however, was somewhat offended, for she thought the song was about herself; you know she and Tomesh are engaged. But just as soon as Barla noticed it, in the twinkling of an eye he made another verse:

'Hush, birdie, hush! thou liest,
'Tis false what thou hast said;
I, too, a lover have,
And yet my cheeks are red.'

We liked the song very much, and the tune was good, too. The girls of Zernov will wonder; they have not heard it yet," added Christina.

Manchinka and Barunka were humming the new song, and just then they rode past the castle. Before the gate stood the youngest chamberlain dressed in black, a fellow not tall and of a sallow complexion. With one hand he smoothed his black whiskers; the other was hung by the thumb in his gold watch-chain, in such a manner as to display all the rings that shone upon his fingers.

When the carriage drove by, his eyes gleamed like a tomcat's watching a sparrow; he smiled graciously upon Christina and waved his hand. The women barely looked at him, and Milo, with much reluctance, slightly raised his otter cap.

"Really, I should prefer to meet Satan himself than that Italian," said Christina. "Now he is again on the lookout for game, and should a few girls come along alone, he would fly among them like a hawk."

"Well, not long ago he got a dressing at Zlitz," began Wenzel; "he came there to the dance, and at once took possession of some of the prettiest girls, as if they had been brought there expressly for him, and the fellow doesn't even know how to speak Bohemian. Still he readily learned to say: 'Pretty girls, I like.'

"Yes, and when he comes to our house he repeats it to me constantly," said Christina; "even if I say ten times over: ' I you *don't* like,' he sticks like the ague."

" The boys dusted his jacket well, and if it were not for me, he would have fared still worse," added Wenzel.

" Let him look out, or else he'll find out what's what somewhere else!" said Milo, making a threatening gesture with his head.

The carriage stopped at the inn. " Many thanks for the ride," said Christina as Milo helped her from the carriage.

" A word more," said Grandmother; " do you know when the Zernov people are going on the pilgrimage to Svatonovitz?"

" I suppose the same time as usual; the first festival to the Virgin following St. John. I am going, too."

" And I, too, that's why I asked," added Grandmother

" This year I'm going with you," said Barunka.

" And I, too," exclaimed Manchinka.

The rest of the children declared they would not remain at home when everybody else went, but Barunka settled that question by telling them they could not walk twelve miles. Wenzel now touched the horses with his whip, and they went to the mill, where Manckinka was left and also several garlands which Grandmother had had blessed in church for the miller's wife.

As they were approaching home, the dogs, Sultan and Tyrol, came running to meet them; they could hardly contain themselves for joy, when they saw their mistress home again. Grandmother thanked God that they were home safe, for she preferred a thousand times to walk than ride; for while those horses went at such a galloping rate she expected every moment that the carriage would capsize and some one would get his neck broken.

Betsey and Vorsa were waiting at the door. " Well, Wenzel, where is your wreath? " asked the talkative Betsey, when Grandmother and the children entered the house.

" O my girl, I have forgotten where I lost it," said Wenzel with a wicked grin, as he turned the carriage toward the road.

" Don't speak with him," said Vorsa; you know he doesn't see into his mouth,* even on the Lord's festival? "

Wenzel, still laughing, struck the horses and in an instant was out of sight. Grandmother hung the fresh wreaths between the double windows and around the pictures, and threw those of last year into " God's fire."

*A common saying meaning that he doesn't perceive how bad his language sounds to others.

CHAPTER VIII.

TO-DAY Grandmother's room is like a garden; wherever a person turns everything is full of roses, mignonette, cherry blossoms, and other flowers; among the rest is a whole armful of oak leaves. Barunka and Manchinka are making bouquets, and Celia is weaving a large garland. On the bench by the stove sit Adelka and the boys, reciting the congratulation.

It is the eve of St. John's, and to-morrow will be father's name's day,* a great day for the family. Mr. Proshek had invited several of his dearest friends to dinner; that always was his custom. That is why there is such a commotion in the house; Vorsa has been scrubbing and cleaning from early morning; Betsey is scalding and cleaning the poultry; Mrs. Proshek bakes kolaches; and Grandmother sees now to the baking, now to the poultry, in fact, is wanted everywhere. Barunka begs her to call John out, because he won't let them alone, and when he is out Betsy and Vorsa complain that he is in their way. Willie wants her to listen to his story, and Adelka pulls at her apron, begging for a kolach, and in the yard the chickens are impatient for their supper.

" For pity's sake, I cannot attend to everything at once? " exclaimed the poor, distracted old lady.

---

* In Bohemia (and in most Catholic countries) one's name's day is celebrated instead of one's birthday. Thus the day of St. John is celebrated by all the Johns named after him.

And now Vorsa gives the alarm: " Mr. Proshek is coming!" There is a rush to hide what must yet remain a secret; Mrs. Proshek locks up the sweet-meats, and Grandmother gives strict orders to the children not to tell anything.

The father enters the yard, and the children run to meet him; but when he says good evening and asks them about their mother, they are embarrassed, fearing to speak, lest they should divulge some secret. But Adelka, who is " Papa's pet," goes to him, and when he takes her up in his arms, she whispers: " Mamma and Grandma are baking kolaches; it will be your name's day to-morrow."

" Wait, won't you catch it for telling? " exclaim the boys as they turn to tell their mother.

Adelka turns red; for a few moments she sits frightened and finally begins to cry.

" Well, don't cry, dear," says the father, sooth-ingly; " I knew it would be my name's day to-morrow, and that mother is baking kolaches."

Adelka wipes away her tears with her sleeve; still she looks with some fear at her mother, who is coming with the boys. She, however, makes everything all right, and the boys find out that Adelka has told nothing that she ought not to tell. But the secret is too much for the children, so that the father hearing does not hear, and seeing does not see. At supper, Barunka must constantly wink at them, and push them for fear they will tell all, and Betsey afterwards calls them " tell-tales."

Finally the work is finished, and everything is in readiness for the morrow; even the smell of the baking is gone. The servants have gone to sleep, and only Grandmother's footstep is heard in the house. She shuts up the cats, puts out the last spark in the stove, and recollecting that there has been fire in the bake-oven outside, and that a spark may have remained there, decides that she had better go out and see.

Sultan and Tyrol sit on the foot-bridge. When they see Grandmother they look up surprised, for she is not accustomed to be out at that hour; but as soon as she pats them on their heads, they begin to rub themselves against her. "I suppose you've been watching for mice, you watermen? This you may do; but don't you meddle with my poultry!" She goes up the hill to the oven, the dogs following close behind her. She opens the oven, pokes among the ashes, but seeing not a single spark shuts it again, and returns homeward. By the foot-bridge is a large oak, whose branches make a convenient roost for some poultry. Grandmother looks up into the branches, hears gentle sighs, low twittering, and peeping. "They are dreaming of something," she says and goes further. What has delayed her by the garden? Does she hear the pleasant warbling of two nightingales in the garden shrubbery, or Victorka's sorrowful and broken melody that resounds from the dam? Or has she turned her eyes to the hill where multitudes of fire-flies are shining like so many twinkling stars? Below the hill over the meadow are hovering clouds like waves of gossamer. The people say they are not clouds, and perhaps she, too, believes that in those transparent silvery gray veils are enrobed the forest women, and is now watching their wild dance by the light of the moon. No, neither this nor that; she is looking toward the meadow that leads to the mill.

From the village inn, across the creek, Grandmother saw a woman running, her shoulders covered with a white wrap. Now she stands and listens, like a fawn that has run out into the open meadow to feed awhile. All is quiet except the song of the nightingale, the rumbling of the mill, the murmuring of the waves under the dark alder bushes. She binds the white wrap upon her right arm and gathers nine different kinds of flowers. Having her bouquet ready, she bends, washes her face with the fresh dew, and turning neither to the right nor to the left, hastens back to the inn. " It is Christina! she is going to make St. John's wreath; I thought she was fond of that youth," said Grandmother, never turning her eyes from the girl. She is now out of sight, and Grandmother remains standing buried in a deep revery.

She sees before herself a meadow, a mountain village, above her the moon and glittering stars; they are the same stars, the same moon, ever young, never changing, and eternally beautiful. She, too, was young when on that St. John's eve she made that fatal wreath of nine kinds of flowers. Grandmother remembers as if it were now, how afraid she was lest some one should meet her and spoil her charm. She sees herself in her chamber, she sees her bed covered with the flowers, she remembers how she placed the wreath under her pillow, how fervently she prayed that God would send her a dream in which she should see him whom her soul had chosen. Her confidence in the fatal wreath was not misplaced; she saw in her dream a tall man of bright, candid expression, whose equal, in her eyes, was not to be found in the whole world. She now smiles at the childish faith with which she went before sunrise to the apple tree, over which she threw the wreath backwards, in order to find out by the distance it fell beyond the tree whether George would return soon or late. She remembers how the rising sun found her in the orchard weeping bitterly because the wreath fell far beyond the apple tree, by which she knew that it would be a long time before she should see George again.

Thus, buried in deep thought, Grandmother stands a long time. Unconsciously she clasps her hands, turns her calm, earnest gaze to the stars, and softly murmurs: "How long, George, how long?" A gentle breeze fans her pale cheek. Are not those the kisses of the departed loved one? She trembles, signs herself with the cross, the tears fill her eyes and fall upon her clasped hands. For some moments she stands in silent meditation, then turns and quietly enters the house.

In the forenoon of the next day, the children stood at the window watching for their parents, who were in town, at church. The father paid for a mass that day, and Grandmother ordered prayers to be said for all the Johns of the family, beginning back several generations. The beautiful wreath, the congratulations, the gifts, — all were ready waiting for the father. Barunka heard one, then another recite his congratulation, but they made so many mistakes that she had them do it all over again. Grandmother's hands were full; still she found time to glance into the sitting room now and then with the admonition: "Be good, don't cut up," and then went about her work again.

Grandmother was going into the garden to cut some parsley, when she saw Christina coming carrying something tied up in a handkerchief. "Good morning, Grandma!" she said with a countenance so bright and happy that Grandmother gazed on her for a moment without speaking.

"Why, child, you look as if you had slept on roses," said Grandmother smiling.

"You have guessed right; my pillowcases are covered with flowers," replied Christina.

"Oh, I see, you do not wish to understand; but no matter, let it be as it will, if only it be well. Is not that so, my dear girl?"

"Yes, yes, Grandma," said Christina, blushing.

"What have you there?"

"A present for John; he liked our doves, so I'm bringing him a pair of young ones, he can raise them."

"Why did you do it? he did not need them."

"Never mind, Grandma; I like children, and children find much pleasure in such things; then why should he not have them? But it seems to me that I did not tell you what happened at our house day before yesterday."

"Yesterday, our house was like the bridge at Prague. * I recollect that you wanted to tell me something about the Italian, but we were too busy to talk. Tell me now, but leave a word out of

* In olden days there was but one bridge in Prague, and as there was a great deal of travel on it, the saying, "Like the bridge of Prague," became proverbial.

each sentence, for I expect our folks home every minute," said Grandmother.

"Now think: that sneak, that Italian came to our house every day to drink his beer. There was no harm in that, for a public house is for everybody. But instead of sitting at the table like a respectable fellow, he rummaged the whole yard like an old broom, and even went into the cow stable; in short, wherever I turned he was at my heels. Father scowled, but you know him; he is good-natured, couldn't harm a chicken, and besides he doesn't like to drive away his customers, especially those from the castle. He thought I was equal to the occasion, so did not interfere. I made short work of the Italian several times, but he acted as though I had said the most loving things to him, and yet I know he understands Bohemian, if he does not speak it. He kept saying constantly: 'Pretty girls I like,' clasped his hands, and even knelt down before me."

"The wretch!" exclaimed Grandmother.

"O, you know, Grandma, that class of men jabber no end of moonshine; it makes one's ears ache to listen to it. What would a person come to if he should believe it? Such nonsense finds no place in my head; but that Italian tired me out. Towards evening we were out in the meadow raking hay, when by chance Milo happened to come along (Grandmother smiled at that "by chance"); we spoke of various matters, and I told him what a nuisance that Italian had become to me. 'Just let him alone, I shall see that he troubles you no more,' said Milo. 'But don't you do anything to offend

my father,' I said, 'for I know you Zernov boys;
when you get started, the deuce himself is to pay.'
In the evening that blessed Italian came again, but
in a few minutes he was followed by the boys;
there were four of them, among them Milo and his
comrade Tomesh, — you know Tomesh, don't you?
He is going to marry Anna Ticanek, who is my
best friend. When I saw them come I was as
delighted as if some one had given me a new gown.
With a merry heart I went to fill their glasses and
drank with each one. The Italian's face grew
dark. I never drink with him. Who can believe
him? He could put in some love potion! The
boys got round a table to play cards, but only for
a blind; for they kept making cutting remarks
about the Italian. Vitkov said: 'Look at him, he
looks like a noodle owl!' Then Tomesh said: 'I
am watching him constantly to see how soon he'll
bite his nose off; that would not be difficult, for it
reaches almost to his chin!' Thus it went on, he
changed color, but did not lisp a syllable. Finally,
he threw the money upon the table, left his beer
standing, and went away without a word. I signed
myself when he left, but the boys said: 'Could he
have stabbed us with his looks, it would be all over
with us now.' As soon as he left, I went about
my work, — you know since mother has been ill,
everything depends upon me. The boys left, too.
I think it was after ten, when I was through with
my work and went to my room. I began to un-
dress, when tap, tap, tap, I heard some one rapping
upon my window. I thought: 'Surely it is Milo,
he probably forgot something.' He always forgets

something. I tell him that sometime he'll leave his head at our house."

"If he has not done it already;" said Grandmother with a smile.

"I threw my shawl over my shoulders;" continued Christina, "and went to open the window; and behold, whom did I see! — That Italian. I banged the window, and was so frightened that I trembled! Then he began to talk and beg, though he well knows that I cannot understand a word he says. At last he offered me the gold rings from his fingers. Then I got mad. I took up my water pitcher and going to the window, said: 'Go away instantly, you miscreant, or I'll dash this over your head!'

"He stepped back from the window, but at that moment out from the shrubbery rushed the boys. They got hold of him, stuffed up his mouth so that he could not scream, and began to mock him. 'Wait, you rascally Italian, we'll teach you manners,' cried Milo. I begged Milo not to beat him, and closed the window, — only partly, for I wanted to know what they were going to do. 'Now Milo what shall we do with him? The fellow is almost gone; he has a hare's heart and trembles as if he had the ague.' 'Let us switch him with nettles,' proposed one. 'Let us tar - and - feather him!' cried another! 'Not that,' decided Milo. 'Tomesh, you hold him, and the rest of you come with me.' They ran off.

In a little while they returned, bringing a pole and some tar. 'Now, boys, take off his boots and turn up his trousers,' ordered Milo. They obeyed, but when the Italian began to kick, they soothed him as if he were a pony: 'Whoa, little one, whoa!

you won't be shod! Don't be afraid. We mean only to grease your feet, so you can run home the faster!' 'At any rate, you'll get a more wholesome smell than comes from those perfumes of yours,' said Tomesh. When they had tarred his feet, so that it seemed as though he had on a pair of boots, they took the pole, and laying it over his breast stretched his arms over it and fastened them on in the form of a cross. He tried to scream, but Tomesh placed his hand over his mouth and held it as in a vice. 'It won't hurt such an idle fellow as you to stretch his limbs a little; otherwise your veins might become contracted!' 'Now, tie his boots together and throw them over his shoulder, and lead him out to the road; let him trot to where he came from,' said Milo. 'But wait, he must have a buttonhole bouquet, so that people may know he's been to see his girl,' said Vitkov, and picked a piece of nettle and a thistle blossom, and put them into his coat. 'Now you are very handsome! Now you may go with your gifts.' Then Tomesh and Milo lead him out to the road.

Presently, Milo returned to the window, told me how furious the Italian was and how he looked running, his arms outstretched and fastened to the pole. I asked how he knew that the fellow was here. He said that the boys and he were passing by, and that he left them waiting at the mill while he ran to my window to bid me good night, and just then espied some one sneaking along the wall like a thief. As soon as he recognized him, he returned to the mill to get his comrades, and all agreed that the Italian ought to have a severe chastisement.

" He said: ' Everything went on as we expected, and I am sure the fellow will trouble you no more.'

" All day yesterday I was amused thinking of the trick the boys had played, but in the evening Watchman Kohoutek came over,— he comes every day, and after drinking several glasses he is apt to tell all he knows. He said that the Italian came home that evening in a fearful condition, having been attacked and maltreated by some villains; that he looked so dreadful that all the dogs ran after him; and that Mrs. Kohoutek worked till morning before she got all the tar away. She got a silver dollar for her trouble, but she was to say nothing of it at the castle. He swore a fearful vengeance upon the boys. I fear for Milo now, for they say those Italians are very bad people. Besides, Kohoutek said that the Italian waits upon Mary, the steward's daughter, and that her folks do not object, since they think that he is likely to be promoted. Milo wanted to serve a year in the manor in order to escape the conscription, but if the Italian sets the steward against him, that plan may as well be given up at once. I have considered all this, and now I wish they had let the fellow alone. Last night's dream comforted me a little, but after all it was but a dream! What do you think of the whole affair, Grandma?"

" It was not a wise thing for them to do; but what can we expect of young men, especially when love is mixed up with their affairs? My George did something very similar and we paid for it dearly."

" What was it?" quickly asked Christina.

" Indeed, would you have me begin the story now? I think our folks are returning from church, for I'm sure I hear the rumbling of wheels? Let us go in. I'll consider what you've told me, and perhaps I may be able to give you some counsel," added Grandmother, as she entered the house.

The children, hearing Christina's voice, ran out into the hall to meet her; and when she gave John the beautiful doves, he threw his arms around her and gave her such a squeeze that a red streak was left upon her white neck. He wanted to take the doves to the dovecot at once, but just then Barunka exclaimed: " Here they are!" Hardly had the carriage entered the yard, when the gamekeeper and the miller followed it, coming to spend the day with the Proshek family.

Mr. Proshek, seeing himself surrounded by loving friends and the family he so dearly loved, and of whose company he was deprived during most of the year, was deeply moved, and when Barunka began to recite the congratulation, his eyes filled with tears. The children, seeing this and observing that their mother and Grandmother were also in tears, hesitated, and finally began to cry. Betsey and Vorsa, listening at the door, covered their faces with their blue aprons and wept, too. The miller turned his snuff box like a water-wheel, and the gamekeeper began rubbing a fine hunting knife over his sleeve (he was in full dress to-day), in order that he might conceal his feelings; but Christina stood at the window, not at all ashamed of her tears, till the miller approached and rapped her on the shoulder with the snuff box, saying: " I suppose you are thinking, ' would that the time were near when I, too, shall be thus congratulated?"

"You, sir, cannot get along without teasing somebody," replied the girl, wiping her eyes.

With the tears still in his eyes, but joy and content in his heart, Mr. Proshek stepped to the table and poured out a goblet of wine. "To the health of all!" he said, drinking the first goblet. Then they all drank to his health, and soon their faces beamed with good cheer. John was the happiest of all; the gamekeeper had given him a couple of rabbits; the miller's wife had brought him an immense cake covered with such sauces as he liked best; and Grandmother had presented him one of those coins she had in the little green bag in her chest. Just after dinner the Princess and Countess came into the orchard, and when the family went out to meet them, the Countess presented Johnny with a beautiful book full of pictures of animals.

"I have come to see how you are enjoying yourself," said the Princess to her equerry.

"With my family, your Grace, and several good friends I am always happy," replied Mr. Proshek.

"Who is with you?"

"My neighbors, the miller with his family, and the Riesenburg gamekeeper."

"Do not let me keep you, return to them," said the Princess, preparing to leave.

Mr. Proshek bowed, not presuming to ask his mistress to remain; but the simple-hearted Grandmother began:

"Oh, indeed! what manners would that be, to let her Grace and Miss Hortense go without even offering them a kolach! Go, Theresa, go bring something. What comes unexpectedly often tastes good. Barunka, you bring a basket and pick some cherries. Perhaps her Grace will accept some cream or some wine."

Mr. Proshek and his wife were much embarrassed, fearing that the Princess would be offended by that simple offer; on the contrary, smiling pleasantly she dismounted, gave her bridle to Mr. Proshek, and seating herself upon the bench under the pear tree, said: "Your hospitality will be acceptable to me, but I do not wish you to neglect your guests; let them come out, too!"

Mrs. Proshek went into the house, Mr. Proshek tied the horse to a tree, brought out a small table, and in a little while the gamekeeper came out, making a profound bow. He was followed by the miller, who showed a great deal of shyness; but as soon as the Princess asked him how his business was prospering, he was in his element and got so far over his bashfulness that he offered her a pinch of snuff. When she had spoken a kind word with each one, she accepted a kolach from Mrs. Proshek and a glass of cream from Grandmother.

While this was going on the children surrounded John, who showed them the pictures in his book. The Countess stood by enjoying their happiness and wonder, and gladly replying to their questions.

"Mamma, look! this is our fawn!" cried Bertie, as John turned the leaves to the picture of a fawn; and the mother and children put their heads together, looking at the pictures.

"Sultan! that's Sultan!" cried Willie, and when Sultan answered the call by running to them, John

showed him the picture, saying: " See, this is you! "
There was also a very large elephant of which
Adelka was afraid. There were horses, cows, rabbits, squirrels, chickens, lizards and snakes, fish,
frogs, butterflies, lady-bugs, and even ants. The
children were familiar with all those creatures, and
Grandmother, seeing the scorpions and snakes, said:
" What will not people make! they paint even those
reptiles! "

When, however, the miller's wife wanted to
see the fiery dragon, whose mouth spits fire, the
Countess said there was no such animal, that it was
only an imaginary monster. The miller, hearing
this, turned the snuff box in his fingers, smiled
mischievously, and said:

" O your Ladyship, it is not an imaginary
monster; there are plenty of such wicked dragons
with fiery tongues in the world, but they belong to
the human race, and therefore are not put here
among these harmless creatures."

The Countess smiled, but the miller's wife rapped him upon the shoulder, saying: " Too many
words, father."

The Princess spoke with Mr. Proshek and the
gamekeeper about various things, till finally she
asked if there were many poachers around.

" I have two such rascals still; there were three
but the most foolish one I fined several times, so
now he stays at home. But the other two are
deuced sharp, I can't catch them unless I put some
shot through their bodies. The master of the
woods tells me to do it; but it is no small matter
to cripple a man on account of a hare."

" I do not wish you to do it," said the Princess.

" I, too, have thought that for such a trifle your
Grace will not come to poverty, and they dare not
enter the ward for larger game."

" I hear that much wood is stolen from my forests. How is that?"

" I have served your Ladyship for many years,
and the damage thus done does not amount to much.
A good deal is said, I know; for example, I could
have several trees cut down during the year, sell
them, and when I could not give a clear record, I
could say they were stolen. But why burden my
conscience with lying and cheating? In the fall
when the women come to rake up leaves and moss,
and the poor people come to collect sticks for fuel,
I am always about and swear till the trees tremble;
but should I half kill some old granny when she
breaks off a few stouter limbs! Your Grace will
not come to poverty for that, and the poor creature
is helped and blesses you a thousand times. I do
not call such things losses."

" You are right," replied the Princess. " Still
there must be some very bad people about; day
before yesterday, in the evening, as Piccolo was
coming from town, he was attacked, and when he
called for help, he was beaten so that he is ill.
Thus I was told."

" That does not seem possible," said Mr. Proshek, shaking his head dubiously.

" In all my life I never heard that there were
robbers about here! " exclaimed the gamekeeper
and miller at the same time.

" What is it that's happened?" asked Grandmother, coming nearer.

The gamekeeper told her.

"That lying scamp," exclaimed Grandmother, in her indignation supporting her hand on her hip. "It is a wonder he isn't afraid that God will punish him. I will tell your Grace how it was." Here she related what Christina had confided to her in the morning. "Not that I would approve of what those boys did; but they cannot be blamed much, for everybody guards his own. If any one had seen that fellow standing by Christina's window in the night, it would have been trumpeted over the whole neighborhood, and her good name and future would have been ruined; people would say: 'O, she shows favor to such lordlings, she is not for us.' But now she is afraid that he will revenge himself upon them," added Grandmother.

"She need not fear, I will manage that," said the Princess, and motioning to the Countess they mounted their horses, graciously bade the company good day, and galloped to the castle.

"Really, no one would venture to talk with the Princess as our Grandmother did," said Mrs. Proshek.

"It is often easier to speak with an emperor than with a secretary, and a word spoken in season may bear good fruit. Had I remained silent, who knows what would have come from it," said Grandmother.

"Now, I always said that our Princess was pale from the lies people told her," said the gamekeeper, re-entering the house with Mr. Proshek and the miller.

In the evening, Kuderna came over, with his hand organ, and as soon as he began to play, the children, Christina, Betsey, and Vorsa began to dance. They also had champagne, which the Princess had sent to be drunk to her health. Even Victorka was not forgotten; as soon as it was dark, Grandmother carried a generous portion to the stump by the dam.

The next day the miller's wife complained to Grandmother that while they were going home in the night, " father talked a great deal of nonsense, and seemed to see things double;" but Grandmother only smiled, saying: " O dear soul, it happens only once a year, and there isn't a chapel without some little preaching."

CHAPTER IX.

FIVE pilgrims are seen wending their way up Zernov hill: they are Grandmother, the miller's wife, Christina, Manchinka, and Barunka. The first two have white kerchiefs tied over their heads and pulled over their faces to a point; the girls have straw hats. Barunka and Manchinka have tucked up their petticoats like the older women, and over their shoulders are hung bundles in which they are carrying provisions for the journey.

"It seems to me I hear singing," said Christina as they reached the top of the hill.

"I, too," cried the girls; "let us hurry up so they won't leave us," and they wanted to start on a run.

"O you simpletons, when the leader knows we are coming, do you suppose he'd leave us?" said Grandmother; and the girls, now satisfied, followed the rest with a slow gait.

On top of the hill the shepherd was watching his flock, and greeted them from afar.

"What do you think, Yoza? shall we get caught in the rain?" asked the miller's wife.

"Have no care, the present state of the weather will continue till day after to-morrow," replied the shepherd. "Remember me with a Pater-noster! A pleasant journey to you."

"God grant it, we will not forget."

"Grandma, how does Yoza know when it will

rain and when the weather will be fine?" asked Barunka.

"Just before rain, worms crawl out of the ground, making tiny cells, the salamanders look out of their holes, but lizards hide, and spiders too; the sparrows fly close to the ground. The shepherds, being out doors all day and having little to do, observe those creatures and thus learn much about their habits. My best calendar was always the hills and the sky. By the clearness in the outlines of the mountains and the color of the sky, I can tell when we are to have fair or foul weather, when winds, hail, and snow," replied Grandmother.

A group of people, men, women and children, were now seen standing by Zernov chapel; they were pilgrims. Several women were carrying babies tied up in pillows. They intended to offer them to the Virgin at the shrine, that she might either restore them to health, or grant them some special blessing.

The leader Martin stood on the steps of the chapel; his tall form towered above the rest, so that he could easily command a view of the whole company entrusted to his care. Seeing Grandmother and the others coming, he said: "Now we are all here, so we are ready to start." But first let us pray *Our Father* for a safe journey!" The pilgrims knelt before the chapel and prayed, and the villagers standing near prayed with them. After the prayer, they sprinkled themselves with holy water, one of the young men took a long cross, upon which Tomesh's bride had hung a wreath, and Christina had tied a pair of red streamers. The men stood near the leader, behind them the women, grouping themselves together according to their ages. But they were not quite ready to start. The careful housewives repeated their directions to their servants to see well to the housekeeping, and the fathers gave strict orders to their help to take good care of the farms. The children begged: "Please bring us something from the shrine!" the old women: "Remember us with a Pater-noster!" Then the leader gave the signal, beginning to sing in a loud voice: "Hail, daughter of God!" The pilgrims joined in full chorus, the young men raised the garlanded cross, and the party started on their pilgrimage to Svatonovitz. At every chapel they stopped and offered a Pater-noster and the creed for the glory and honor of God; by every tree .upon which some pious hand had hung the picture of the Virgin, by every cross that marked the spot where some accident had happened, they knelt and prayed.

Barunka and Manchinka gave good heed to the leader and sang with the rest. But when they came to Red Hura, Barunka all at once asked Grandmother about the deaf and dumb girl from Turyn.

This time her questioning met with a sad rebuff, for Grandmother replied: "When you go on a pilgrimage, you must turn your mind to God, and not think of something else. Sing or silently pray!" The girls sang again.

They now came into the woods. Here and there strawberries were seen in the grass. It was a pity to let them go to waste; they preferred to pick them. Their hats fell, their petticoats came down and had to be tucked up again, and finally they remembered the buns in their bundles and began to

break off bits and eat. Neither Grandmother nor
the miller's wife noticed it, for they were deeply
buried in their devotions; but Christina and Anna
did, and reproved them several times. " Much
good your pilgrimage will do you, and great reward
you will merit if you keep on like this," they said.

The pilgrims reached Svatonovitz before dark;
before entering the village, the women stopped to
put on their shoes and arrange their clothing.
When they entered the village, the first thing they
did was to go to the sacred well, whose waters gush
out in seven streams from under a tree upon which
is hung a picture of the blessed Virgin. There
they knelt down and prayed, then each one took
a drink of the water and moistened his face and
eyes three times. That clear, cold water is said to
possess miraculous powers of healing, and by it
thousands of people have been restored to health.

From the well the pilgrimage went to the well-
lighted church, from whose walls was heard the
murmur of different melodies; for processions kept
coming in from different parts of the country, and
each sang a different hymn.

"O Grandmother, how beautiful it is here!"
whispered Barunka.

The child knelt down beside her Grandmother,
who bent her head almost to the floor and sent forth
fervent prayers to the most holy mother of Christ,
whose image upon the altar, gleaming in the light
of thousands of candles, was decorated with garlands and bouquets, the gifts of pious maidens and
brides, who came hither that she might grant success to their love. The image was covered with a
magnificent robe, decked with costly jewels, the

offerings of those who, afflicted with diseases, had
sought and received help at her feet.

The prayers being ended, the leader arranged
such matters as were necessary with the sexton, and
led his little flock to their lodgings. He did not
have to seek these, for as the swallows coming in
the spring seek their old nests, so the pilgrims went
where year by year they had received, if not a rich
hospitality, still a pleasant welcome, bread and salt,
and a clean bed. The miller's wife and Grandmother were in the habit of staying at the house of
the steward who was in charge of the iron mines
in the neighborhood. They were old people, holding to the good old ways, and for this reason Grandmother felt at home with them. The stewardess
hearing that Zernov pilgrims had come, sat on a
bench before her house waiting to welcome them.
Before they went to bed she exhibited to them her
treasures, whole rolls of linen and dimity and skeins
upon skeins of yarn. This was her own work, to
which she added some each year.

"For whom, my good woman, are you saving
this, seeing that your daughter is married?" asked
the miller's wife.

"O, but I have three grandchildren, and linen
and yarn never come amiss."

With this the other women fully agreed; but
when the steward came along, he said: "Well,
mother, you are again spreading out your wares;
shall I have the drums beat for an auction?"

"Wait a while, till I have saved some more,"
she replied.

It worried the stewardess not a little that she
could not entertain Grandmother with anything

else than bread, for when the latter went on a pilgrimage, she lived only on bread and water. This vow was sacred to her, and nothing would induce her to break it. The miller's wife enjoyed it very much at the steward's and when she sank down in the soft feather beds filled with down, she would say with great satisfaction: "Dear soft bed, it feels as if a person were lying in a snow bank."

Christina and Anna went to a certain widow who owned a little house with a garden. They used to sleep in the garret on the hay, where a bed was made for them. They would have slept soundly upon a rock. This night they did not remain in the garret, but climbed down the ladder into the garden.

"Isn't it a thousand times better here than up there?" said Christina. "This garden is our chamber, the stars our candles, 'And the green sward, love, our bed shall be,'" she sang, wrapping herself up in her petticoat and lying down under a tree. "There I shall slumber, there I shall slumber, sweetly with thee," replied Anna, lying down beside her. "But listen! how Mrs. Fouskek snores; it sounds just as if one were emptying a bag of stones," she said laughing.

"Wouldn't it be delightful to sleep beside her. Say, Anna, do you think they will come to-morrow?" asked the girl, turning to her mate.

"Of course they will come," said Anna, with great assurance. "Tomesh is sure to be here, and that Milo should not come is not to be thought of. Why, he likes you."

"Who knows, we have not spoken of it yet."

"And why should you speak of it? one knows

that without speaking; I really can't say whether
Tomesh ever told me that he liked me, and yet we
are very fond of each other, and the wedding day
has been set."

" When will it be? "

" Father wants to give us the homestead and go
to live in the new house he is building. When the
house is finished, we shall be married; that will be
about St. Katherine's. It would be very pleasant
if you and I could have our wedding the same day."

" O, go away! You talk as if the arm were
already in the sleeve, and yet all is still behind the
mountains."

" If it is not, it can very easily be. Jacob Milo's
folks would be very glad to have him marry into
your business, and your father could not get a better
son; no one could suit him better. As to yourself,
why, there is no question. No one can deny that
he is the handsomest fellow in the village, and I
think the squire's daughter, Lucina, would mourn
for him."

" You see, that is another stone in our path,"
sighed Christina.

" Indeed, there is more than one stone, for
Lucina is solid enough herself, and to her weight
her father will add a bag of Rhine dollars."

" So much the worse! "

" But do not worry your precious head about
that. If her father is the squire, he is not the
Lord, and Lucina, with all her dollars, cannot hold
a candle up to you, and Milo has good eyes."

" But if they all go against him, if he does not
get that place on the manor farm, and if he is
taken into the army? "

" Do not borrow trouble; should the steward look dark, his eyes can be brightened with coin, you understand ? "

" That could easily be done, but it does not always work; yet on St. John's night I dreamed Milo came to me. But a dream is a dream, and Grandmother says we should not put any faith in such superstitions, nor tempt God to reveal to us the future."

. " But Grandmother is not the Gospel.

" I believe her as I do the Scripture; she always gives one good counsel, and everybody says she is a most estimable woman. What she says is the most sacred truth."

" I believe that, too, but I would bet my little finger that when she was young she believed as we do. That is the way all old people are; my mother is forever complaining that the young people are not as they used to be, that all they care for are dances and merrymakings, and that they haven't a grain of sense. That was not the way they acted when she was young, and I know positively that our great grandmothers were no better when they were young than we are, and when we get old, we will sing the same tune they do. But now let us commend ourselves to the care of the Blessed Mother and go to sleep," added Anna, pulling the petticoat tight around herself, and in a little while, when Christina looked into her face she was fast asleep.

In the garret one of the women that slept there was trying to quiet her baby, which, however, kept on crying.

" What! mother, does that child cry this way

every night?" asked the other woman waking from her sleep.

"For two whole weeks, every night," she replied. "I have given it everything that people advised, but to no purpose. The blacksmith's wife says it has been overlooked and that it has gone to its bowels. I decided to offer it upon the altar of God that it might get well, or that the Lord would take it to himself."

"To-morrow, place it under the stream, so that the water shall go over it three times; that helped my little girl," said the woman, turning over and going to sleep.

In the morning, when the pilgrims gathered before the church, shaking hands with the usual greeting, "Let us forgive each other," — they were going to communion, — two familiar voices were heard behind Christina and Anna: "May we be forgiven, too?"

"We grant you absolution without confession," replied Anna, giving her hand to Tomesh; Christina, blushing, gave hers to Milo. The young men, putting themselves under the command of Martin, entered the church with the rest.

After the service all went to the baths, where the old men and women were usually cupped, that being also one of the duties of the pilgrims. After the bath, they went to the numerous stands and booths to buy presents for those at home. The miller's wife bought a great many pictures, rosaries, images, and other gifts; for she said: "I have my help, the people come in with the grist, and each expects something from the pilgrimage, so I must have a goodly supply."

Not far from Grandmother stood Mrs. Fousek who wanted to buy a bladder-nut rosary; but when the shopkeeper told her it was twenty kreutzers, new coin, she laid it back, saying it was too dear.

" Too dear!" exclaimed the excited shopman, "you never saw a bladder-nut rosary in your life, if you say this is too dear. You had better buy a gingerbread one."

" Well, sir, it may not be too dear for others, but it is too dear for me, for twenty kreutzers is all the money I have in the world," she replied, sadly.

Mrs. Fousek went away, but Grandmother followed her, and advised her to go to another stand, where everything was a great deal cheaper. And behold! that shopman seemed to sell everything for a song, just as Grandmother wanted it, so that the twenty kreutzers paid not only for the bladder-nut rosary, but also for pictures and various knicknacks.

When she left the stand, Barunka said: " Grandma, you paid the shopman what was lacking; I saw how you winked at him, when Mrs. Fousek was not looking."

" Suppose you saw, that is no reason why you should tell. The left hand must not know what the right hand doeth," replied Grandmother.

Christina bought a silver ring with two flaming hearts, and Milo seeing this at once bought one that had two clasped hands. All these things the pilgrims had touched with relics or blessed; and a rosary, ring, picture, or prayer book so " touched " or blessed was kept as a precious memento.

All the duties being performed, the pilgrims thanked their friends for their hospitality, prayed once more by the sacred well, and commending themselves to the care of the Mother of Christ, began the homeward journey. After going some distance, they reached Hertin forest, and being weary sat down to rest near a spring of water not far from The Nine Crosses. Being thirsty and seeing that Christina gave Milo some water from the palm of her hand, they asked her to give them some too, which she willingly did. The older people sat down in the grass, and began to examine one another's purchases, and to discuss the other processions. The girls went into the woods to gather flowers for garlands, and the boys went to put in order a large grave upon which were the nine crosses.

"Nannie, please tell me why those nine crosses are here," asked Barunka, arranging the flowers for the bouquet Anna was making

"Listen then, I'll tell you. Not far from here is the ruin of an old fortress which is called Vizemburg. In olden times a squire dwelt there who was called Herman; he was in love with a girl from one of the villages. Another suitor tried to win her, but she did not like him and gave her hand to Herman. On the morning of her wedding day Herman's mother brought him a red apple, and asked him why he was so sober. He replied that he did not know. The mother then begged him not to go to the wedding, because she had had bad dreams; but he hastily arose, bade his mother farewell, mounted his steed, and started. The steed refused to go through the gate; the mother again begged him: 'My son, remain at home; this is a bad omen, some misfortune will happen.' But he would not obey; putting spurs to his steed, he reached the bridge. The steed reared on his hind legs and again refused to go; and the third time the mother begged him not to go; but he gave no heed to her words and went to meet his bride. When the wedding party reached this place, they were stopped by the other young man with his comrades. The two rivals began to fight and Herman was killed. When the bride saw her lover killed, she plunged a knife into her heart. The wedding guests killed the rival, and it was said that nine persons perished in that battle. They were buried in the same grave and nine crosses were placed here to their memory. These crosses are kept in repair by the pilgrims, and when we come here, in the summer, we hang garlands upon them and offer a Pater-noster for their souls."

Anna finished the tale, but Mrs. Fousek who was near, gathering mushrooms, and who had heard part of it, shook her head and said: "Your story is not quite correct, Anna. Herman was a squire from Litobor, and not from Vizemburg, and the bride was from Svatonovitz. He was killed, together with his attendants, before he reached the bride; she looked for him, but he never came. She sat down to the table, when suddenly she heard the tolling of the bell; she asked her mother three times for whom the bell tolled; but she would not tell her the truth, saying it was for this one or that one, till finally they took her to the chamber where Herman was laid out. Filled with despair she stabbed herself through the heart. They buried them all here. That is the way I heard it," added Mrs. Fousek.

"Who can decide which story is the true one,

since it happened so long ago. No matter how it happened, it is a pity it ever happened. It would have been better could they have been married and lived happily."

"In that case no one would ever have heard of them; we could not decorate their graves with flowers," said Tomesh fixing the fir cross that was broken down.

"Yes, but what does that amount to? I should not want to be such a bride," replied Anna.

"Nor I," said Christina, coming with the finished garlands.

"Well, I should not want to be killed on my wedding day," said Milo; "but after all Herman was more fortunate than his rival. It must have been dreadful for him to see the maid he loved carried to the home of another. For that reason we ought to pray the more fervently for him, for he died guilty and unhappy, while Herman was happy and in God's grace."

The girls hung the garlands upon the crosses, scattered the rest of the flowers over the moss covered mound, and having offered up their prayers returned to the rest of the pilgrims. Presently the leader took his cane, the boys raised the cross, and singing they turned their steps homeward. Not far from Zernov, at the crossroads the villagers were already waiting for them. As soon as the villagers heard the song and caught a glimpse of the red streamers, the children rushed forward to meet them. Before they reached the village, the boys blew their new trumpets, whistled on new whistles, and chased about with wooden horses; the girls carried dolls, little baskets, pictures, and gin-

gerbread hearts. After praying in the chapel, the
pilgrims thanked their leader, the cross was placed
in the chapel, the garland with streamers was hung
upon the altar, and the pilgrims scattered to their
respective homes.

At parting, when Christina was giving her hand
to Anna, the latter noticed the silver ring that was
glistening on Christina's finger, and smiling she
asked: "That is not the one you bought?"

Christina blushed, but before she could reply,
Milo whispered to Anna: "She gave me her
heart, I gave her my hand."

"A good exchange, may God bless you," replied Anna.

At the mill, by the statue under the lindens sat
the Proshek family and the miller; from time to
time they turned their eyes to Zernov hill; they
were waiting for the pilgrims. When the sun was
sending its last rays upon the hills, and bathing the
tops of the oaks and ash trees in a flood of golden
light, white kerchiefs and straw hats gleamed
through the green branches, and the children, who
had been watching the hill most intently, cried out:
"They are coming!" and started to meet them.
Mr. and Mrs. Proshek and the miller slowly followed. The children hung about Grandmother and
kissed her as if she had been gone a year. Barunka,
with much pride, declared that she was not at all
tired. Grandmother asked the children if they had
missed her, and the miller's wife asked her husband: "What's the news?" "Our old goose lost
her shoes," he replied, and added, very soberly:
"It was a great calamity, mother."

" There is no talking with you," she replied, giving him a smart stroke upon the hand.

" When you are at home, he teases you; but when you are away he goes about like a wet chicken," remarked Mrs. Proshek.

" That is the way, those men appreciate us only when they miss us."

Thus the conversation began, but it proved to be unending. The pilgrimage to Svatonovitz was to the inhabitants of this quiet hamlet an event of the greatest importance. It furnished a theme for conversation for at least two weeks. When one of the neighbors had occasion to go to Vamburg, it was discussed six months before and six months after, and a pilgrimage to Maria Zell was talked of for a whole year.

CHAPTER X.

THE Princess is gone, and with her the Countess; the father is gone, and the merry swallows, whose homes were under the eves, are gone, too. For several days it has seemed at Proshek's as it does after a funeral; the mother's eyes are often red from weeping, and the children seeing this weep, too.

"Now, Theresa, dry your eyes," Grandmother would say. "What good does it do to cry? You knew what you had to expect when you married, so now have patience. And you, children, rather than shed tears, pray God to keep your father in good health, so that when spring comes he may return to us."

"When the swallows return, Grandma?" asked Adelka.

"Certainly, my dear," replied Grandmother, and the child dried her tears.

Around the Bleachery it was sad and quiet. The foliage in the forest grew less and less dense; when Victorka came down the hill she could be seen from afar. The hill grew yellow, the wind and streams carried away heaps of dried leaves no one knew whither. The wealth of the orchard was hidden in the store-room, and in the garden only asters and kitchen and French marigolds were seen; and the fireflies played their games near the dam in the meadow saffron. When the children went out walking, the boys took their kites to let them fly on the top of the hill. Adelka followed them, catching upon a switch the fine threads of gossamer that floated in the breeze. Barunka gathered viburnum and haw berries for Grandmother, which she used in her medicines, and hips for culinary purposes; or she picked mountain ash berries to make bracelets and necklaces for Adelka. Grandmother loved to sit with the children on the top of the hill behind the castle. Before them spread a beautiful valley, where a herd of cattle was grazing; they could see even to the village, and at their feet was the castle, built upon a small elevation and surrounded by a park. All was now changed. The green curtains were drawn, no flowers were seen on the balcony, and the roses on the sides of the balustrade were faded; instead of attendants in livery, common laborers were seen in the garden, covering the plants with branches of evergreen. No beautiful flowers were seen, but the germs of them were hidden beneath the covering, and in due time would delight the eye of their mistress. Rare exotics, deprived of their green robes, were rolled up in straw; the fountains, sending forth silvery streams of water were protected with moss and lumber, and the golden fishes had hidden in the bottom of the pools whose surface, at other times so clear, was now covered with leaves, duck weed, and green slime. The children looked down to the castle and thought of the time when they walked with Hortense in the garden; they remembered how beautiful everything was when they breakfasted with her, and wondered where she was now. Grandmother, however, preferred to look beyond the opposite hill, beyond the villages, wards, groves, and forests, to the new town, clear to Dobrau, where dwelt her son, and beyond Dobrau, among the hills, to the little village that held so many souls dear to her. When she turned her eyes to the east, there lay before her a beautiful half garland of the Riesengebirge, from the rough, projecting back-bone of Heyshov to the summit of the snow cap. Pointing to Heyshov, Grandmother said: " There I know every nook; there in those mountains is Kladrau, where your mother was born, there is Vamberitz and Varta; in those regions I spent many happy days."

She fell into a deep reverie, out of which she was awakened by Barunka's question:

" Is Varta the place where Sybilla sits upon that marble horse ? "

" They say it is upon a hill near Varta. She sits upon a marble horse,— herself made of marble, —and has her hand raised up to heaven. When she sinks into the ground so that not even the end of her finger will be visible, her prophecy will be fulfilled. My father said he saw her, and then the horse was in the sand clear to his breast."

" Who was that Sybilla ? " asked Adelka.

" Sybilla was a wise woman, who could foretell the future."

" What did she foretell ? " asked the boys.

" I have told you already several times," replied Grandmother.

" We have forgotten."

" But you should not forget."

" Grandma, I remember some of it," said Barunka, who always listened with great attention;

" Did not Sybilla prophesy that much misery was to come to Bohemia, that there would be wars, famines, and plagues, but that the worst time would come when the father did not understand the son, the brother his brother, when the given word or promise would not be held sacred; that then the Bohemian land should be carried over the earth upon the hoofs of horses?"

" You have remembered well, but God forbid that any such thing should ever happen!" sighed Grandmother.

Barunka, kneeling at Grandmother's feet, her clasped hands upon her knees, her bright eyes fixed confidently upon that old dignified face, asked further: "What was that prophecy you told us about the Blanik Knights, St. Vaclav and St. Prokop?"

" That is the prophecy of the Blind Youth," replied Grandmother.

" O, Grandma, sometimes I am so afraid that I cannot even express it; you would not want our country to be carried over the earth upon the hoofs of horses, would you?"

" Dear child, how could I wish such a misfortune! do we not pray every day for our country, because it is our mother? Well, if I saw my mother going to destruction, could I be indifferent? What would you do, if somebody wanted to kill your mother?"

" We should cry and scream," quickly replied the boys.

" You are but children," smiled Grandmother.

" We should have to help her, shouldn't we?" asked Barunka, her eyes brightening.

" That's right, my child, that's right; that is the proper thing to do; crying and screaming profit little," said she, laying her hand upon her grand-daughter's head.

" But, Grandma, we are so little, how could we help?" asked John, vexed that her opinion of him was so unfavorable.

" Don't you remember what I told you about the young David, how he slew Goliath? You see even the little one can accomplish much when he has faith in God, — don't you forget this. When you grow up, you will go into the world, see good and evil, be enticed and led away into temptation. Then think of your Grandmother and what she used to tell you. You know that I gave up a good living which the king of Prussia offered me, and preferred labor and great hardships rather than see my children estranged. Therefore, you, too, must love your country as you love your mother; work for her as dutiful children, and the prophecy you fear will never be fulfilled. I cannot hope to see you grown up, but I believe you will remember my words," she added, with a voice trembling with emotion.

" I shall never forget them," said Barunka, hiding her face in Grandmother's lap.

The boys stood silent; they did not understand their grandmother's words as Barunka did. Adelka, clinging close to her asked with a voice broken by sobs: " You are not going to die, are you!"

" My dear child, everything in the world is only for a time, and some day God will call me," she replied, pressing the little one to her bosom. They were silent for some time; Grandmother was buried in thought, and the children did not know what to say. The silence was broken by the rustling of wings, and when they raised their eyes, they saw a flock of birds sailing in the air above them.

"These are wild geese," said Grandmother; "they always go in small flocks consisting of one family only, and their way of flying is different from that of other birds. Observe! two fly in the front, two behind, and the rest go in single file, either lengthwise or crosswise, unless they make a half circle. Jackdaws, crows, and swallows go in large flocks. Several go in front, these seek a place of rest on their journey. In the rear and on the sides fly the guards, which in time of danger protect the female birds and the young; for often they meet an unfriendly flock and then a battle is fought."

"But, Grandma, how can they fight a battle when they have no hands in which to hold swords and guns?" asked Willie.

"They fight in a manner peculiar to themselves; they peck with their bills, and strike with their wings as cruelly as people do with sharp weapons. In such a battle many fall to the ground dead."

"How foolish they are," cried John.

"My boy, God has endowed man with reason, and yet how often for mere trifles men will fight till they destroy one another," said Grandmother, rising from the bench and preparing to go. "Look! the sun is about to set, the west is scarlet, to-morrow it will rain." Turning to the mountains, she added: "and Snowcap has a hood."

"Poor Mr. Beyer! what hard times he will have when he must travel through the woods," said Willie, thinking of the gamekeeper of the Riesengebirge mountains.

"Every occupation has its hardships; but when one chooses it, he must be willing to suffer the evil with the good, even should it be a matter of life and death," replied Grandmother.

"I shall be a gamekeeper, anyhow, and go with Mr. Beyer" said John courageously, and letting his kite fly he ran down the hill, Willie following; they heard the call for the cattle which the cowherd was driving home from the pasture, and the children loved to look at those beautiful cows that went in front of the herd, with red straps on their necks, upon which were hung brass bells, each having a different sound. One could see that they understood, for they proudly tossed their heads from side to side. Adelka seeing them coming, began to sing:

> "Heigh—ho! the cows come home,
> Through the meadow, by the stream,
> Bringing us both milk and cream.

Grandmother was looking for Barunka, who still stood upon the hill, gazing upon the beautiful sunset. Here the outlines of the hills were seen in huge sketches upon the bright background; then the small elevations, upon whose tops were castles and churches, were set against the sky. From the level plain stretched up slender pillars connected by arches, like Gothic architecture, and all the dark figures were bordered by golden hieroglyphics and arabesques. These mountains, forests and castles disappeared, and forms even more strange appeared in their places. Barunka was so delighted that she called her grandmother to come up once more to see the beautiful sight; but she said her feet were not so young as they once had been, so Barunka came down to the rest of the party.

On All Saints' day the children, as usual, going out to meet Grandmother coming from church, said: " To-day we shall get some candles from church." And Grandmother brought the candles.

" When we cannot go to the graveyard to offer them for the souls, we will light them at home," she said. Thus in their own home each year they celebrated the festival for the dead. On All Souls' day, * in the evening, they set up the candles on the table, and as they were lighting them named the souls for whom they were offered. At last they lighted several without any name saying: " Let those burn for the souls that are un-remembered."

" Grandma, may I light one for that unfortunate wedding in Hertin forest? " asked Barunka.

" Yes, yes, my child; our prayer will be acceptable to them." One more was lighted. Grandmother and the children knelt around the table and prayed as long as the candles burned. Grandmother ended the prayer with the words: " Let the Eternal Light shine for them, and may their souls rest in peace!" to which the children said: " Amen."

A week after All Souls' day, when Grandmother called the children in the morning, she told them that St. Martin had come upon a white horse. They jumped out of bed and ran to the windows,— and lo! everything was white. Not a single trace of green leaves was seen upon the hill side, nor on the willows by the river, nor on the alders by the pond. The only green things in the woods were

---

* On All Souls' day the graves are decorated and candles lighted for the souls of the dead.

the firs and balsams, the branches of which bent down beneath their loads of snow. Upon the mountain ash, which stood near the house and had still a few bunches of frozen berries, a crow sat, and the poultry in the yard stood quiet, looking with wonder upon this strange sight. The sparrows, however, hopped about merrily, picking up the grain that the chickens had left. The cat, returning from the chase, at each step shook the snow from her paws, and hastened to her favorite place upon the oven. The dogs, wet to their knees chased each other playfully in the snow.

"Snow! snow! That is good! we shall ride down the hill!" shouted the children, welcoming the winter which brought them new pleasures. St. Martin brought them good rolls, and after St. Martin would come the feather bees.* They liked the spinning bees much better, for then they had more liberty. When the women got around the long kitchen table, and on it appeared a great heap of feathers, like a snow bank, then Grandmother kept driving Adelka and the boys away. Once, while John was at the table, he fell into the feathers, and the rumpus thus made can easily be imagined. From that time Grandmother did not think it advisable to allow the children to come near the table. Indeed, they did not dare to play near it or blow, or open the door too wide, for in that case they got a scolding at once. The only pleasant things about the feather bees were the puchalka,† and the stories about ghosts and robbers, about lights and fiery men. On long, foggy evenings, as the women

* Gatherings at which feathers are stripped.
† Pease first soaked and then roasted.

went from village to village, it often happened that one was frightened here and another there; and when once they started to talk about it, there was no end to the stories, for each one knew several similar instances. The Kramolna thieves, going to prison in the spring and returning in the fall,— people said they had been at school, for they always learned something,— often furnished topics for conversation. Speaking of them, they began to talk of thieves in general, and then they related stories of bands of robbers. The children sat as still as mice, but for the whole world they would not have ventured out of doors. For this reason, Grandmother was never pleased with such conversation; still she could not stem this general current of thought.

After St. Martin's there was a market in town. Mrs. Proshek, taking Betsey and Vorsa with her, went there to buy crockery, and whatever else was needed for the winter. The children awaited their mother's return with the greatest impatience, for she always brought them some toys and ginger-bread; and Grandmother got each year woolen stockings, a pair of fur-lined shoes, and half a dozen strings for her spinning wheel.

As she was putting them away in the side drawer in her chest, she would say to John: " If it were not for you, one string would be all I'd want."

This time Adelka got a wooden block on which was the alphabet. " To-morrow, when the school-master comes, you can begin to learn; you don't know what to do with yourself while the others are studying; and since you remember the Lord's prayer and various songs, you can learn the *a, b, c,* too," said her mother.

The child skipped for joy, and immediately began to examine the letters with great attention; the clever Willie offered to teach her *a, e, i, o, u,* but she hid the block behind her back, saying: " I don't want to learn from you, you don't know it as well as the schoolmaster."

" As if I didn't know my letters when I can read from a book," said the boy, much hurt.

" But the letters are not the same as in the book," replied the sister.

" O, how foolish you are," exclaimed Willie, clasping his hands in astonishment.

" I don't care," said Adelka with a toss of her head, and went with her letters to the window.

While these two were quarreling over the letters, John, together with Sultan and Tyrol, was making a concert in the kitchen; he blew the trumpet and beat the drum which his mother had brought him from the market. The dogs did not seem to appreciate his music, for Sultan barked and Tyrol howled in a way that was fearful to hear. Grandmother was in the storeroom with her daughter putting away the purchases; hearing this music they both rushed into the kitchen. " Didn't I say so? it is that reprobate of ours; there isn't a good bone in his body. Say, will you stop! "

John took the trumpet out of his mouth and, as if he had not heard what Grandmother said, laughed, saying: " Look at those dogs, how mad they are; they do not seem to like my music."

" If those dogs could speak they would tell you to go to the Old Nick with such music, you understand? Put those things away instantly. If you will be such a bad boy, this year, I shall surely complain of you to St. Nicholas, and he'll not give you anything," threatened Grandmother.

" That would be a good thing; they say that St. Nicholas brought a whole wagonload of toys to town, and that he will be very generous this year,— to those who are obedient," said Vorsa, who, standing in the door, heard Grandmother's words.

The next day, as soon as the schoolmaster came, Adelka got her block and sat down with the rest of the children; she gave good heed, and in an hour she came running to Grandmother with great joy, saying she knew all the letters in the first row, and read them, together with the signs that the schoolmaster had made to help her to remember them. Both her mother and her Grandmother were well pleased with her, especially when the next day she still remembered them; and since Grandmother was obliged to hear her recite them so often, she finally learned them herself. " Well, well," said she to herself, " never in my life did I think I could yet learn the *a*, *b*, *c*, and now I have learned it. With children one must again be a child."

One day, John rushed into the room with the words: " Children, children, come see, Grandma has brought down her spinning wheel from the garret."

" What of it?" said the mother, as she saw all, even Barunka, rushing out of the door.

Certainly it was nothing, but she did not consider what pleasures were brought with the spinning wheel. With it came the spinners, and with them beautiful stories and merry songs. The mother, indeed, found no pleasure either in the stories or in the songs; she preferred to remain in her sitting room and read books from the castle library, and when Grandmother said: " Tell us something from those histories," the mother complied with her request; but the children were not half so interested as when she told them about the life in Vienna; and when the spinners said: "How beautiful it must be in such a city," not desiring, however, to see it, the children thought: "Oh, that we were grown up, so that we could go there, too."

All, except the mother, liked best to listen when Grandmother told stories about princesses with golden stars upon their foreheads, about knights and princes turned by enchantment into dogs and lions, or even into stones, about nuts, in whose shells were folded whole wardrobes of magnificent garments, about golden castles and seas, at whose bottom lived water nymphs. The mother never suspected, while she combed Barunka's hair, that the child, buried in deep reverie, and gazing out of the window, saw upon the bare hillside and the snow-covered valley, a garden of paradise, a palace of costly stones, birds of brilliant plumage, ladies, whose hair of pure gold, came down to their feet; that the frozen river changed for her into a blue, billowy sea, upon whose waves nymphs sailed in pearly shells. Sultan, who lay snoring stretched upon the floor, never dreamed of the honor the boys gave him when they looked upon him as an enchanted prince. How pleasant it was in the room as soon as it was dusk! Vorsa closed the blinds, the pitch pine cracked in the stove, in the middle of the room a large wooden candlestick was placed, in whose iron arms were burning faggots, around it were benches for the spinners, for whom Grandmother always had ready a basket of dried apples and prunes, "just for a bite," as she said. With what impatience the children waited to hear the click of the door latch in the hall when the spinners entered the room. During this time Grandmother would not begin to tell anything, but waited until all the spinners were present. In the day time she sang Advent hymns.

When, as yet, the children did not know her well, her good and ill humor, they thought they could tease her till she told them a story. But she disposed of them quickly. Sometimes she began to tell them about the shepherd who had three hundred sheep, and who, driving them to pasture, came to a footbridge over which only one could go at a time; "Now we must wait till they cross," she said, and became silent. In a little while the children asked: "Are they over?" She replied: "What are you thinking of? it will take at least two hours." They knew what that meant. Another time she said: "You think I have seventy-seven pockets and a story in each. Very well, out of which pocket do you want one?" "Perhaps from the tenth," said the children. "Very well. In the the tenth pocket is this story

"There was once a king, who had a ring, in which he rolled a tomcat bold. Now listen, for it will be very long," and that was the end of that story

The worst story was about Red Ridinghood. The children could not endure that one, and usually ran away; with every other story they could coax Grandmother to keep still or talk about something else, but here they did not dare to say a word unless they wanted to hear it repeated.* The children finally learned to wait patiently for the spinners. The first who came were Christina and Milo, then Celia Kuderna, the friend of Betsey and Vorsa; sometimes the miller's wife came, too, with Manchinka and the gamekeeper's wife, and once a week Christina brought with her Anna, who was now the wife of Tomesh. When the spinning was over, her husband came to see her safe home.

While the women were warming themselves and getting ready for the work, they spoke of various things. One told the news from the village, another that which had been heard in town; or if there happened to be some holiday, with which there was connected some national custom or some superstition, this also furnished a topic of conversation. For example, on the eve of St. Nicholas, Christina asked Adelka if she had her stocking hung up, for St. Nicholas was already going through the village. "Grandma will hang it up for me, when I go to bed," said the child.

"You must not hang up your own stocking, it's too small. Ask Grandma to lend you hers," suggested Christina.

*This story about Red Ridinghood is not the one commonly known in America as well as in Europe. The story teller begins by saying: "Now I'll tell you the story about Red Ridinghood." Most probably the listener will say: "Very well," upon which the teller says: "I wasn't going to tell a story about 'very well' but about Red Ridinghood," and so on, each time repeating what the listener says.

"That won't do, for the rest of us would be cheated," said John.

"You won't get anything anyhow but a switch," teased Christina.

"Oh, but St. Nicholas knows that Grandma has had one hidden since last year and that she never whips us," replied John. Grandmother, however, remarked that it was not because he had not deserved it.

Lucie's day was very disagreeable to the children. The superstition was, that on this night, Lucie a tall woman in white, with long, disheveled hair, went about seeking disobedient children. "Cowardice is folly," said Grandmother, who was not at all pleased when the children were taught to be afraid. She used to teach them to fear nothing except God's displeasure; but she could not, like their father, prove to them that no such things existed as watermen, fiery dragons, will o' the wisps, fiery men that roll before the observer like a bundle of straw; for her own belief in them was too deeply rooted in her mind. To her, the various forms in nature were animate with good or evil spirits; she believed in a wicked infernal spirit, that God sends upon the earth to try the souls of his people. She believed it all, but was not afraid; for she possessed a firm living faith in God, in whose power is the whole earth, heaven, and hell, and without whose permission not a hair falls from our heads.

This confidence in God she tried to instil into the hearts of the children. So, when on Lucie's day Vorsa began to talk about the woman in white, Grandmother told her to be quiet, for she had never heard that Lucie ever harmed any one.

Milo was the most welcome visitor, for with his jack knife he made the boys little sleighs, plows, and wagons, or prepared the faggots for lighting, and the boys did not stir a step from him. When the spinners related ghost stories, and Willie clung to him, he would say: "Don't you be afraid, Willie; against the devil we will take the cross, and a cane for the ghost, and we'll beat them both."

This pleased the boys and they would have gone anywhere with Milo, even at midnight. Grandmother agreeing with him said: "A man is a man."

"Yes, indeed, and Milo is not afraid even of the devil, nor of the steward, who is worse than the devil," said Christina.

"How is it, Milo, is there any prospect of your getting work on the manor farm?" asked Grandmother.

"I fear not, they are pressing upon me from two directions, and several malicious women are meddling with my business," replied Milo.

"Do not speak in this way, perhaps it may yet be arranged," said Christina sorrowfully.

"I desire it as much as you; but, really, I see no way out of the difficulty. The steward's daughter can never forgive me for that trick I played upon the Italian. They say she was in love with him, and when, on account of that trouble, he was discharged by the Princess, the young lady's plans were brought to naught. Now she uses all her influence to induce her father not to take me into service. That is one enemy, the other is Lucie, the Squire's daughter. She has taken it into her head that I shall be her king on Long Night,*

*A festival held by the spinners.

and as I cannot accept that distinction her father will be angry, and when spring comes I suppose I shall sing:

> " ' Alas, no longer am I free,
> For soon a soldier I must be.' "

As Milo began to sing, the girls joined in, but Christina burst into tears.

"Never mind, my girl; it is long before spring, and who knows what God has in store for us," said Grandmother, trying to comfort her.

She wiped her eyes, but remained sad the rest of the evening.

"Don't worry about it; perhaps, after all, father will be able to manage the matter," said Milo, sitting down beside her.

"Could you not be that king without compromising yourself?" asked Grandmother.

"Of course I could, Grandma; some fellows wait on two and even three girls at the same time, before they select one for good, and girls do the same. I should not be Lucie's first admirer, and should not be obliged to be the last; and yet among us it is an unheard-of thing that a fellow should woo two girls at once, and when one is the 'King,' it is almost the same as if he went to the wedding."

"In that case you do well not to go," replied Grandmother.

"What has possessed Lucie, that she wants only you, as if there were not plenty of other boys in the village," scolded Christina.

"The miller would say 'There is no accounting for tastes,' " replied Grandmother smiling.

When the Christmas holidays were drawing near, the conversation was varied with talks about the baking of Christmas rolls, discussions about the fineness of the flour and how much butter each intended to use; the girls also talked about melting the lead, the children, of the good loaves, the sailing of candles in nut shells, and the little Jesus * bringing them presents.

* In Bohemia there are two festivals when presents are given. St. Nicholas day, on the 6th of December, and Christmas day. The children believe that on the latter day, the child Jesus makes them presents.

CHAPTER XI.

IT was the custom at the mill, the gamekeeper's lodge, and The Old Bleachery, that whoever came on Christmas eve or Christmas day had all he wanted to eat and drink; if no one had come Grandmother would have gone to the cross roads to look for somebody. Her joy can be imagined when, unexpectedly, her son Caspar with her nephew from Olesnic came the day before Christmas. For a whole half day she wept with joy, and every few moments she left her baking and ran into the room to look at them, to ask her nephew how this one and that one were doing in her old home; and again and again she said to the children: "Your grandfather looked exactly as you see your uncle here, only he was a great deal taller." The children examined their uncle and cousin from all directions, and were much pleased with them, especially since they replied pleasantly to their endless questions.

Every year, the children wanted to fast the day before Christmas, so that in the evening they might see the golden pigs;* but they never succeeded in keeping the fast the whole day. Their intentions were good, but their wills were weak. On Christmas eve everybody received a goodly share of dain-

* The children are told that if they will fast the whole day, in the evening they will see beautiful golden pigs running about the room. As no child ever succeeded in keeping the good resolution the promised pigs are never seen.

ties, and even the poultry and cattle were not forgotten when the Christmas loaves were cut. After
supper, Grandmother took a part of the contents of
each dish, half of which she threw into the stream
that the water might remain pure, and buried the
other half under a tree in the orchard that the
ground might be fertile. She brushed the crumbs
up carefully and threw them into the fire, so that it
should do no damage.

After the work was done, Betsey took a branch
of sweet elder and shaking it, recited:

> "Sweet elder I shake, I shake!
> Tell me, ye dogs that wake,
> Where is my lover to-night."

Then she listened to ascertain in what direction
the dogs were barking.

In the sitting room the girls were melting together wax and lead,* and the children were sailing candles in nutshells.

John secretly pushed the pan of water so that it
moved, and the shells, which represented the ships
of life, sailed from the edge to the center of the
water; then he cried joyfully: "Look, look, I shall
get far, far into the world!"

"My dear boy, when you get into the current
of life, among its eddies and rocks, when the waves
dash your boat hither and thither, then you will
think with longing of the quiet haven from which
you sailed," said the mother in a low tone, cutting
his apple, "for luck," through its wide part. The
seeds made a star, three of its rays being clear and
sound, two imperfect and worm-eaten. Laying it

* A species of fortune telling, the form which the wax and lead assume on cooling indicating what will happen to the person during the
coming year.

aside with a sigh, she cut Barunka's, and again the star was imperfect. She said to herself: "Neither one will be completely happy!" Then she cut Willie's and Adelka's, and in those the stars were clear and sound, but had only four rays. "These perhaps may be happier," thought the mother, when Adelka interrupted her by complaining that her boat would not go from the shore, and that her candle was almost burnt down.

"Mine, too, is going out, and did not get very far," said Willie.

At that moment somebody pushed the pan, the water was covered with waves, and the boats in the middle went down.

"See, see, you'll die before we do!" cried Adelka and Willie.

"No matter, since we shall go far," replied Barunka, and John agreed with her; but the mother looked sadly at the extinguished candles, and a presentiment took possession of her soul, that perhaps, after all, this innocent, childish play was the foreshadowing of their future.

"Will the child Jesus bring us something?" whispered the children to Grandmother, when the table was cleared.

"I cannot tell you that; you will hear, if he rings," replied Grandmother. The smaller children took their post at the window, thinking that when Jesus went by they would hear him. "Don't you know that Jesus can neither be seen nor heard?" said Grandmother. "He is in heaven sitting upon a shining throne, and sends his gifts to good children by angels, who bring them down upon golden clouds. You will hear nothing but the bells."

The children looked out of the window, piously listening to all Grandmother said. Just then a bright light gleamed past the window, and the sound of bells was heard. They clasped their hands, while Adelka whispered: "Grandma, that was the child Jesus, was it not?" Grandmother nodded. Then the door opened, and the mother entered, telling the children that Jesus had left gifts for them in Grandmother's room. When they saw a beautiful lighted tree, their joy knew no bounds. Grandmother was not familiar with this custom, it not being common among the villagers, but she· was much pleased with it, and, long before Christmas, was careful to see that a tree was provided, and helped her daughter to trim it.

"In Niesse and Kladrau this custom is celebrated; do you recollect, Caspar? You were quite a boy before we left," said Grandmother addressing her son. She then seated herself beside him, leaving the children to enjoy their tree and their presents.

"Of course I remember," replied Caspar; "it is a good custom and you did well, Theresa, to introduce it here. The recollections of these domestic festivities will be dear to the children when they find themselves adrift in the world. When one is away from home, one loves to think of this day. I found it the case when I lived among strangers. My masters were not hard, so that I had good times; and yet I always thought, 'Oh, that I could be at home with my mother, to eat pudding with honey, buns with poppy-seed sauce, and pease with cabbage. I would have gladly exchanged all the good things I had for that homely fare."

"Our own victuals," smiled Grandmother, nodding: "but you forget the mixture of dried fruit?"

"Yes, but you know I never cared for it. I have thought of something else that we all love to hear; at Dobrau they call it 'music.'"

"Oh, I know what you mean! the shepherds' Christmas carol; we have that here, too, you'll hear it before long," said his mother, and hardly had she spoken, when the shepherd's horn was heard near the window. First the melody of the carol was played upon the horn and then the shepherds sang:

> "Arise! ye shepherds, arise!
> Glad tidings to you we bring;
> To day a Savior was born to us
> In a manger in Bethlehem."

"You are right, Caspar. If I did not hear this song, it would not seem like Christmas to me," said Grandmother, listening to the rest of the song with much pleasure. Then she went out and loaded the shepherds with Christmas dainties.

On St. Stephen's, the boys went to sing Christmas songs at the mill and at the gamekeeper's; if they had not come, the miller's wife would have thought that the ceiling must have come down, and she herself would have gone to The Old Bleachery to see what had happened. Afterwards Bertie and Frank came down to sing in return.

The Christmas holidays were over; the children began to talk of the next holiday, of the Three Kings or Wise Men of the East. Then the schoolmaster came and sang of Christ's birth, and wrote the names of the Three Wise Men upon the door. After the Three Kings, the spinners celebrated their festival of the "Long Night." To be sure, at The Old Bleachery and at the mill it was not as in the village, where there were many young people; there they chose a king and queen, had a dance, trimmed the spinning wheel, and crowned the queen.

In The Old Bleachery a good supper was prepared, the spinners came, sang, ate and drank, and if by chance the hand organ was heard behind the door, they danced in the kitchen. Tomesh, the miller, and the gamekeeper, and several others came, and the party was complete. The floor of the kitchen was of bricks, but the girls did not mind it, though some of them, who were too careful of their shoes, took them off and danced barefooted.

"What do you say, Grandma, couldn't we have a little hop together?" said the miller, who had entered the kitchen among the young folks, where Grandmother was watching the small fry who, together with Sultan and Tyrol, were constantly getting in the way of the dancers.

"O, my dear miller, there were times when I did not care though my feet were full of bloody blisters, if only I could dance. As soon as I showed myself at the tavern, or in the summer on the threshing floor, the boys would say: 'Madaline is here, play Kalamajka, Vertak!* Hurrah! Now for it!' and Madaline flew into the circle. But now, good heavens! I'm like the steam over the kettle."

"Indeed, I do not doubt it, for you are still as smart as a quail; come, let us try just a little dance."

*Slavonic dances.

Here is a dancer, who can turn like a spindle," laughed Grandmother, taking the hand of Anna, Tomesh's wife, who happened to be standing behind the miller, listening to the conversation.

Gayly the young woman took the miller's arm, told Kuderna to play the first tune slowly, and began to get her step ready for the dance. The miller, willing or unwilling, had to start, while the young people clapped their hands and shouted, till the miller's wife, hearing the noise, came to see what was going on. Tomesh, seeing her, offered her his arm, and she was soon following her husband, and thus the old people also had a hop, and Grandmother laughed at the miller's expense.

" Hardly was the Long Night over, when there was merry making in the mill. A fat hog had been killed, sausages were made, fried cakes were cooked, and a sleigh was sent to get the friends from the mill and the gamekeeper's. Later, the feast was at the gamekeeper's, and at last at Proshek's.

Shortly after this, the young people came to play Dorothea. Vaclav Kuderna acted the part of King Diocletian, his sister Lida was the maid Dorothea, the two courtiers, the judge, the executioner and his assistants were boys from Zernov. The courtiers and the assistants carried bags for such edibles as they hoped to receive. The pond before Proshek's house furnished a good skating place; here the actors stopped to have a good time, while Dorothea, the maid, shivering with cold stood by and watched them. She urged them to go, but her voice was drowned in the general shouting, and they did not start until they had had their fill of skating, rolling, and tumbling over one another. Then they entered the house, where the dogs met them with a terrible barking; but the children welcomed them with the greatest delight. They remained near the door, where they laid down their bags and put themselves in order for the play. Their clothes were quite simple. The maid Dorothea had on her brother's boots, a white dress that Manchinka had lent her, and beneath her paper crown she wore her mother's white kerchief. The boys wore paper caps, and to complete their costumes they had white shirts over their other clothes, fastened around the waist with bright colored handkerchiefs. King Diocletian also had a crown, and the beautiful cloak that hung so gracefully from his shoulders was his mother's best Sunday apron, which she had lent him as a special favor. As soon as they had warmed themselves by the fire, they took their stand in the middle of the room to recite their parts; the children heard it every year but never got tired of it. When the heathen king, Diocletian, condemns the Christian maid Dorothea to death, the assistants take her by the arms and lead her to the block, where the headsman stands with his sword raised up high, and says with terrible pathos:

> " Thou maid, Dorothea, kneel,
>   My sword do not thou fear;
> Now bravely bend thy head
>   In a second, thou art dead! "

Dorothea kneels, bends her head, the headsman cuts off her crown, and the assistant raises it in the air. Then all bow, Dorothea picks up her crown and puts it back upon her head, and takes her stand in the corner of the room, by the door.

"How well those children recite!" exclaimed Vorsa; "I could listen to them the whole evening."

Grandmother, too, was not chary of her praise, and the actors, with well-filled bags, sallied into the yard. When they got behind the house they examined the contents of their bags. The food was at once divided equally among them, but the money the king put into his own pocket, saying that he had a right to do so, since as director of the troupe he had assumed all the expenses and the responsibility. After this just distribution of profits, the party started for the gamekeeper's. For several days the children kept reciting the verses and acting the part of Dorothea, but the mother could not comprehend how any one could enjoy such egregious nonsense.

One Sunday morning some time after this, a handsome sleigh was seen in Proshek's yard. When the horses stirred, their bells jingled so loudly that the crow, the winter boarder in the poultry yard, flew away to the top of the mountain ash, and the chickens and sparrows eyed the team curiously, and seemed to say: "What in the world can this mean?" It was Shrovetide, and Mr. Stanicky had come to take the Proshek family to town to spend the day with him.

Grandmother, however, would not go; she said: "What should I do there? leave me at home, such company is not for me." The Stanickys were good, pleasant people; but as they kept a hotel, all sorts of people met there, some from afar and quite stylish, and this was no company for our lowly Grandmother

In the evening, when the family returned home, the children related all they had seen and heard, and what nice things they had eaten. Here, however, Grandmother was not forgotten, for Mrs. Stanicky never neglected to send her a large package of good things. The children praised the music and told her who were there.

"Guess, Grandma, whom we saw?" said John.

"Well, whom?" asked Grandmother.

"The peddler, Vlach, who comes to our house and gives us figs! But you would not have known him; he was clean, dressed up like a prince, and had a gold watch chain!"

"One can afford to be extravagant when one has a plenty; besides, you, too, do not go out among people in your every day clothes. A person owes it to himself and to society to dress as well as he can afford."

"But he must be rich, do you not think so, Grandma?"

"As I never looked into his chest, I cannot tell. Doubtless he is, for he is a good business man."

On the last day of Shrove-tide the masqueraders came along with great parade, at their head Shrove-tide himself. He was covered with pea straw, so that he looked like a bear. Wherever he came, the house-wife tore off a piece of the straw and saved it to put into the nest the following spring, when the goose was set, so that the eggs should hatch well.

Shrove-tide passed by and with it all the winter merry-makings. At her spinning Grandmother

15

sang Lenten Hymns; when the children sat near her, she told them stories from the life of Christ, and the first Sunday in Lent she put on mourning. The days grew longer, the sun shone with greater power, and the warm wind carried away the snow from the hillsides. The poultry cackled gayly in the yard; and when the housekeepers met, they talked of setting hens and of sowing flax, and the men prepared the ploughs and harrows. When the gamekeeper wanted to come from the woods opposite to The Old Bleachery, he could not cross the river, for the ice was cracking and, as the miller said, " piece after piece was taking leave of its fellows."

The Sundays came, " the Black," " the Social," "the Sneezing," and, finally, the long expected " Death Sunday." The children cried: " To-day we will carry Death away," and the girls added: " Now it is our turn to be waits." * Adelka had been saving eggshells all the week, and now Grandmother took these, together with some gay streamers, and trimmed up a switch for her; this was called " summer." The girls prepared for the spring merry-making. In the afternoon they met at the mill to dress " Death." Cilka Kuderna made a straw dummy, and each girl contributed some article of clothing; for the handsomer Miss Mawlikin was, the greater was the credit which the girls received. When she was dressed, two girls took her by the arms, the rest formed a procession behind, and dancing as they went, they sang:

> " Death from the village now we carry,
> New season come, and do not tarry."

* Usually boys or men go out on the eve of festivals or holidays to sing under the windows, but on Easter it is the privilege of the girls to do the singing, or be " waits."

A few of the villagers followed them out some distance, but the boys came close to them, making gestures of contempt and trying to jerk off poor Miss Mawlikin's cap; but her escort protected her well. Reaching the dam, they disrobed her and with shouts of joy flung her into the water, and then both boys and girls sang:

> "Death is floating down the stream,
> A new season is drawing near,
> Bringing eggs and Easter cheer."

Then the girls sang alone:

> "Oh summer, summer so sweet,
> Where hast thou been delayed?"
> "To wash my hands and feet,
> In the forest's deepest shade.
> The rose and the violet blue
> Cannot bloom without God's dew."

Then the boys burst forth with their song:

> "St. Peter at Rome, be thine
> The good will to send us some wine.
> Thy praises we'll drink, and sing
> Till the woods with merriment ring."

"Come in, come in, ye waits!" called Mrs. Proshek, who had been outdoors listening to the songs of the young people; "we cannot give you wine, but we have something with which to make you merry."

The party still singing, entered the house, where for some time they enjoyed themselves to their heart's content.

On the morning of Palm-Sunday, Barunka went down to the river to pick some pussy-willows. "They are already in blossom, as if they knew they were wanted," thought the child. When she went with Grandmother to early mass, each carried a bunch to be blessed.

On Ash-Wednesday, when Grandmother had finished her spinning and was carrying the spinning wheel up into the garret, Adelka cried: "Oh, my! the spinning wheel is going up to the garret. Grandma will now use the spindle."

"If God grants us life and health, next winter we'll bring it down again," replied Grandmother.

On Maundy-Thursday the children knew they would have nothing for breakfast but Judases * with honey. At The Old Bleachery they had no bees; but every year the miller sent them some honey, and had promised them that as soon as a good swarm was ready to leave, he would give it to them; for he once heard Grandmother say that she desired nothing so much as a beehive near the house. "Everything seems more cheerful," she said, "when one sees those bees flying about so busily all day long."

"Rise, Barunka, the sun will soon be up!" called Grandmother early on Good-Friday, gently rapping her grandchild on the forehead. Barunka opened her eyes, and seeing Grandmother standing by her bed she recollected that she had asked to be awakened for early prayers. She jumped out of bed, put on her petticoat, and throwing a shawl over her shoulders was ready to accompany Grandmother to the hill. Vorsa and Betsey were awakened, too, but not the little ones, for Grandmother said they did not understand it yet. As soon as the kitchen door squeaked, the poultry and cattle began to stir, and the dogs jumped out of their kennels.

---

* A kind of flat biscuit baked only in Passion week.

Grandmother pushed them aside as she said: "Have patience till we have said our prayers." When Barunka, at Grandmother's suggestion, had washed her face in a stream of water, they went upon the hillside to say nine Pater-nosters and nine Ave Marias, so that God would grant them for the whole year cleanliness of body. Grandmother knelt down, clasped her hands, and prayed fervently, her confiding gaze turned to the crimson sunrise.

Barunka knelt beside her, fresh and rosy as a bud. For a while she, too, prayed fervently; but soon her gaze wandered from the east to the woods and over the meadows and hillsides. The river still carried along with it pieces of snow and ice, and the snow still lingered in the valleys; but here and there were seen patches of green grass, the early daisies were whitening the hillsides, the trees and bushes were beginning to bud, and all nature was awakening to a new life. The red clouds were scattered in the skies, the golden rays rose higher and higher behind the mountain, gilding the tree-tops, till finally the sun showed itself in all its glory, pouring a flood of light upon the whole hillside. The opposite hillside was still in a dim light, behind the dam the mists fell lower and lower, and above them upon the opposite hill, the women of the mill were seen kneeling in prayer.

"Look, Grandma! how beautiful the sun rises," said Barunka, all wrapped in wonder at the glorious sight. "O that we were now on the top of Snow Cap!"

"All places are sacred to worship, for the earth is the Lord's," replied Grandmother, making the sign of the cross and rising from her prayers.

When they turned, they saw a woman's figure standing on the top of the hill leaning against a tree. It was Victorka. Her disheveled hair, damp with the dews of night, hung about her face, her throat was bare, her black eyes, gleaming with a strange light, were fixed upon the rising sun, and in her hand she held a primrose. She did not seem to observe them. "Poor child, where has she been wandering?" said Grandmother, pityingly.

"And where could she have found that primrose?" said Barunka.

"Somewhere upon the top of the hill. Why, she knows every nook and corner," replied Grandmother

"I am going to ask her for it," said Barunka, and was already running up the hill. Just then Victorka seemed to awake from her reverie and turned to flee; but when Barunka called: "Please, Victorka, give me that flower!" she stopped, and with her eyes turned away gave the child the primrose. The she turned abruptly and flew down the hill. Barunka came down to Grandmother.

"It is a long time since she came to get some food," said Grandmother.

"O, no! Yesterday, when you were gone to church, Mamma gave her a loaf of bread and some Judases," said Barunka.

"Poor creature! The summer will soon be here, and then she will be better off; but heaven knows whether she has any feeling left. She wears such thin garments the whole winter long, and goes barefoot, and often she can be tracked by the bloody marks which she leaves upon the snow. How gladly would the gamekeeper's wife give her something warm to eat every day; but she won't accept anything but bread, or some other cold victuals. Unhappy girl!"

" Grandma, I don't think she is cold in that cave; if she were she would go somewhere else. Why, we have asked her many times to stay with us."

" The gamekeeper says that it is warm in such underground places, and since Victorka never enters a room warmed by a fire, she is not so sensitive to cold as we. God orders things thus; he sends guardian angels to protect children from evil, and Victorka is a poor child, too," said Grandmother, entering the house.

Usually the bell from the village chapel called the family to prayers and to dinner; but this time, John and Willie ran into the orchard with clappers and clapped till the sparrows were frightened out of their nests. In the afternoon, Grandmother and the children went to the village to see the Lord's tomb, and on their way they stopped for Manchinka and her mother. The miller's wife took Grandmother into the store-room to show her the great basket of colored eggs which she had prepared for the Easter singers. There was also a long row of coffee-cakes covered with various kinds of sauce, and a fat lamb ready to be roasted. She gave each of the children a little roll, but none to Grandmother; for she knew that from Maundy-Thursday, she never took a mouthful till the evening before the Resurrection Day. She herself fasted on Good Friday, but not so strictly as Grandmother. The latter said: " Every one must act according to his own conscience. As for myself, it seems to me if I'm going to fast, I must fast during all of these days. She examined and praised all the baking, and added: "We are going to bake to-morrow, everything is prepared; but to-day is devoted to prayer!" This was the custom at Proshek's, for there Grandmother's word was law.

The Saturday before Easter, from the earliest dawn till the close of the day, The Old Bleachery reminded one of the bridge at Prague; in the sitting room, in the kitchen, in the yard, at the oven, everywhere busy hands were constantly meeting each other, and each one of the women to whom the children turned with their difficulties declared she didn't know where her head was. Even Barunka had so much to do that she forgot one thing in the effort to remember another. But by evening the house was in apple-pie order, and Grandmother, with Barunka and the mother, went to the service of the Resurrection. When they entered the brilliantly lighted church filled with devout people, a full chorus burst forth with the hymn beginning:

"This day our Savior arose! Hallelujah!"
Barunka was carried away by a powerful feeling, her breast heaved, and she felt impelled to rush out into the open air that she might give free vent to the inexpressible emotions that filled her soul. The whole evening she was filled with a quiet joy, and when Grandmother came to bid her "good night," she put her arms around her neck and burst into tears.

"What is the matter, my child?" asked Grandmother.

"Nothing is the matter, Grandma, only I am so very happy," replied Barunka. Grandmother bent down, kissed her grandchild on the forehead, but said not a word,— she understood her Barunka.

On Easter Sunday, Grandmother took a cake, some eggs, and some wine to church to be blessed. When she returned, she cut up the cake and gave each one a piece, and also a little wine. The poultry and cattle also got their extra portion of food as on Christmas, so that they would become attached to their home and return good profits.

Easter Monday was a bad day for the women, for then the waits came to sing and to switch them. Hardly were they awake at Proshek's, when they heard a voice behind the door singing: "A little wait am I," and somebody knocked at the door. Betsey opened it very carefully, fearing it might be one of the boys come to give her a switching; but it was the miller, the earliest of them all. He came as meek as a saint, and wished them a merry and happy Easter; but all at once he pulled out a switch from beneath his coat and began to apply it vigorously. He spared no one, and even Mrs. Proshek and Adelka and Grandmother were struck several times across their petticoats "so the fleas shouldn't bite" as he said. He was treated the same as any other wait, he got his Easter egg and an apple. "Well, boys, have you done your duty this morning?" he asked.

"They are nice fellows! other days one can hardly get them out of bed; but to-day I was hardly in the sitting room when they began to switch me," complained Barunka, and both the miller and the boys laughed at her.

The gamekeeper, too, and Milo and Tomesh came down to switch the women; in short the girls had no rest the whole day, and as soon as they caught a glimpse of some new comer, they covered their bare shoulders with their aprons.

CHAPTER XII.

SPRING was coming on apace. The people were working in the fields; upon the hillsides lizards and snakes basked in the sun, so that the children, going out to gather violets and lilies of the valley were often frightened by them; but Grandmother told them they had nothing to fear, for before St. George's such creatures were not poisonous, and could be handled with impunity; but when the sun was high, then they had poison in them. In the meadow behind the dam were seen blossoming the ox-eye daisies and larkspurs, on the hillside liver wort and the golden primroses. The children gathered young leaves for soup and brought nettles for the goslings; and whenever Grandmother entered the stable she promised Spotty that she should soon be taken out to pasture. The trees quickly put on their green leaves, the mosquitoes sang merrily in the air, the lark winged his way high up into the clouds, so that although the children often heard the little singer they never could see him; they also listened to the cuckoo and called into the woods: "Cuckoo, cuckoo, tell us how many years we shall live?" Sometimes she would coo, but sometimes she refused, and Adelka scolded, saying that it was just out of spite. The boys taught Adelka to make willow whistles; when her whistles wouldn't sound they told her it was because while knocking the bark to loosen it she had not said the words right. "You girls can't even make a whistle," laughed John.

"That isn't our business; but you can't make a hat like this," said Barunka, showing her brother a hat made of elder leaves and trimmed with daisies.

"Hm, that's nothing!" said John, with a toss of his head.

"Nothing for me, but a good deal for you," laughed Barunka, making a doll out of the pith of elder to match the hat.

John placed the switch on his knee and said to Adelka: "Now, listen and watch how I'm going to do it!" and striking the switch with the handle of his knife, he recited:

> "Hark! hark! hark!
> And quickly loosen thy bark;
> If thy bark thou wilt not free,
> It shall be ill with thee.
> Our prince will come full soon
>   And give thee a blow
>   Till thou shalt go
> Right up to the silver moon?
>
>   Clip! clip! clip!
> At first thou wast only a whip,
> But with my little knife
> I'll give thee a new life;
> A new life so sweet and good,
>   That at my word
>   Thou wilt sing like a bird,
> Like a little bird of the wood."

The bark was loosened, the whistle made, and when John tried it, it gave out a pleasant sound; but Willie said that it did not whistle nearly as well as Wenzel's old whistle that he used when he watched the cattle. He got tired of making whistles and made a wagon instead, to which he hitched himself, and started to race about the meadow with the dogs after him.

Barunka, giving her sister the pith doll, said: " Here, you may have this, but you must learn to make them yourself? Who will play with you when we are gone to school? You will be here alone."

" Grandma will be here," replied the child with an expression that said that although it would not be pleasant to be left alone, still if Grandma was with her she would have everything.

Just then the miller came along and handing Barunka a letter, said: " Take it to your mother and tell her one of my men was in town, and the postmaster gave it to him."

" It's from papa! " exclaimed the children running into the house. Mrs. Proshek read the letter with a face beaming with joy, and having finished it, told the children that their father would come home about the middle of May, and the Princess, too.

" How many times shall we sleep? " asked Adelka.

" About forty times," replied Barunka.

" O, my! that is so long yet! " said the little girl, much disappointed.

" Do you know what I'll do? " said Willie; " I will make forty chalk marks upon the door, and every morning when I get up I will rub one out."

" That is a good idea, the time will pass away more quickly," said his mother.

The miller was going from the dam and stopped at Proshek's. His face was sober, the habitual grin was gone, and he held his snuff box in his hand, but did not turn it; instead of that he tapped the cover with his fingers. " Do you know what's the news, my friends?" he said as he entered the room.

" What has happened?" asked Mrs. Proshek and Grandmother at the same time, seeing that the miller was not in his usual mood.

" The mountain water is coming."

" God grant that it be neither sudden nor heavy!" said Grandmother, much frightened.

" I am not a little alarmed," said the miller. " For several days we have had south winds; then there have been heavy rains in the hilly regions, and the farmers tell me that the streams are flooded and the snow is rapidly thawing. The outlook is not inviting. I shall hurry home now and put everything out of the way of the evil visitor. I should advise you to do the same; we cannot be too careful. In the afternoon I will come to see how things appear. Watch how the water rises, — and you, little linnet, don't you go near the water!" he added, pinching Adelka on the cheek; then he left the house.

Grandmother went to look at the dam. On each side the banks were protected by oak piles, among which brakes had grown. She saw that some of the lower brakes were already beneath the water. Pieces of wood, sod, and branches of trees were carried away across the dam by the muddy current. She returned to the house with an anxious face. When the ice broke, it sometimes stopped at the dam, and the current rushed into the sluice and flooded the house. This was always a time of anxiety to the miller, and his men were constantly on the watch to arrest every threatening danger, by separating the floes that were accumulating in heaps. This, however, could not arrest the progress of the mountain flood. Like a mad charger it came plunging down the sides of the mountain, carrying with it everything that lay in its path. The banks of oak were torn asunder, houses were overthrown, and all this happened so suddenly that the people scarcely had time to think what to do. Grandmother, who had once experienced this, no sooner entered the house than she advised the immediate removal of the furniture to the garret, which was done at once.

In the meantime, the gamekeeper came over. Going from the woods past the saw mill, he had heard of the coming of high water and had noticed the rise of the river. " Those children will only be in your way, and when the worst comes, what will you do with them? I will take them with me up above." Mrs. Proshek gladly accepted his offer. Everything was packed and put away, the poultry was taken to the top of the hill, and Spotty to the gamekeeper's.

" You two go to the gamekeeper's, so his wife shall not have everything on her own hands," said Grandmother to her daughter and Betsey, when everything was in order. " Vorsa and I will remain here. Should the water come into the house, we will go up into the garret, and, God protecting us, we hope it will not be so bad that the house will be carried away; it is not so low here as at the mill; they, poor souls, will have a harder time."

For some time Mrs. Proshek would not consent to her mother's remaining there; but when she could not persuade her to go, she finally went without her. " Don't let the dogs get away," she said, as she was leaving.

" Never fear for them; they know where their safety lies, they will not leave us." And, truly, Sultan and Tyrol were constantly at Grandmother's heels, and when she took the spindle and sat down by the window, out of which she had a good view of the river, the dogs lay down at her feet. Vorsa, accustomed constantly to be doing something, began to clean out the empty pens, not thinking that in an hour, they would be filled with mud and water.

It grew dusk, the water rose higher and higher, and reached almost to the edges of the sluice; the meadow behind the dam was already under water, and where the willows did not obstruct the view, although the house lay low and the banks of the river were high, Grandmother could see the dashing of the waves. She laid aside her spindle, clasped her hands, and began to pray. Vorsa entered the room, and said as she brushed the dust from the bench by the window: " The water roars till one is filled with terror; all living creatures have hid themselves as if they knew something was going to happen; not a sparrow is to be seen."

The sound of a horse's hoofs is heard on the main road leading from the dam, and a rider gallops along at full speed; he stops at the house and shouts: " Save yourselves, people; the flood is upon us !" Then he gallops on to the mill and from the mill to the village.

" God be with us. Up above they are in peril; they've sent a messenger," said Grandmother, turning pale. Still she told Vorsa not to be afraid, and went again to see if all was safe, and to note how much the water had gained. She caught sight of the miller. He had on a pair of high boots and was examining the condition of the water; he showed her that it was already overflowing the side of the sluice.

Milo and Kuderna came to offer their assistance and to stay with her; she sent Kuderna home, saying: "You have children, and if some misfortune should befall them, I should always blame myself. If any one is to stay, let it be Milo; at the inn he is not needed; there they have nothing to fear, except that the water may get into their stable." Thus they parted.

By midnight the house was surrounded with water. On Zernov hill the people went about with lanterns; the gamekeeper, too, came near the house, upon the hill, and thinking that Grandmother could hardly be asleep called and whistled, till Milo replied that they were all right, that Mrs. Proshek need have no fears for her mother. Then the gamekeeper went away again. In the morning the whole plain was one vast sheet of water. Down stairs they had to walk on planks, and with great difficulty Milo got to the top of the hill to the poultry; the water rushed with such force as almost to knock him over. At daybreak everybody came down from the gamekeeper's to see how it was at The Old Bleachery. The children seeing the house, in the middle of a lake, and Grandmother walking about on planks, began to cry and lament at such a rate that they could scarcely be quieted. The dogs were looking out of the door of the garret, and when John called them they barked and howled, and would have jumped down, had not Milo held them back.

Kuderna came and related what damage the water had done below. In Zlitz it had carried away two houses, in one of which there was an old woman, who, not heeding the warning of the messenger, delayed till it was too late. Bridges and trees were carried away, in short everything that lay in the way of the flood. At the mill, they lived in the upper rooms.

Christina came to Proshek's to see if it was possible to bring them something warm to eat; but she saw that it was not to be thought of, and when Milo boldly started to cross over, she herself begged him to remain where he was.

The danger lasted two days; the third day the water began to subside. How the children wondered when they returned to the house. The garden was flooded, the orchard was covered with debris, deep gullies were washed out in many places, and the willows and alders were half buried in mud. The foot bridge was carried away, deep caves were worn out under the pens, and the dogs' kennels were nowhere to be seen. Adelka and the boys went to look behind the house. They had some trees there which they had brought from the woods, and which Grandmother had planted for them,—birches for the girls, and firs for the boys. They stood there unharmed. Under the pear tree they had made a little cottage, and around it a garden with a fence and a small ditch, in which were mills that turned when a rain had filled it with water. There also an oven there in which Adelka baked her mud buns and kolaches.

Not a trace was left of this little establishment. "You simpletons," said Grandmother, laughing when she heard the children bemoaning their loss, "how could you expect your plaything would stand before the force of those angry waters that in their course overturn houses and root up trees centuries old!"

Before many days passed the sun dried the fields, meadows, and roads, the wind carried away much of the debris, the grass grew more lush, the damages were repaired, and hardly a trace remained of the destructive flood; but the people spoke of it for a long time. The swallows returned, and the children welcomed them gladly; they hoped that Mr. Beyer, too, would soon come, and after him their father.

It was the evening of Philip and James' day. Grandmother took chalk that had been blessed upon Three Kings' day,* and made three crosses upon every door, not only of the house, but of the stables, pens, and chicken coops, as a protection against witches. This being done, she went with the children to the hill near the castle, the boys carrying an old broom upon their shoulders. Christina and Jacob Milo were already there, as well as the young people from the manor and from the mill. Wenzel Kuderna, with his brothers, was helping Jacob to cover the brooms with pitch, and the others were arranging the wood for the bonfires.

The night was beautiful. A gentle breeze swept the young grain into small billows, and carried the fragrance of the flowers and blooming

*Festival of the three wise men that came to Bethlehem at the birth of Christ.

fruit trees over the whole hill. The hooting of the owl was heard from the forest, a blackbird chirped from a tall poplar by the roadside, and the nightingale's sweet song resounded from the park. Suddenly a flame was seen to shoot up from Zlitz hill; in an instant more one appeared on Zernov hill, and along the hillsides lights were seen moving in all directions. Further off, upon the hills of Nachod and Newtown, were seen bonfires and dancing lights. Then Milo set fire to the pitched broom and threw it upon the heap of leaves and faggots, and presently the whole was in flames. The young people shouted, and each seized his pitched broom, lighted it, and hurling it high into the air cried: "Fly, witch, fly!" Then they fell into line, and began to dance wildly about, holding the burning torches; but the girls made a ring and, singing, danced round the burning faggots. When the heap fell down, they scattered the pieces and jumped over them, each trying to outjump all the others.

"See," said Milo, "this old witch must fly the farthest," and seizing a broom,* he threw it up with such force that it whizzed through the air and flew almost to the green field where the lookers-on were standing.

"How she spits!" laughed the boys, running for the crackling broom, while the others applauded. From the other hills also were heard singing and laughter. Around the red flames people moved hither and thither, their dark forms producing a fantastic effect; from time to time a witch flew up out of their midst into the air, shook

---

*The brooms commonly used are made of birch twigs, hence are heavy and well adapted to the use described.

her fiery mallet till it rained a thousand sparks, and then fell down again amid the shouts of the people. "Look! how high she flies!" said Manchinka, pointing toward Zernov hill. One of the women, however, pulled down her hand, saying that she must never point at a witch, lest one of the fiery darts pierce through her finger.

It was late when Grandmother returned home with the children. "Grandma, don't you hear something?" whispered Barunka, stopping in the middle of the blooming orchard, "it seems to me I hear something rustling."

"It's nothing but the breeze playing with the leaves," replied Grandmother, and then added: "That breeze does much good."

"Why, Grandma?"

"Because it bends the trees together. They say that when blossoming trees embrace and kiss each other, there will be an abundant harvest."

"O, Grandma, what a pity that now, when there will be cherries and strawberries, and everything will be gay, we must be shut up in the school-house all day," said John sorrowfully.

"That cannot be otherwise, my boy; you cannot always remain at home and play. Now you are beginning to have new tasks and new pleasures."

"Oh, I shall be glad to go to school," said Barunka, "only I shall be so lonesome not to see you all day, Grandma!"

"I shall miss you, too, my children, but it must be so; the tree blossoms, the child grows; the fruit ripens and falls, the child grows up and leaves. It is God's will. While the tree is sound, it bears fruit; when it dies they cut it down and cast it into the fire, and the ashes fertilize the soil out of which new trees grow. Thus your Grandmother will finish her tasks, and you will bear her away to her eternal rest," said she, almost in a whisper.

The nightingale began to sing in the garden shrubbery; the children said he was their nightingale, because he came every spring and built his nest there. From the dam came the sad sound of Victorka's lullaby. The children wanted to remain outdoors a little longer, but Grandmother said: " Don't you know school begins to-morrow, and that you must get up early? Come to bed, lest your mother be angry;" and she pushed them one after another into the house.

In the morning at breakfast, Mrs. Proshek gave all the children except Adelka, who was still asleep, some excellent counsel. She told them how to behave at school and on their way home, and how to improve their time. She admonished them with so much earnestness that they could scarcely refrain from weeping.

Grandmother prepared their lunches. " Here you have each your share," she said, laying three great slices of bread upon the table. " Here is a jack-knife for each, the same that I put away for you. Don't you see, Johnny, that if I had not hidden it, you would have lost it long ago, and now with what would you have cut your bread?" And taking three red-handled knives out of her pocket, she gave one to each of the children. Then she cut a piece of bread out of the middle of each slice, filled the hole with butter, covering it up with the bread that she had cut out, and putting one slice into Barunka's wicker basket, she placed the other two in the boys' leathern satchel. She also added some dried fruit. Breakfast over, the children were ready to start on their journey. "Go in the name of the Lord, and don't forget what I have told you," said the mother, standing in the door.

They kissed their mother's hand, while their eyes filled with tears. Grandmother did not bid them good-bye yet; she went with them across the orchard, and Sultan and Tyrol followed. "Now, boys, you must mind Barunka; you know she is older than you," said Grandmother, on the way. "Don't play any of your foolhardy tricks, lest you hurt yourselves! Improve your time well in school; if you do not you will regret it when you are older. Greet respectfully every one you meet and keep out of the way of teams. You, Willie, don't try to pet every dog you meet; some are cross, and you might get bitten. Don't go into the water, and when you are warm, do not drink. And Johnny, don't you eat your lunch before dinner time, and then gape at the others. Now, good-bye. Adelka and I will come to meet you about four o'clock."

"And Grandma, don't forget to leave us some dinner, — a part of everything you have," begged John.

"You foolish boy, how should we forget!" said Grandmother. Then she blessed each one with the sign of the cross, and they turned to go, when she thought of something else. "Should a storm come up — I don't believe it will — then don't be afraid; go your way quietly and pray, but don't stop under a tree, for lightning is very apt to strike into a tree. Do you understand?"

"Yes ma'am, Papa told us so once, too."

"Now good-bye, give the schoolmaster our best regards!"

Grandmother turned around quickly, so the children should not see the tears in her eyes. The dogs sprang about, thinking that they were going out walking with the children, but John drove them back. At Grandmother's call they followed her, but turned back several times with wistful looks, thinking that perhaps some one would call them. Grandmother, too, looked back several times, and only when she saw the children turn to the bridge where Manchinka was waiting for them, did she turn and go home without stopping. The whole day she seemed somewhat absent-minded; she went about the house as if she were looking for somebody. Hardly had the cuckoo in the clock sung four o'clock, when she put the spindle under her arm and said to Adelka: "Come, my dear, let us go to meet our little scholars; we can wait for them at the mill. So they went.

By the statue under the lindens sat the miller, his wife, and several farmers who had brought in grist. "You are coming to meet the children, are you not?" called the miller's wife from afar; "we, too, are looking for Manchinka. Come, take a seat among us."

As Grandmother sat down she asked: "What's the news?"

"Just before you came, we spoke of the conscription; it takes place this week," replied one of the farmers.

"May heaven comfort our young men," said Grandmother.

"They will need to be comforted. I fear there

will be great lamentations, and Milo's heart is beginning to fail him," said the miller's wife.

" That is the way it generally goes when a person is well favored," said the miller, half closing his eyes as he spoke. " If that were not the case with Milo, he never would be taken into the army; but that deuced jealousy of Lucie and the spite of the steward's daughter have settled it for him."

" Will not his father help him?" asked Grandmother. " Milo had hoped so, when last Christmas the steward refused to give him work at the manor."

" We heard," began one of the farmers, " that Old Milo would gladly devote one or two hundred guilders to that purpose."

" Two hundred! my dear sir, that isn't enough," said the miller; " their farm is not large, and there are several more children. The only way I see out of the difficulty is for him to marry Lucie, but there's no disputing of tastes. I know that if he still has the choice, he will prefer to be a soldier rather than marry the daughter of our squire."

" Well, one evil is as great as the other," said one of the farmers with a shake of his head. " Whoever gets Lucie need never say: 'Lord, chastise me!' he will be chastised enough."

" I am very sorry for Christina," said Grandmother; " how that girl will take on!"

" Never mind the girl," said the miller with half closed eyes; " she will weep a while and groan and sigh, and that's all; but poor Milo, he will suffer worse."

" There is no doubt of it. He who doesn't like to be a soldier, finds it very hard; but he must get accustomed to it as to everything else. I know by experience how that is. My husband,—may God grant his soul eternal rest,—was obliged to get accustomed to worse than this, and I with him; but with us it was not as with Jacob and Christina. George got permission to marry and we lived together contented. In this case it may not be, and it is no wonder that he doesn't want to go, when we remember that they would be obliged to wait for each other for fourteen long years! But perhaps he will escape after all." At this moment her whole face brightened up, for she espied the children coming; they in turn, seeing her, started on the run to meet her.

"Well, Manchinka, are you not hungry?" asked the miller, when his daughter greeted him.

"Indeed, I am, Papa, and all of us are. Why, we haven't had any dinner to-day!"

"That large slice of bread, those dried apples and buns, that was dew?" asked the father as he turned round his snuff box.

"Oh, that was no dinner, that was only a lunch," laughed the girl.

"To walk such a distance and study besides makes one hungry, does it not?" asked Grandmother, and putting the spindle under her arm, she added: "Come let us hurry home lest you die of starvation!" They bade each other good-night. Manchinka told Barunka she would wait for them the next morning again, and hastened into the house. Barunka took her grandmother's hand. "Now tell me how you got along at school, what you studied, and how you behaved?"

"Just think, Grandma, I am bankaufser," said John, skipping before her.

"What in the world is that?" asked Grandmother

"You see, Grandma, he who sits at the end of
the bench watches those that sit near him, and
when they do not behave he puts down their
names," explained Barunka.

"It seems to me that in our village they called
him a monitor, but the monitor was always one of
the best boys in the whole school, and this honor
was not conferred upon any one the first day he
came to school."

"Indeed, and didn't Anton Kopriva twit us with
it on our way home and say that if we were not
Proshek's children, the schoolmaster wouldn't
make such a fuss over us," complained Barunka.

"Don't you believe that!" said Grandmother,
"the schoolmaster will make no exceptions with you;
when you deserve it he will punish you as quickly
as he would Anton; he showed you this favor to
make you like to go to school, and to have you behave well. What did you learn?"

"*Dictando,*" replied Barunka and the boys
together.

"What's that?"

"The schoolmaster reads to us and we write it
down, and then we must translate it from German
into Bohemian and from Bohemian into German."

"Do those children understand German" asked
Grandmother, who, like the Princess, wanted to
know the why and wherefore of everything.

"Well, Grandma, nobody knows any German
but us, because we studied it at home and Papa
speaks to us in German; but it makes no difference,

if one does not understand it, if only the exercise is correctly written," explained Barunka.

" But how can they do it, when they don't even know how to look in German?"

" Indeed, they are punished enough for not doing it right; the schoolmaster puts their names in the 'black book,' or they must stand on the dunce-block, and sometimes he strikes their hands with the ferrule. To-day, Anna, the daughter of the squire, was obliged to stand on the floor; she never knows the German *dictando*. At noon she told me, while we sat outdoors, that she didn't know how to write the exercise. She was so afraid that she did not eat her dinner. I wrote it out for her, and she gave me two cheeses for it."

" You should not have taken them from her," said Grandmother.

" I did not want to take them, but she said she had two more; she was delighted that I wrote the exercise for her, and promised that she would bring me something every day, if I would only help her with the German. Why shouldn't I do it?"

" You can help her, but you must not do it all yourself, for then she will not learn anything."

" What of it! she need not know that; we study it only because the schoolmaster wants us to."

" Because the schoolmaster wants you to know something; for the more one knows, the easier one can get along in the world; and, after all, the German language is very necessary; you see how hard it is that I cannot speak with your father."

" But papa understands all you say, and you understand him, though you do not speak German. But in Zlitz, only Bohemian is spoken; therefore,

Anna need not know any German. She said that if she wanted to learn German she could go to Germany. But the schoolmaster will have it his own way. Indeed, Grandma, nobody likes to learn the German *dictando*, it is so hard; if it were Bohemian; oh, my! it would be as easy as the Lord's prayer!"

"You don't understand this yet, but you ought to obey and learn all things willingly. How did the boys behave?"

"Quite well, until Johnny began to cut up with the other boys when the schoolmaster left the room. They even jumped over the benches, till I told him ——"

"*You* told me? indeed, I stopped because I heard the schoolmaster coming!"

"I'm learning nice things about you! You should watch others and you misbehave yourself; how is that?" asked Grandmother.

"O Grandma," said Willie, who till then was silent, but was busily engaged showing Adelka a piece of sweet wood and a tiny book made of gilt paper, which he got from some boy at school in exchange for a kreutzer. "O Grandma, those boys in school are so bad; why they jump over the benches and fight, and the monitor acts as bad as the rest."

"For the Lord's sake, what does the schoolmaster say to that?"

"That's while he is out of the room. When he is coming they jump back to their places, put their hands on the desks, and all is quiet."

"The little wretches!" exclaimed Grandmother.

"But the girls play with their dolls; indeed, I saw them," said John.

"You seem to be blossoms from Satan's own garden; the schoolmaster must have the patience of Job to stand it all." The children related much more about the school, and what they had seen and heard on their way; it was their first journey from home, and they felt as proud as if they had returned from Paris. "Where are your cheeses, did you eat them?" asked Grandmother, fearing that they might have indulged their appetites too much.

"One we ate, the other I wanted to bring home; but while I was writing at the blackboard, Anton Kopriva smuggled it out of my hand bag. He sits behind me. If I had said anything to him he would have beaten me on my way home. He is a fine fellow!"

Grandmother did not take the children's part, but in her soul she thought: "We were not any better." They knew that she was a great deal more lenient than their mother; she winked at many a caper that the boys cut up, and did not object when Barunka engaged in some boisterous game. For this reason the children confided in her much more than in their mother.

CHAPTER XIII.

ONE Thursday, several days after the first of May, there was no school and the children were helping Grandmother to water the flowers and grape vines, whose green leaves were already decorating the walls; they also went to water their trees. They had a great deal to do; for three whole days Barunka had not examined her dolls, the boys had not driven their horses, and the wagons, guns, and balls had lain in the corner untouched; they had not been to visit the dove-cot, and Adelka had fed the rabbits. All this neglect was to be atoned for this Thursday.

Having watered the plants, the children were allowed to go to their own occupations, while Grandmother seated herself upon the turf bench under the lilac bushes and began to spin, for she was accustomed to be busy all the time. To-day she was sad; she neither sang nor noticed the black hen that came into the garden through the open gate, and, when no one interfered, began to scratch up one of the beds. The gray goose was feeding close by, while her yellow goslings thrust their heads through the holes in the fence, impertinently looking into the garden. Grandmother liked them very much, those pretty goslings; but now she did not even notice them. Her thoughts wandered in several directions. A letter had come from Vienna, saying that the Princess would not come in the

255

middle of May, for Countess Hortense was very
ill. Should God be pleased to restore her to health,
perhaps the Princess would make a short visit to
the castle, but this was quite uncertain. When
Mrs. Proshek read the letter she could not restrain
her tears, and the children, seeing their mother
weep, wept also. Willie had only a few more
marks to erase, and now all their bright hopes were
dashed to the ground. And that the dear, good
Hortense should die seemed dreadful to them. At
their prayers, they never forgot to offer a Pater-
noster for her restoration. The children, however, were soon comforted, but Mrs. Proshek, who
usually spoke little, now spoke still less; and
whenever Grandmother entered her room, she
saw that her daughter's eyes were swollen from
weeping. She therefore sent her out to visit the
neighbors and so forget her sorrows. She was
always glad when Mrs. Proshek went, for she knew
that after all her daughter was very lonely in that
isolated little house, and would have preferred to
live in the busy city, to which for so many years
she had been accustomed. She had been very
happy in her marriage, but the one unpleasant thing
about her life was that her husband spent the
greater part of the year in Vienna, and she was
obliged to live in fear and anxiety without him.
And now she was not to see her husband, nor the
children their father for a whole year! " A life
for a life," said Grandmother. Johanna, Grandmother's second daughter was to come home with
John; she wanted to see her mother, to have a long
visit with her, and to get her advice, for she was
about to be married. Grandmother had looked

forward to this with great anticipations, but now she, too, was doomed to disappointment. Besides this, Milo's fate worried her not a little. Milo was a good-hearted, worthy young man, Christina was a good girl, and Grandmother loved them both and wanted to see them happy in each other's love. " When equal meets equal, there is concord, and God himself rejoices over such a marriage," she used to say. But a cruel blow seemed to await this hope, for that morning Milo had gone with the others to the conscription. All this lay upon Grandmother's mind and consequently she looked very sober.

" Grandma, just look, Blackie is scratching here! Wait, you monkey, Vsh-sh-sh!" Grandmother, hearing Barunka's voice, raised her eyes and saw the black hen flying out of the garden, and noticed a large hole in one of the beds.

" That vixen, how quietly she came! Take the rake, Barunka, and smooth the bed. And the geese are here, too! The poultry are calling; it is time for them to go to roost. I forgot myself. I must feed them." Saying this, she laid aside her spindle and went to get the basket of grain. Barunka remained in the garden smoothing the bed.

Shortly after Christina came. "Are you alone?" she asked, looking into the garden.

" Come in, Grandma will be here presently; she went to feed the poultry," replied Barunka.

" Where is your mother?"

" She went to town to visit Godmother; you know she grieves so because Papa will probably not come home this year. So Grandma sends her out visiting that she may be comforted a little. We all looked forward with such joy to the return of Papa and the Countess, and now we are all disappointed. Poor Hortense!"

After these words Barunka, resting one knee in the path, leaned her elbow against the other, and laying her head in the palm of her hand remained buried in deep thought. Christina sat down under the lilacs, dropped her clasped hands in her lap, and her head fell upon her bosom. Her eyes were red and swollen, and she was the picture of misery.

" That fever must be a dreadful disease. If she should die, — oh heavens! You never had a fever, Christina? " asked Barunka after a pause.

" No, I never was ill in all my life; but now I fear that I shall lose my health," sorrowfully replied Christina.

Not till then did Barunka look at her, and seeing her changed countenance, she jumped up, ran to her and asked: " What is the matter? Is Milo a conscript? " Instead of replying, Christina began to sob aloud. At this moment Grandmother came back. " Have they returned ? " she quickly asked.

" Not yet," replied Christina, shaking her head; " but all hope is vain. Lucie has sworn that if she doesn't get Milo, I shan't get him either. What she wants the squire will do, for he is very proud of her; and the steward will do a great deal to please the squire. The steward's daughter cannot forget that her lover was disgraced by Milo; she too, adds some gall, and there are various other things, dear Grandma, that undermine my hopes."

" But Milo's father was at the courthouse and,

as I hear, had with him quite a sum of money; there is some hope then?"

"True, that is our only hope; since they listened to him, they will perhaps help; but it has often happened that they listened but did not help; if they said it could not be done, one had to be satisfied."

"I hope that it will not be so in Milo's case; but if it should be, then it seems to me his father ought to take the money he intended to use as bribes, your father should add to it, and then they could pay Milo out according to law."

"Yes, if there were not so many ifs, dear Grandma. In the first place, the money his father has already paid is gone; then my father has no more ready money than he needs in his business; and if he liked Jacob, and had no objections to my marrying him, still he would prefer to have his son-in-law bring something into the business rather than carry something out. And granted that he would do it, Milo is of a proud disposition; he will accept no favors from any one; he would not allow my father to pay him out."

"I suppose he thinks: 'A wife with a dowry large, will be sure to govern the barge;' and that is something that every proud spirited man would avoid. But, under the circumstances, it would not be any disgrace for him to accept the favor. Yet, why trouble ourselves for something that most probably will not be needed, and if it should be, would be quite difficult to do?"

"It's a great pity that that affair ever happened with the Italian; then I laughed at it, now I could weep. If it had not happened, Milo would have had a place on the castle farm, he could have worked there two years, and thus have been freed from the army. It grieves me the more when I think that it was all on my own account."

" My dear girl, why should you blame yourself? would this daisy at your feet be to blame if two, wanting it, should quarrel over it? I, too, should have to blame myself that I brought my husband into a similar difficulty, — the case was almost like yours. Dear child, do you suppose that when a person is carried away by anger, jealousy, love, or any other passion, he has the time to take counsel with reason? At that moment he doesn't care if he should die! And besides the best and noblest characters have their weak moments."

"Grandma, last year, on Mr. Proshek's holiday, you told me that your husband did something similar, and that he suffered for it, and now you've referred to it again. I forgot all about it. Please tell me about it now. Our time will pass away, our thoughts will be turned to other matters, and it is so pleasant to sit here under the lilacs."

" Well, perhaps I will," replied Grandmother. " Barunka, go see that the children do not go near the water."

Barunka obeyed, and when she was gone, Grandmother began:

" I was a grown up girl when, in 1777, Maria Theresa began that war with the Prussians. They had a misunderstanding about something, and the Emperor Joseph came with an army to Jarmirn, and the Prussians took their stand on the boundary. The fields around us were full of soldiers, and the villages, too. We had several privates and an officer quartered at our house. The officer was a man

of lax morals, one of those men that have no scru-
ples about entangling in their snares every girl they
meet. I disposed of him quickly, but he paid no
attention to my words,—shook them off as if they
were dew. Since he would not listen to me, I
arranged my work outdoors in such a manner that
I should never be obliged to meet him.

"You know how it is; a girl has occasion to be
out many times during the day, now in the field,
now to cut grass,* and often her folks are all gone,
and she must be in the house alone.

"In short, neither is it the custom nor is it necessary that any one should guard a girl; she must
guard herself, and thus many opportunities can be
found by an ill-disposed person to persecute her.

"But God protected me. I went to cut grass
early in the morning while everybody still slept. I
was always an early riser, for my mother used to
say: 'Who is up with the sun, his fortune is begun.'
She was right, and if I had had no other profit, the
pleasure was ample reward. When in the morning
I entered the orchard or went out into the fields
and saw the beautiful green grass covered with
dew, my heart was filled with joy. Each little
flower stood there like a maiden, with head erect
and bright, smiling eyes. The birds, dear little
creatures, hovered over me, praising God with their
songs; otherwise a holy stillness was around me.
Then when the sun rose behind the hills, it seemed
to me that I was in the house of God. I sang, and
my work seemed but play.

"Once, while I was thus cutting grass,—it

* Since there are but few pastures, the women must spend several
hours each day cutting grass for the cattle.

was in the orchard, — I heard a voice behind me: 'God bless your work, Madeline!' I turned around to reply: 'God grant it!' but I was so surprised that I could not utter a word, and the sickle fell from my hand."

"It was that officer, was it not?" asked Christina, interrupting her.

"Not so fast, my dear," continued Grandmother; "it was not that officer, for then I should not have dropped the sickle. It was a joyous surprise. George stood before me! I must tell you that I had not seen him for three years. You remember that George was the son of our neighbor, the widow Novotny, the one who was with me when I spoke with the Emperor Joseph."

"Yes, I remember; you also told me that he became a weaver instead of a priest."

"Yes, his uncle was to blame for that. Learning was as easy to him as play; his father heard nothing but good reports of him whenever he came home for the vacations. He was so fine a reader, that when he was at home he would take father's place in reading the Bible to the neighbors every Sunday. We all liked to listen to him, and his mother used to say: 'I seem already to hear him preach.' We treated him as if he were already ordained, and whatever delicacy any of us had we sent it to him; and when his mother objected, saying: "Dear Lord, what can I give you in return?' we replied: 'When George is a priest he will give us a blessing.'

"We grew up together. What pleased one pleased the other; but when he came home for the second and the third vacation I began to feel somewhat shy; and when he followed me into the orchard as he often did, and in spite of all I could do carried my grass for me, I thought it was wrong for me to allow him to do it. I told him such a thing was not becoming for a priest to do; but he only laughed, saying that much water would yet flow away before he would preach. It often happens that man proposes, but God disposes.

" Once when he was at home for the third vacation, a message came from his Uncle George, at Kladrau, requesting that he should come to visit them. This uncle was a skillful weaver, who made beautiful goods by which he had gained quite a sum of money, and not having any children of his own, he thought of his nephew George. Mrs. Novotny did not want to send him, but father himself urged her to let him go, saying that it would be for his good, and that his father's brother, after all, had some claim to him. He went; Mrs. Novotny and my father accompanied him, going on a pilgrimage to Vamberitz.

" They returned, but George remained with his uncle. We all missed him, especially his mother and I, only she spoke of it often, while I kept it all to myself. His uncle promised that he would care for him as if he were his own son. Mrs. Novotny, therefore, thought that he attended school at Kladrau; she was full of hope that he would soon receive his first ordination, when behold! George came home in a year a weaver by trade! His mother grieved dreadfully, but what was to be done? He begged her not to take it so hard, and confessed that although he should have been glad to continue his studies, he had no desire to become a priest.

He said that his uncle persuaded him to give it up,
telling him that he would suffer much want, would
knock about from school to school, from official to
official, before he could earn a mouthful; that a
trade, on the contrary, had a golden bottom, and
that it was so much the better for him, if he was
likewise educated. In short, George listened to
his uncle and learned the weaver's trade; and because he always did everything with a good will,
he prospered in this also.

"In a year he finished his apprenticeship, and
his uncle sent him to travel, to gain more experience
by working with different masters. His first journey was to Berlin, and on his way there he stopped
with us in Bohemia, and on that occasion brought
me this rosary."

So saying, Grandmother pulled from her bosom
a bladder-nut rosary. She looked at it for a moment, kissed it, hid it in her bosom, and continued:

"My father did not blame George for learning
the trade; he told Mrs. Novotny not to mind it,
saying: 'Who knows to what good this may lead?
Let him alone; as he has sowed, so shall he reap.
Though he should weave tow, if he understands
his business and remains a good and honest man,
he will be as worthy of honor as any lord.' George
was glad that his god-father was not offended with
him, for he thought as much of him as if he were
his own father. Finally, his mother became reconciled,— how could she help it when he was her
only child, whom she dearly loved? She could not
desire that he should feel unhappy in his occupation.
He remained with us a few days, and then went
out into the world, and for three years we did

not see him, and hardly heard from him until that morning when he suddenly appeared before me.

"You can imagine how glad I was. I recognized him instantly, although he had changed much; he was unusually tall, and withal so well proportioned that it would have been hard to find his equal. He bent down to me, took my hand, and asked me why I was so frightened? 'How could I help it,' I said. 'You appeared as suddenly as if you had fallen from the skies. Whence came you and when?'

"'I came direct from Kladrau. Uncle is afraid, since they are collecting troops everywhere, that I also might be impressed into service. I had hardly reached home, when he sent me here, where he thinks I can hide more easily. I got through the mountains without any mishaps, and here I am.'

"'For heaven's sake! suppose they should find you here, what does your mother say?'

"'I have not seen her yet. I got here at two o'clock this morning, and did not want to wake mother up. I thought to myself: "You can lie down on the grass under Madeline's window; she is an early riser. You will wait till she comes, and then you can go home." In truth, it is not in vain that the people of the village say of you: "Ere the lark sings Madeline brings home the grass." The day had hardly dawned before you were cutting the grass. I saw you at the spring washing yourself and combing your hair, and I could hardly restrain myself from coming to you; but when you were praying, I did not want to interrupt you. But, now Madeline, tell me, do you still love me?'

" Thus he spoke; what else could I say than that I did, for I had loved him from childhood, and never had thought of any body else. We talked a while longer, then he went to see his mother and I went into the house to tell father that he had come. Father was a prudent man, and he was not at all pleased that George had come at this dangerous time.

" 'I don't know whether he'll escape the white coat * here,' he said, 'but we will do what we can to hide him; do not tell a single soul that he is here!'

" His mother, although very glad to see him, was greatly alarmed; for he had been enrolled among the conscripts, and had escaped thus far, because no one knew where he was. For three days he was hidden in the garret upon the hay. Through the day, only his mother was with him; but in the evening I came, too, and then we had long, pleasant talks together.

" I was so afraid lest he should be discovered, that I went about like a lost sheep and forgot to keep out of the way of that officer, so that we met several times. He, probably thinking that I wanted to make up with him, began to sing his old tune; I let him talk, but was not so sharp to him as before, for I feared for George. As I said, George was hidden; besides my family and his mother, no one knew that he was in the house.

" The third evening I remained a little longer than usual with him, and when I went home every thing was quiet and it was dark, when all at once that officer stood in my path. He had discovered that I went to Mrs. Novotny's every evening, and

* Conscription.

had waited for me in the orchard. What was to be done? Had I called, George would have heard me, but I was afraid to have him come down. I depended upon my own strength, and when the officer would not listen to my words, I prepared to use my fists. Do not smile my child, do not look at me, as I am now; I was not tall but thick set, my hands, accustomed to hard work, were solid and strong. I could have withstood him, but in his rage he began to curse and swear. In that way he was discovered and all at once, like a clap of thunder, George was between us, holding the officer by the throat. He had heard the cursing, and looking down through the garret door recognized me and jumped down. It was a wonder that he did not break his neck. Did he stop to consider? No indeed; he would have jumped down had the faggots of a funeral pile been burning below him.

"'What mean you, sir, by attacking an honest girl here in the night?' he cried.

"I tried to calm his anger, and begged him to remember his situation; but he, trembling with rage, held the officer as in a vise. Finally, I succeeded in persuading him to let him go.

"'In another place and time we should settle this matter differently, but listen to me and remember what I say. This girl is my bride; if in the future you do not let her alone, you shall hear of me again. Now go!'

"With that he threw him over the gate as if he were a ball. Then he turned to me, and putting his arms around my neck, said: 'Madeline, dear, remember me, greet my mother for me, and now farewell, for I must away this moment, or else I shall be taken. Do not fear for me, I know every path and I shall get to Kladrau, where I can hide. I beg you, come on a pilgrimage to Vamberitz; there we shall meet!'

"Before I could collect my thoughts, he was gone. I hastened to his mother to tell her what had happened, then we both went to my father's house. And now it seemed as if we had lost our senses. Every noise frightened us. That officer sent out his soldiers on all the roads; he did not know George, but he thought he was from some village near by and that they would capture him; but he escaped out of their hands. I avoided the officer as much as I could, but when he could not revenge himself in any other way, he slandered me in the village as if I had been a girl of loose morals. Everybody knew me, so he was not successful in that. Fortunately, orders came that the soldiers should depart, as the Prussians had crossed the frontier. Nothing at all came from this war. The farmers called it the 'kolach war,' because after the soldiers had eaten all the kolaches in the villages, they returned home."

"And what became of George?" asked Christina, who had been listening with breathless attention.

"We heard nothing of him till spring, for in those stormy times there was little travel.

"We were full of anxiety. The spring came, still no news. I prepared to go on the pilgrimage as I had promised George. Several of the villagers were going, I joined their party, and as the leader had been at Kladrau several times, he promised my father that he would take me there.

"When we reached the town the leader said; 'we will stop awhile at Mrs. Lidushka's to rest.' Every one who came from Bohemia stayed with Mrs. Lidushka, for she was our countrywoman. In those days Kladrau was almost entirely Bohemian, but one prefers to go to some one that he has known before. Mrs. Lidushka welcomed us very cordially, took us into her private parlor, and after telling us to make ourselves at home went out to get us some wine soup.

"My heart was full of the conflicting emotions of joy and of fear; joy that I should meet George, and fear less something had happened to him. Suddenly I heard a familiar voice greet Mrs. Lidushka, and then she said: 'Come in, George, there are some pilgrims here from Bohemia.'

"The door opened, and there stood George, but glancing at him I stood dumbfounded. He had on a soldier's uniform? All grew dark before my eyes! He gave me his hand and then taking me into his arms, said in a broken voice: 'Wretched man that I am! hardly had I learned my trade, shaken off one yoke, when I put on another. I ran away from the rain and got under the eaves. Had I remained in Bohemia, I should at least, have served under my own Emperor, while now I must serve a foreign ruler.'

"'For heaven's sake, George, what have you done?' I asked.

"'Done? my dear girl, I have acted like a fool! refused to listen to my uncle; when I came here, I was lonesome, restless, could find no peace anywhere. One Sunday I went with several comrades into a saloon, against the earnest advice of my uncle. We drank till we became intoxicated, and then the officers seeking for volunteers came in.'

"'Those villains!' interrupted Mrs. Lidushka, who just then entered the room with the soup. 'Had George remained with me, this would never have happened. I never put up with their deceitful ways; his uncle never goes anywhere, forsooth, except to Lidushka's. Well, well, these young people,—what can one do, when they have no sense? But never mind, George, you are a handsome fellow. Our King likes tall soldiers; he will not leave you long without shoulder straps.'

"'What's done can't be undone,' began George. 'We did not know what we were about, and when we became sober, Lehotsky, my dearest comrade, and I were soldiers. I thought I should go mad. Uncle, too, was sorry enough. Finally he began to consider what could be done to lessen the evil I had brought upon myself. He went to the commander and was so far successful in his errand that I remained here. I shall soon be a corporal, and—but of that we will speak by-and-by. Now, do not grieve my heart, for I am so glad to see you.'

"We comforted each other as well as we could. Afterwards he took me to his uncle, who was very glad to see me. In the evening his friend Lehotsky came over; he was a good man. He and George remained faithful friends till death. Both have gone to their reward, while I am still here," said Grandmother, and paused, overcome by the feelings that these recollections awakened.

"You did not return home; Grandpa married you then, did he not?" asked Barunka, who in the meantime had returned and was listening to Grandmother's story.

"Yes, he would not have it otherwise. His uncle had obtained permission for him to marry, and they were waiting till I should come on the pilgrimage. After we had discussed everything, George went away for the night, while I remained with his uncle. He was a dear, good old man,—may God grant his soul eternal rest! The next morning George came over very early, and he and his uncle engaged in an earnest conversation, after which George came to me and said:

"'Madeline, tell me truly, upon your conscience, do you love me so that you could endure hardships for my sake, and forsake your father and mother?'

"'Yes,' I replied.

"'Then remain here and be my wife,' he said, and throwing his arms around my neck, kissed me.

"He had never kissed me before. This was not the custom among us; but, poor fellow! he was beside himself with joy and did not know what he was doing.

"'But what will your mother say, what will my parents say?' I asked, while my heart beat fast with joy and anxiety.

"'What should they say? Do they not love us? would they want me to die of grief?'

"'But for heaven's sake, dear George, we must have our parents' blessing!'

"He did not reply, but his uncle stepped to us, and sending him away said to me:

"'Madeline, I see you are a pious girl; I like you, and know that George will be happy, and

that he had good reason to lament when he thought
he had lost you. If it were somebody else I should
object, but George is headstrong. If it had not
been for me, he would have given way to despair;
but I succeeded in comforting him, because I
obtained permission for him to marry. I cannot
deceive you, he dare not return to Bohemia; and
should you go without him, who knows but that
they might try to dissuade you from this step.
After you are married, we will go together to Olesnic, and your parents will not refuse you their blessing. We will send a letter by the pilgrims. To-
morrow you will be married in the soldier's chapel;
I shall take the place of your parents, and assume
the whole responsibility. Madeline, dear, look at
me; my head is white as snow; think you I could
do anything for which I could not answer before
God?' Thus he spoke to me, while the tears
flowed down his cheeks.

"I consented to all. George could scarcely contain himself for joy. I had no more clothing with
me than what I had on. George bought me a
new skirt, a jacket, and a garnet necklace for the
wedding; the rest was furnished by his uncle. The
garnets were the very same ones that I still wear;
the linsey-wolsey skirt was of a violet color and the
jacket sky-blue. The pilgrims returned home, and
uncle gave them a letter, in which he said that I
would remain there a few days and then return
with him. He wrote nothing more. 'It will be
better to tell it than write it,' he said.

"The third day we had our wedding; the priest
of the regiment performed the ceremony.

"The only guests were Mrs. Lidushka, Mr.

Lehotsky, who acted the part of groomsman, his sister, who was my bridesmaid, and George's uncle and another citizen, who were witnesses. Mrs. Lidushka was the wedding matron and made the wedding dinner. We spent that day in joy and in God's fear, regretting only that those at home could not be with us. At the table Mrs. Lidushka constantly teased George, saying: 'Look at that cross soldier of ours! one hardly knows him to-day, but it is no wonder; he has something to make his face beam with joy!' Thus they talked as people do on such occasions.

"George wanted me to live with him at once, but his uncle would by no means allow it; he said this must not be till I had returned from Bohemia.

"In a few days we went home. I cannot describe to you the astonishment of all when they heard that I was married, nor mother's grief when she heard that George was a soldier. She wrung her hands, wept, said that I wanted to leave her to follow a soldier in a strange land, and was so affected that I myself became almost distracted with grief. At length, father put an end to those lamentations. He said:

"'This is enough, as she has made her bed, so she shall lie in it. They love each other, let them suffer together; you know, wife, that you, too, left your father and mother for my sake, and that is the lot awaiting every girl. Who of us can help this misfortune that has befallen George? But the service there is not long, and when that task is over he can return home. Mother, cease your lamentations. George is a sensible young man. He will not be homesick, he has himself provided against that. Madeline, my child, dry your tears. May God bless you and grant that he with whom you have gone to the altar may also go with you to the grave?' With these words he gave me his blessing, while the tears filled his eyes.

"Mother also wept. Dear mother, always so thoughtful of everything! she had her hands full. 'What were you thinking of?' she said; 'you have n't a single piece of bedding, no furniture, no clothing, and yet you get married! Since the day I was born, I have never heard of such thoughtlessness!' I got a good outfit, and when I had everything in readiness, I returned to George and remained with him till his death. If it had not been for that unfortunate war, he might be here still. You see, my dear girl, that I know what joy and sorrow, youth and folly are," said Grandmother with a smile, laying her withered hand on Christina's round arm.

"You suffered enough, Grandma, but still you were happy,—you got what your heart desired. If I knew that after all my trials I, too, should be happy, I would endure all in patience, even if I had to wait for Milo fourteen years," said Christina.

"The future is in God's hands. What is to happen will happen, we cannot avoid it. The best thing we can do is to place our trust in God."

"I know that is best, but one cannot always control one's feelings, and if Jacob is taken, I shall mourn. With him will depart all my happiness, my protection, and my support."

"What do you mean, Christina, have you not a father!"

"I have a good father,—may God preserve him

to me for many years; still he is old and unreasonable. This summer he gave me no peace, because he insisted that I should get married so that he might have somebody to help him in the business. What shall I do when Jacob is gone? But I will not have anybody else, even if they all set themselves against me. I will work like a slave, and if that is not enough to please father, why then, he must remain displeased, for I shall not marry. O my dearest Grandma, you have no idea what I must put up with in that inn? It is not the hard work, —that troubles me the least,—but it is what I must listen to from those men."

"Can't you prevent it?"

"How can I? I often say to father: 'Why do you allow such things in your own house?' But he is afraid to say anything lest he should drive away his customers. He often says: 'My dear girl, have patience. Don't you know our living depends upon them?' He doesn't want me to be rough, and when I am amiable, every good-for-nothing thinks he may take my name in his foul mouth. I shall never be as happy and full of song as I used to be! If it were those common fellows only, it would not be so bad; but the steward and the secretary from the castle are bitter pills; they poison my whole existence. I am ashamed to tell you how that old wretch, the steward, follows me. I know it as well as if some one whispered it to me, that he will leave nothing undone to put Milo out of his way; for he knows that he is my protector. He acts sometimes as though he wanted to please the squire, then again as if he were seeking to revenge his daughter; but the old fox thinks of no one but himself. Father fears him, and mother, poor soul! seems scarcely to belong any longer to this world. I cannot harass her with my troubles. If I were married all would be changed. Even now, when Milo is with us, if any one molests me, I have only to tell him and he watches the fellow so that he either leaves or no longer dares look at me. O Grandma, if you only knew how we love each other! but that cannot be expressed." And Christina rested her face in her hands and remained buried in deep thought.

At that moment, quietly and unobserved, Milo entered the garden. His handsome face was distorted with grief, his bright eyes were dim, the dark brown curls that were wont to hang about his forehead were cut off; in place of his jaunty, high otter-skin cap, he wore a soldier's cap, in which was stuck a twig of balsam. Barunka was frightened; Grandmother's hands fell into her lap, her face turned pale, but she whispered: "God comfort you, my boy!"

But when Christina raised her head, and Milo, giving her his hand, said in a hollow voice: "I am a soldier, in three days we depart for Koniggratz!" she fell senseless into his arms.

CHAPTER XIV.

THE next day when, as usual, Grandmother went to meet the children, her first words were, "Guess who is at our house?"

The children were surprised, and for the moment could not think of any one until Barunka exclaimed: "Oh, I know; Mr. Beyer!"

"Right," replied Grandmother, "and his son is with him."

"Oh, I am so glad!" exclaimed John, "let us run to see him;" and both he and Willie rushed to the house as fast as their legs could carry them.

Grandmother called after them not to go like wild beasts, but like human beings; but they were already beyond hearing. All out of breath, they bounded into the room; their mother was about to reprove them, when Mr. Beyer stretched out his long arms toward them, and raising one after the other, embraced and kissed them. "How have you been all the year?" he asked in a deep voice that re-echoed through the small space. The boys did not reply immediately; their eyes fell upon a boy, about Barunka's age, who was standing beside Mr. Beyer. He was a handsome lad, the image of his father, though he had not as yet the latter's muscular strength; his face was ruddy, and childish happiness beamed from his eyes. "Aha! you are looking at my boy; well, take a good look and shake hands, so as to become good comrades. This is my Orel."

Thus saying he pushed his son forward, who without any bashfulness stepped up and shook hands with the boys. Just then Barunka came, together with Grandmother and Adelka. "My boy, here you see Barunka, who I told you is always the first to bid me good morning when I stay here over night. This year I see it is different; you attend school, and so Johnny must rise as early as his sister. And how do you like it at school, Johnny, would you not prefer to roam about in the woods? You see, my Orel must go with me everywhere, and soon he will know how to shoot as well as his father," continued Mr. Beyer.

"O, do not tell such things," said Grandmother; "John will get wild and will want to see Orel's gun."

"Well, why should he not see it? Go, Orel, show him your gun; it is not loaded."

"No, for you remember I fired the last charge at that buzzard," replied the boy.

"Yes, and killed it, too. You can show it to the boys." The boys ran outdoors delighted, but Grandmother was not satisfied; she followed them, although Mr. Beyer assured her that Orel would be careful.

"Why, you have a name like a bird," said Adelka to Orel,* while John and Willie were examining the buzzard.

"My name is really Aurel, but father prefers to call me Orel, and I like it too," replied the boy, smiling at Adelka's question. "The eagle is a fine bird; father once shot an eagle."

"Very likely, but wait," said John, "I will show

* "Orel" in Bohemian means Eagle.

you an eagle and many other animals; I have pictures of them in a book that I got as a present upon
my namesake's day. Come with me." With these
words he dragged Orel into the house, where he
showed him the pictures in his book.

Orel was much pleased with the pictures, and
even Mr. Beyer looked on with great interest.
"You did not have that last year, did you?" he asked.

"I got it as a present from the Countess on my
namesake's day; besides that, I got a pair of doves
from Christina, rabbits from the gamekeeper, a silver dollar from Grandma, and a suit of clothes
from my parents!" said John proudly.

"You are a lucky boy," said Mr. Beyer, who
was looking into the book; and seeing a fox, he
smiled and said: "Wait, you rascal, I'll make you
come to time yet!" Willie, thinking he meant
the one in the book, looked up with surprise; upon
which Mr. Beyer said: "Don't you be afraid. I
don't mean this fox in the book, but one in the
mountains that resembles this one and that must be
caught, because it does us much damage."

"Perhaps Peter will catch it; I helped him set
the trap before we started," said Orel.

"O my boy, a fox is ten times more cunning
than Peter; he is up to tricks that a man would
never think of, and especially if, like this one, he
has once been caught. The wretch! I set a nice
roast for him, thinking I should catch him; he was
hungry, but what did he do? Just bit off his broken
leg and escaped. Now he will hardly allow himself to be caught a second time. Man learns wisdom by experience, and a fox seems to be as wise
as a man."

"People say very appropriately 'as cunning as a fox,'" said Grandmother.

"This is the eagle!" cried the children, looking at a beautiful bird with wings outstretched, just as if he were about to light on his prey.

"Just like the one that I shot! It was a beautiful bird and I was almost sorry to shoot it, but what was to be done? one does not meet such an opportunity every day. I hit it well, — that is the principal thing, — so that the creature did not suffer."

"That's what I always say," spoke up Grandmother.

"But are you not sorry for those poor animals, Mr. Beyer. I could not shoot any of them," said Barunka.

"But you could cut a creature's head off," smiled Mr. Beyer; "and which is better: to kill it at once, when it is not suspecting danger, or first to frighten it while you are catching it, then to spend some time in preparation, and finally to cut its neck, sometimes so clumsily that it escapes still alive?"

"We never kill the poultry," protested Barunka; "Vorsa, who doesn't pity them, does it, and then they die instantly." For a while longer, the children amused themselves with the pictures, and then Mrs. Proshek called them to supper.

Heretofore, when Mr. Beyer had come, he had no rest from the children; they wanted to know about the mountains, whether he had not wandered into Ryberzol's garden, and many other things. This time, however, they questioned Orel, and listened with great wonder when the boy told them of the perils which he had shared with his

father and of the game he had shot, when he described to them the great masses of snow that lie on
the tops of the mountains, sometimes rolling down
their sides and burying whole villages, till the people have no outlet but their chimneys, and each one
is obliged to make his own path from his house to
that of his neighbor.

All this did not discourage John; he still wished
to be old enough to go and live with Mr. Beyer.

" When you are with us, father will send me to
the Riesenburg gamekeeper, so that I may have
experience in easier gamekeeping," said Orel.

" That will be too bad, if you are not there,"
said John, quite vexed.

" You will not be lonesome; we have two other
apprentices, and brother Chenek is as tall as you,
and Sister Mary will like you," said Orel.

While the children, seated in the yard, were
listening to Orel and looking through the crystals
which he had brought them, Mr. Beyer was
listening to Grandmother, who told him of the
flood and all the other events that had happened
during the year.

" Are the family of my brother at Riesenburg
well? " asked Mr. Beyer.

" Quite well," replied Mrs. Proshek. " Anne is
growing fast; the boys attend school at Red Hura;
it is nearer for them than the town school. I am
surprised that the gamekeeper isn't here yet; he
said he would drop in to welcome you when he
went to watch. He was here this morning and
brought me news from the castle, that a letter had
come from Vienna. I went to the castle and
learned that the Countess is better, and that most

likely the Princess will come during the harvest festival, to remain a fortnight, and then go to Florence. I have hopes that my husband will remain with us during the winter; they say she will not take the attendants with her. Thus after waiting so long we shall be together again."

For many days Mrs. Proshek had not spoken so much; for many days she had not been so happy as to-day, after she had heard the good news of her husband's home-coming.

" Thank God that the Countess is restored to health. It would be a thousand pities to lose that dear, good child," said Grandmother. " We remembered her in our prayers every day, and but yesterday Celia Kuderna was here and wept for her."

" She might well weep if the Countess should die," remarked Mrs. Proshek.

Mr. Beyer asked what they meant, and Grandmother told him about her visit to the castle, and how the Countess had helped the organ grinder's family.

" I heard," said Mr. Beyer, " that the Countess was the daughter of ——"

At this moment somebody tapped at the window.

" That is the gamekeeper, I know his knock. Come in," called Mrs. Proshek.

" People have evil tongues," returned Grandmother, replying to Mr. Beyer's remark. " He who goes in the sun is followed by the shadow; how could it be otherwise. What matters it whose daughter she is."

The Riesenburg gamekeeper entered the house and was heartily welcomed by Mr. Beyer.

"What kept you so long?" asked Grandmother, casting a timid glance at the rifle he was hanging up.

"I had a precious guest, the steward; he wanted some wood; he sold his deputat,* and now wants wood in advance, and would inveigle one into crooked dealings. He can't come any such game on me. My suspicions were at once aroused, for he came like a saint. I told him what's what. I also gave him a thrust for Milo; I am sorry for that boy and for Christina, too. I stopped at the inn this morning for a glass, and she frightened me, she looked so ghastly. That conf——," here the gamekeeper struck his lips, recollecting that he sat near Grandmother—"steward has that to answer for."

"What has happened?" asked Mr. Beyer, and Grandmother quickly informed him of Milo's conscription and the causes that led to it.

"That's the way it goes in the world; wherever one turns, nothing but misery and sorrow among the great and small, and he who has none, will make some for himself," said Mr. Beyer.

"The soul is purified by misfortune and sorrow, as gold by fire. Without sorrow there can be no joy. If I knew how I could help that girl,— but it is impossible. She must bear it as well as she can. The worst trial will be to-morrow when Milo goes away."

"He goes, then, to-morrow?" questioned the gamekeeper. "They seem to be in a great hurry. Where does he go?"

"To Koniggratz."

*An allowance in kind in addition to the salary.

" Then we have the same destination, only I travel by water and he goes by land."

Just then the boys ran into the room; John and Willie showed the gamekeeper a buzzard that Orel had shot, and the latter told his father that they had been at the dam and had seen crazy Victorka.

" Is that poor creature still alive?" wondered Mr. Beyer.

" Yes, indeed, though it would be better if she were under the ground," replied Grandmother. " But she is failing fast; it is very seldom that we hear her sing, except on bright moonlight nights."

" But she still sits by the dam and looks into the water, often till after midnight," replied the gamekeeper. Yesterday I went past her; she was breaking off willow twigs and throwing them over the dam into the water; it was late, I asked: " What are you doing here?" She made no reply. I repeated the question. She turned, looked at me, and her eyes flashed. I thought she was going to spring upon me; but she must have recognized me, for she turned away and began again to cast twig after twig into the water. One cannot do anything with her. I feel sorry for her and should be glad to know that her miserable life is ended, and yet if I did not see her at the dam, and hear her song when I watch in the night, I should miss her and feel lonely," said the gamekeeper holding the buzzard in his hand.

" When a person becomes accustomed to a particular object it is hard to give it up," replied Mr. Beyer, putting a bit of glowing fungus into his short, wired* clay pipe, and after taking several

*A common method of mending broken stoneware is by a lace work of wire, after which it lasts longer than the unbroken article.

deliberate puffs he continued: "be it man, beast, or aught else. Thus, I have become accustomed to this pipe while going on a journey; my mother used to smoke from one just like it. It seems to me I can see her sitting on the doorstep."

"What, did your mother smoke?" cried Barunka, greatly surprised.

"In the mountains many women smoke, especially old grandmothers; but instead of tobacco they use potato tops, and, when they can be obtained, cherry leaves."

"I shouldn't think that would be good," said the other gamekeeper, filling his pipe, a beautifully painted porcelain one.

"Thus I have certain favorite places in the woods," again began Mr. Beyer, "where I stop unconsciously. These have become dear to me, because they remind me either of certain persons or of pleasant or unpleasant events in my life. If from those places a single tree or shrub were taken away, I should miss it. In one place, upon a precipitous height, stands an isolated fir. It is an old tree; its branches on one side hang over a deep precipice, in whose fissures, here and there, are tufts of ferns or juniper shrubs; and down below, a stream hurries along over rocks, forming cataracts and waterfalls. I don't know myself how it happened, but whenever some grief oppressed my mind, or some misfortune befell me, I always found my way to that spot. Thus it was when I used to go to see my wife, and imagined I should not get her; her parents were unwilling, and it was not till later that they gave their consent.

"It was the same when my oldest son died and

when my mother died. Each time I started from the house, went without any purpose, looking neither to the right nor to the left, and unconsciously my feet carried me into that wild dale; and when I found myself over the precipice by that gloomy fir tree; when I saw before me the summits of the mountains, one above the other, my burdens seemed to fall from me, and I was not ashamed of my tears. When I embraced its rough trunk, it seemed to me that it had life, that it understood my sorrows, and the rustling foliage seemed to sigh as if it wanted to tell me of similar griefs."

Mr. Beyer made a long pause, his large eyes were turned to the light burning upon the table, and instead of words little clouds of smoke passed from his mouth and went up to the ceiling like visible thoughts.

" Yes indeed, it often seems that those trees have life and consciousness within them," said the Riesenburg gamekeeper. " I know this from experience. Once, — it happened several years ago, — I selected some trees for felling. The forester could not go, so I was obliged to see to it myself. The woodcutters came and were preparing to fell a beautiful birch; there wasn't a flaw in her, she stood there like a maid. I fixed my eyes upon her and it seemed to me, — it is laughable, but it was so, — as if she were bending to my feet, as if her branches embraced me, and something sounded in my ear: 'Why do you wish to destroy my young life? what have I done to you?' Just then the sharp teeth of the saw creaked over her bark and entered her body. I don't remember whether I cried out, but I know that I wanted to stop the men from cutting further;

but when they looked at me with astonishment, I
was ashamed of myself, and left them to their
work and went away into the woods. I wandered
about for a whole hour, followed by the thought
that the birch begged me to spare her life. When
I composed my feelings and returned to the spot,
she was down; not a leaf stirred on her, she lay
there like a corpse. I was seized with remorse, as
if I had committed murder. For several days I
was almost ill, but I did not tell any one the cause,
and if we had not happened to speak of such things
to-day, I suppose I never should have mentioned
the incident."

"Something similar happened to me," began
Mr. Beyer in his deep voice. " I was to furnish
the game for my master. I went hunting. A fawn
came in my path, — a handsome creature, with hair
as smooth and even as if it had been trimmed.
She looked about her gayly and here and there
cropped the grass. I was moved with compassion;
but I thought: ' How simple I am?' I fired, but my
hand trembled, and I hit the fawn in the side; she
fell and could go no further. My dog rushed to
her, but I called him back, for something told me I
must not let him harm her. I went to her, and I
cannot tell you how that creature looked at me, —
so mournfully, and so imploringly! I pulled out my
knife, and thrust it into her heart; her limbs quiv-
ered and she was dead. But I burst into tears and
since that time, — well, why should I be ashamed
of it?"

"Father won't shoot at a fawn," quickly cried
Orel.

" Quite true. Whenever I aim, I see before me

the wounded fawn with her mournful eyes, and fear lest I might miss my aim and only wound the animal; so I don't shoot at all."

"You should shoot only the bad animals and leave the good ones alive," said Willie, his eyes filled with tears.

"There is no animal so good that it is not also bad, nor any so bad that it is not sometimes good, as is the case among people. It is a mistake to suppose that the animal that has a pleasant, mild face must therefore be good, and that the one with a repulsive face is bad. The face is often a great liar. It often happens that that which is repugnant to a person and does not interest him is less pitied than that which is agreeable and interesting, and thus great injustice is often done.

"Once I was at Koniggratz before the execution of two criminals. One was a handsome man, the other hideous and disagreeable. The first had murdered his friend because he believed that he had seduced the girl he loved. The second one was from our neighborhood; I went to him, after he was condemned, to ask him if he had no word to send home, and said that I would gladly deliver any message. He looked at me, laughed wildly, then shook his head and said: 'I send a message, a greeting! to whom? I know nobody.'

"He turned from me, buried his face in his hands, and remained silent for some time; then he sprang up, stood before me with his hands folded over his breast, and asked: 'Will you do for me what I ask?' 'Most willingly,' I replied, giving him my hand. At that moment such agony was depicted in his countenance that I would have done anything in the world for him; his face lost its repulsiveness and awoke only pity and sympathy. He must have read my heart well, for he seized my hand quickly, pressed it, and with a trembling voice said: 'If you could have given me your hand thus three years ago, I should not be here. Why did we not meet? Why did I only meet people who trampled me into the dust, who ridiculed my face, who fed me with wormwood and poison? My mother never loved me, my brother drove me away, my sister was ashamed of me, and she, who I thought loved me, for whom I would have risked my life, for whose smile I would have brought down the stars, for whom I regretted that I did not have ten lives that I might offer them for her love, she only mocked me, and when I wanted to hear from her own lips what all others told me, she drove me out of her door with her dog.' Then this savage man wept like a child.

" After a while he dried his tears, took my hand and added quietly: 'When you come to Marsovward, go into that deep, wild glen. Above the precipice stands an isolated fir; give it my greeting and greet those wild birds that fly about its head, and those high mountains. Under its branches I slept many a night, to it I told what nobody knows. Then I was not such a wretched being; I was——.' He stopped, sat down on the bench again, and said no more, nor did he look at me again.

" I left the prison full of pity for him; the people condemned him, cursed him for a hideous monster, said that he deserved death, that villainy looked out of his eyes, that he would see no priest nor anybody else, that he made faces at people and went to his execution as to a feast. The handsome man was pitied by all; they fought for the song that he had composed in prison, and every one wished that he might be pardoned, since he had killed his friend through jealousy, but the other one, they said, had shot a girl out of pure maliciousness,— a girl who had never done him any harm.

"Thus each judges according to his own feelings. 'So many heads, so many opinions;' to each eye things appear different, and therefore it is hard to say: 'This is thus and cannot be otherwise.' Only God knows the world. He looks into the innermost depths of the human heart and judges it; He understands the language of animals; before Him is unfolded the chalice of every flower; He knows the path of every worm; the rustling of the wind is according to His commands; the streams flow the way He has pointed out."

Mr. Beyer again made a long pause; his pipe had gone out, his eye sparkled with animation, his face resembled a mountain dale lighted up with the soft light of the autumn sun, and upon whose bosom there is still green shrubbery and flowers, even though the top of the mountain is already covered with snow.

All turned their eyes upon him, until Grandmother spoke out: "You are right, Mr. Beyer; one loves to listen to you, it seems like a Scripture lesson. But the little folks must go to bed; your son must be tired after his journey, and you, too. To-morrow we will finish our conversation."

"That buzzard you can give to me for my owl," said the gamekeeper to Orel.

" Most willingly," replied the boy.

" May we take it to your house to-morrow morning early," begged the boys.

" But you must go to school."

" I told them they might have a holiday to-morrow, so that they can enjoy your son's visit," said the mother.

" Why, then, I must let those blue jays of mine stay at home, too. Now, come. Good night! Farewell!"

" The dear brother of the lowlands," as Mr. Beyer sometimes called the Riesenburg game-keeper, shook hands with his friends, called Hector and departed. In the morning, before the children were dressed, Orel was out on the river upon the floating logs. After breakfast Mr. Beyer and the boys went to the gamekeeper's, while Grand-mother, together with Barunka and Adelka, went to the inn to bid Milo good-bye. The inn was already crowded; mothers and fathers came to see their sons depart; friends, relatives and acquaint-ances were there. Although one tried to encourage another, although the innkeeper and his daughter had so much to do that even Milo was called on to assist at the bar, although the young folks joined in many a gay song, it was all of no avail; not one drank too much, as had been the case when they went to the conscription. Then they trimmed their caps with evergreens, shouted gayly, drank and sang so as to smother their fear and anxiety. Each one, even the straightest, the handsomest young man, cherished still a little hope. Then they were flattered by the sorrow of the girls, they were pleased with the love of their parents, which on such occasions gushes out like a stream which has been hidden in the bosom of the earth; they were proud of the opinions expressed by their friends: " Oh, he'll not return,—such a man, grown like a fir tree, as solid as if he were cast from metal, —they delight in such soldiers!" With such sweet drops, vanity tried to lessen the bitterness of the cup which necessity placed before them; on the other hand, that which comforted the strong, handsome men only embittered the hearts of those who had nothing to fear, who were conscious of their physical defects; many a vain fellow felt this burden so grievous that he would have preferred to be a soldier rather than hear remarks like the following:

" Your mother need not weep for you; you will not swear on a drum, you'll do to put into a dog's garter," or " Why, boy! join the cavalry; your legs are like the horns of an ox!" and other equally cutting remarks.

Grandmother entered the inn, but she did not venture into the bar-room, not because the air there was close and oppressive, but because she was startled by the heavy cloud of grief that had settled upon every countenance. She knew how those unhappy mothers felt. Here, one wrung her hands in mute agony; there, another was weeping quietly; while still another gave vent to her grief by loud lamentations. She understood the feelings of those girls, who were ashamed to make their grief visible and yet could not, without tears, look upon the pale faces of their lovers, who even while drinking became only sadder, and whose voices failed them when they tried to sing. She felt with those fathers who, seated around the table, spoke of nothing, thought of nothing, except what they should do without the help of their industrious boys, who had been as their right hands; how they should miss them, and how they were to live without them for fourteen long years!— Grandmother sat down with the children in the orchard.

After a while Christina came out, haggard, with swollen eyes, and pale as a sheet. She wanted to speak; but a stone lay upon her breast, and her throat was drawn together so that she could not utter a word. She leaned against the branch of a blossoming apple tree. It was the same tree over which on St. John's eve she had thrown her wreath. The wreath had fallen on the other side, and now, when her fondest hopes should have been realized, she must part with her lover. She covered her face with her white apron and began to weep aloud. Grandmother did not try to stop her. Milo came. What had become of that ruddy face, those bright eyes? He seemed to be carved out of marble. Without a word he gave his hand to Grandmother, embraced the girl so dear to him, and drawing from his pocket an embroidered handkerchief, which every girl works for the youth she loves, wiped away the tears from her cheeks. They did not say to each other how deep was their grief, but when a stanza of the well-known song resounded from the inn:

> " When, dear love, I part with thee,
>   Two faithful hearts shall broken be;
>   Two faithful hearts and four eyes bright,
>   Shall mourn and weep both day and night,"

Christina threw her arms around her lover and, sobbing violently, hid her face upon his bosom.

That song was the echo of a melody that was heard in their own hearts.

Grandmother arose, and the tears rolled down her cheeks; Barunka also wept. Grandmother placed her hand upon Milo's shoulder, and said in a deep voice: "God go with you and comfort you, Jacob! Do your duty willingly, and it will not seem so hard. If God grants success to my plan, your parting will not be for long. Hope! You, my child, if you love him, do not make this parting so much more grievous by your lamentations! Farewell!" Thus saying she blessed Milo with the cross, pressed his hand, and turning quickly took the little girls by the hands and hurried home, having the sweet consciousness that she had comforted the sorrowing.

The lovers, into whose hearts Grandmother's words fell like dew upon a perishing flower, quickening it to new life, stood under the blossoming apple tree clasped in each other's arms. A wagon was heard entering the yard; it came for the soldiers. Somebody called from the inn: "Milo!—Christina!" But they did not hear. What cared they? what was the whole world to them? Each held his whole world in his arms.

In the afternoon, Mr. Beyer, too, bade his kind hostess good bye. Mrs. Proshek, as usual, loaded him and his son with food for the journey. Each of the boys gave Orel something as a keepsake, and Barunka presented him with a band for his hat. When Adelka asked Grandmother what she should give, she told her to give the rose that the Countess had given her.

"But, Grandma, you said I should keep it till I am grown up and then wear it in my belt."

"What you value the most, you must bestow upon your friend, if you wish to do him honor. Give it to him; it is becoming for girls to present flowers."

Adelka put the pretty rose into Orel's hat.

"O my dear Adelka," said Mr. Beyer, "I don't know how long that rose will keep its beauty. Orel is a wild bird, the whole day long he flies over rocks and hills, in wind and rain."

Adelka turned her questioning eyes to Orel.

"Do not think so, father," said the boy looking with great pleasure upon the gift; "during the week while I am in the mountains, my rose shall be put away; I shall wear it only on Sundays and holidays, and then it will always stay pretty."

Adelka was pleased. No one thought that she herself would be the rose for which, some day, Orel would long, which he would carry off into the snow-covered mountains, and there in the seclusion of the forest keep and cherish for his delight; that her love would become the light and bliss of his whole life.

CHAPTER XV.

THE Pentecost holidays were over; Grandmother called them green holidays, probably because everything both inside and outside the house was decorated with foliage; so that whether they sat at the table or slept on their beds, they were "under the green." Corpus Christi and St. John the Baptist's were also gone. The voice of the nightingale was heard no more in the thicket, the swallows under the eaves were leading forth their young, on top of the oven with the old cats lay a May kitten, which Adelka loved to pet. Her black hen was leading about a brood of half-grown chickens, and Sultan and Tyrol were again jumping into the water to catch water rats, which gave occasion to the old spinners to start the report that the foot bridge at The Old Bleachery was haunted by a waterman.

Adelka used to go with Vorsa to watch Spotty in the pasture; she also helped Grandmother collect herbs, or sat with her in the yard under the old linden, whose blossoms they dried for tea. Here also she recited her lessons to her. In the afternoon, when they went to meet the children returning from school, they took a stroll in the fields, where Grandmother stopped to see how her flax was doing. She loved to look at the broad, manorial wheat fields, for their full heads were fast turning yellow, and when the wind swept them into billows, it was such a beautiful sight that she could scarcely turn

away her eyes. When she met Kuderna, who was
watching the fields, she would say: "God blesses
the country with abundant harvest; may he also
keep it from all damage!"

"Yes, there is some reason to fear; the weather
for several days has been unusually hot," he replied
as he turned his eyes to study the clouds.

Whenever they passed the field of peas, Kuderna
picked Adelka's apron full of nice green pods;
quieting his conscience by observing that the
Princess would not object, seeing she was so fond
of Mr. Proshek's children.

Barunka did not bring Adelka any more gum
or sweet wood from school, for as soon as the
cherry woman took her stand near the schoolhouse,
she brought each day a kreutzer's worth of cherries; or when she took the path through the oak
grove, she gathered strawberries for her little
sister, putting them in a little birch-bark basket that
she had made for the purpose. Later in the season
she brought huckleberries, and finally hazel nuts.
Grandmother gathered mushrooms and taught the
children to know the good from the poisonous.
July was over, and at the beginning of August the
Princess would come, and also their father. In addition to these pleasures, vacation was close at hand.
Mrs. Proshek went to the castle to see that all was
in readiness for the arrival of the mistress, and the
gardener almost ran his legs off in his anxiety lest
the garden should not be in the best possible condition. He scrutinized the sward to see that no blade
of grass was higher than another; he raised up the
leaning branches of the plants for fear some weed
might still be hidden beneath them. Preparations

were made everywhere for the coming of the mistress. Those to whom her arrival would bring some gain rejoiced, while others were vexed. Among the latter was the steward, who grew more and more humble each day, and when the report was circulated that she would be in the castle the next day, he became so meek that he returned the greeting of the forester quite respectfully, something that he never did in the winter, when he regarded himself the first person on the estate of the Princess.

Grandmother at all times wished well to the Princess, and always remembered her in her prayers; but if with her coming had not been connected that of Mr. Proshek, it would have been all the same to her whether she came or not. On this occasion, however, she could hardly restrain her impatience; she had something on her mind that she confided to no one.

The harvest began in the early part of August, and the Princess came with all her attendants. The steward's daughter was expecting the Italian, but was disappointed, for he had been left in Vienna. Mrs. Proshek's face beamed with joy, for the children had their dear father with them. Grandmother's face, it is true, grew somewhat sad when she saw that Jóhn came without Johanna. He brought her a letter, in which her daughter sent her a thousand greetings from Aunt Dorothy and from Uncle, but said, that on account of her uncle's illness she could not come, for she could not leave her aunt to care for the sick man and see to the housework besides. She wrote that her lover was a worthy young man, that her aunt was satisfied with him, and that she would make a wedding for them on St. Katherine's, and that they were only waiting for Grandmother's consent. " As soon as it is possible, after we are married, we will come to Bohemia to receive your blessing, dearest mother, and to make you acquainted with my George, whom, however, we call Jura. He is not a Bohemian, his home being somewhere on the Turkish boundary, but you can speak with him, for I have taught him Bohemian more quickly than Theresa taught John. I should have preferred one of our nationality, for I know you would have been more pleased; but, dearest mother, what can one do? The heart will not be constrained, and I have chosen my Krobat." Thus the letter ended.

Theresa read the letter. John was present and said: " It sounds as if I heard her, our joyous Hannah; she is a good girl, and Jura is a worthy young man. I know him; he is the foreman at Uncle's, where Hannah is, and whenever I entered the blacksmith shop I loved to look at Jura, — a fellow like a mountain! it would not be easy to find his equal."

" There was one word there, Theresa, that I did not understand, somewhere near the end; read it for me again," said Grandmother.

" It was ' Krobat,' was it not?"

" Yes, that's it."

" That is what they call a Croat in Vienna."

" Is that what it means? May God grant her happiness! But who would have guessed from what remote regions they would come to meet each other! And his name is George, the same as her father's!"

With these words she brushed away the tears that came into her eyes, folded the letter, and went to hide it in the side drawer of her chest.

The children were delighted to have their father with them. They never grew weary of looking at him, and each interrupted the other in trying to tell him all that had happened during the year, which, however, he already knew from their mother's letters. " Now you will stay with us the whole winter, won't you, Papa? " asked Adelka, coaxingly, stroking his beard, which was her favorite way of caressing him.

" And, Papa, when it is sleighing, you'll give us a ride in that beautiful sleigh, and hang the bells on the horse? Our Godfather from town came for us once in the winter; we went there with Mamma; Grandmother would not go. How it went, and how the bells jingled! People ran out to see who in the world was coming," cried Willie, and before the father could put in a word John said: " Papa, when I am big, I shall be a gamekeeper. When I leave school, I shall go to Mr. Beyer's to learn, and Orel will go the Riesenburg gamekeeper to learn."

" Very well, only you must first be very diligent in school," said the father smiling, but leaving the boy full freedom of choice.

His dear friends, the gamekeeper and the miller, came to welcome Mr. Proshek. The whole household grew happier, and even Sultan and Tyrol rushed out to meet Hector with unwonted glee, as if they wished to tell him some good news. Mr. Proshek liked them; they had not been whipped since they had killed the goslings, and whenever they came to meet him he patted them on the head. Grandmother seeing their joy, said that animals knew well who was kind to them, and never forgot it.

"And is the Countess quite well?" asked the gamekeeper's wife, who also came to welcome Mr. Proshek home.

"They say she is, but I think she is not. Something must prey on her mind. She was always delicate, but now she seems only a spirit, and her eyes seem to look down from heaven. I could weep when I see her; she is an angel. The Princess is filled with sorrow and anxiety, and from the time the Countess was taken ill, there have been no merrymakings in our house. Just before her illness she was about to be betrothed to a certain Count. He comes from a wealthy family, and the Princess thinks a great deal of his parents, and was very desirous to have this marriage take place. I don't know what to think of it," added Mr. Proshek, shaking his head dubiously.

"And what does the Count say?" asked the women.

"What should he say? He must be content to wait till she gets well. If she dies he can put on mourning, if he really loves her. They say he wants to follow her to Italy."

"Does Hortense like the Count?" asked Grandmother.

"Who can tell! If she hasn't given her heart to any one else, she could learn to like him; he is a handsome man," replied Mr. Proshek.

"That is, if she doesn't like any one else," said the miller, passing his open snuff box to Mr. Proshek; "there is no disputing of tastes." This was his favorite saying. "Now, our bar-maid from the tavern could be married, and not go about as if she had been put under the water, if those deuced fellows had not taken away what she liked," continued the miller taking a pinch of snuff, and casting a side glance upon Christina who was there also.

"I was sorry for both of you, when I learned from Theresa's letter what had happened," said Mr. Proshek, looking kindly upon Christina's pale face. "Has Milo become somewhat reconciled to his lot?"

"What can he do? he must be reconciled. It is hard enough for him," replied Christina, turning to the window to hide her tears.

"Yes, indeed," said the gamekeeper; "shut a bird up in a golden cage, and he will still prefer the woods."

"Especially if his mate is pining there without him," said the miller, with a mischievous smile.

"I, too, was a soldier," began Mr. Proshek: a smile played about his lips as he said this, and his blue eyes turned to his wife.

She smiled in return, as she said: "Yes, and what a hero you were!"

"Don't you laugh, Theresa; when you and aunt Dorothy came to the fortifications to see us drill, you wept, both of you."

"And you with us," laughed Mrs. Proshek; "but at that time nobody was in a laughing mood, except, perhaps, those who observed us."

"I must confess," said the tender hearted Mr Proshek, "that it was all the same to me whether they called me an old woman or a hero. I had no longing for the latter distinction. The whole of those fourteen days that I was a soldier I spent in sighs and tears; I scarcely ate or slept, so that when I was discharged, I was but a shadow."

"So you were a soldier only fourteen days! Hm! that would suit Milo, if they would count his days as years," observed the miller.

"But I should not have suffered so much, had I known that a good friend was trying to pay me out, and, that my brother was offering to act as substitute. It came to me wholly as a surprise. My brother liked a soldier's life, and was in every way better adapted to it than I; still, I do not think that I am a coward! If it were necessary to guard family and home, I should be the first in the ranks. We are not all alike; one is adapted to this, another to that. Is it not so Theresa?"

Thus speaking, he placed his hand upon Theresa's shoulder and looked lovingly into her eyes.

"Yes, yes, John, you belong with us," replied Grandmother for her daughter, and all agreed with her, knowing Mr. Proshek's gentle disposition.

When the company was about to leave, Christina slipped into Grandmother's room, and drawing a letter from her bosom, upon whose seal was the impression of a soldier's button, said almost in a whisper: "From Jacob!"

"Indeed! And what does he write?" asked Grandmother.

Christina unfolded the letter and began to read slowly:

"My dearest Christina, I greet and kiss you a

thousand times. But alas! I should prefer to kiss you once in reality than a thousand times on paper; but a great distance lies between us, so that we cannot come to each other. I know that many times each day you think: ' I wonder how Jacob is? What is he doing?' I have enough to do, but such work! The body works while the thoughts are elsewhere. Were I free like Anton Vitkov, perhaps I might learn to like a soldier's life; my comrades are becoming accustomed to it, and soon they will not be so lonesome. I, too, learn everything and find no fault; but nothing seems to interest me, and instead of becoming accustomed to it, it seems harder every day. The whole day long I think only of you, my dear dove, and if I knew you were well, if I had a single greeting from you, I should be happy. When I stand guard and watch the birds flying in the direction of our village, I think: ' Why can't they speak, so that they can carry my greeting to my love?' or rather I wish that I myself might be a bird, and fly away to you. Doesn't Proshek's Grandmother say anything? What did she mean by saying that perhaps our parting would not be for long? Do you know? When I feel the worst I think of her last words, and it seems as if God himself came to me, pouring fresh hope into my soul, and that she will find some way to help us. She never speaks in vain. Send me a few lines to comfort me; some one can write them for you; tell me everything, you understand? Did you get the grain in dry? Harvest has begun here, too. When I see the reapers going into the fields, I want to fling everything aside and run away. I beg you, Christina, don't go alone to the socage,* they will question you and grieve your heart, don't go. And that good-for-nothing.— that clerklet—— "

" How foolish he is! Does he think that I could—— " frowned Christina, but began reading further: " would not let you alone. Stay near Tomesh. I charged him before I left to be your right hand. Give him my greeting,— and Anna, too! Remember me also to my folks, to Grandmother and the children, and to all my friends. I could say so much more, that it could not be put upon a piece of paper the size of Zernov hill; but I must go to stand guard. When I stand guard at night, I sing:

'Ye stars so beautiful, how small you are.'

You remember we sang it together the evening before I left; you broke down and wept. O, heavens! how those little stars used to cheer us up; but only God knows whether they will ever cheer us again. May God bless you. Good bye! "

Christina folded the letter, and turned her questioning eyes to Grandmother's face.

" You can be comforted; he is a good boy; give him my greeting and tell him to trust in God; tell him the darkest days pass away and the sun shines again, and his sun, too, will shine. I cannot tell you positively, it is thus or so, as long as I am not certain. When it is necessary, go with the reapers; I want you to present the garland to the Princess at the harvest festival, for since you work in her fields, it will be becoming for you to do it ? "

Christina was comforted by these words, and

*Service due the lords from their tenants, being usually work in the fields.

promised to do everything according to Grandmother's advice.   Since Mr. Proshek's return
Grandmother had asked him several times when
the Princess was likely to be at home, and what
were her accustomed places of resort, till Mr. Proshek was surprised.   " Never before has she been
curious to know what was going on in the castle;
the castle did not seem to exist for her, but now she
asks and asks.   What does she want?"   But she
did not tell them.   They did not wish to question
her; therefore they learned nothing, and ascribed
her queries to inquisitiveness.

In a few days Mr. Proshek took his wife and
children to town; he wanted them to have a good
time.   Vorsa and Betsey went into the fields, while
Grandmother watched the house.   She took her
spindle and went into the yard under the linden as
was her custom.   Something seemed to weigh upon
her mind, for now and then she shook her head,
then nodded, and finally, as if she had decided what
to do, she said aloud: " That is the way I'll do it."
At this moment she saw the Countess coming down
the hillside past the oven and over the footbridge.
She had on a white dress and a round straw hat;
she walked as lightly as a fairy, and her feet, en-
cased in satin gaiters, hardly touched the ground.
Grandmother arose quickly and welcomed her
with joy; but her heart ached, when she looked
into the girl's face, so pale that the skin seemed
transparent, and so resigned and full of deep pain
that no one could gaze on her without pitying her.

" Alone! and so quiet here," said Hortense, after
returning Grandmother's greeting.

" Yes, all the rest have gone to town with their

father; they cannot enjoy him enough after having missed him so long," replied Grandmother as she brushed the dust from the bench with her apron before asking the Countess to be seated.

"Yes, indeed, that was a long time, but I was to blame."

"Is one to blame, dear Countess, when God visits one with illness. All of us were so sorry for you and prayed every day that God would restore you to health. Health is a precious treasure that one is apt to value only when it is lost. It would have been a great pity to lose you, you are so young, and her grace, the Princess, would have been over-whelmed with grief."

"I know that well," sighed the Countess, placing her clasped hands upon a beautifully bound album that was lying in her lap.

"You are so pale, dear Countess, what ails you?" asked Grandmother, with great sympathy, looking upon Hortense, who seemed the embodi-ment of sorrow.

"Nothing, Grandma," replied the Countess, with a forced smile, which, however, only revealed the pain it was meant to conceal.

Grandmother did not venture any more ques-tions, but she felt sure that physical illness was not the only thing that troubled the Countess.

After a moment of silence, the Countess began to inquire what had been going on in the cottage during her absence, and whether the children thought of her. Grandmother gladly told her, and in turn asked how the Princess was and what she was doing.

"The Princess rode to the gamekeeper's," replied the Countess. "I got permission to remain here so that I might sketch this vale, and make you a visit. She will stop for me on her way back."

"Really, it seems as if God himself sent her!" rejoiced Grandmother; "I must put on a clean apron; one gets all dusty from this flax. Excuse me, if you please, I will return presently!"

Grandmother hurried into the house, and before long returned with a clean apron, and clean kerchiefs both on her head and neck, and bringing white bread, honey, butter, and cream.

"Perhaps, your Grace would relish a piece of bread; it was baked yesterday. But let us go into the orchard, it is pleasanter there. When I am alone, I prefer to sit here under this linden, for I like to have the poultry about my feet."

"Then, let us remain here, I am quite comfortable," said the Countess, taking the refreshments Grandmother brought. She did not wait for Grandmother to urge her to eat, but took some bread and a glass of cream. She knew that if she accepted nothing, Grandmother would feel hurt. Then she opened the album and showed Grandmother what she had sketched.

"Oh, dear Lord!" exclaimed Grandmother, "here we have the whole country above the dam; the meadows, the hillside, the woods, and here is Victorka, too!"

"She suits this lonely region well. I met her on the hillside; she looked bad. Cannot anything be done for her?" asked the Countess in a voice full of pity.

"Oh your Grace, her body could be helped, but her trouble is not there. Her mind is wandering;

what she does, she does as in a dream. Perhaps God out of pity took away the remembrance of her sorrow, which must have been heavy, indeed. Should her reason return, she might in despair lose her own soul, as — well, God forgive her if she sinned; she has suffered enough," said Grandmother, turning over another leaf. A new wonder. " In all my life! why this is The Old Bleachery, the yard, the linden, — here am I and the children, and the dogs, — everything! Well, well, in my old age what wonders do I see! What would our folks say!" exclaimed Grandmother, more and more astonished.

" I never forget people that once were dear to me," said the Countess, " but that I may retain a clear image of their faces, I usually paint them. It is the same with places in which I have spent happy days. I love to transfer them to paper, so that I may have a pleasant remembrance of them. This vale here is most charming. If you would not object, Grandma, I should like to paint your picture for your grandchildren."

Grandmother blushed, shook her head, and said: "Such an old woman as I, why that wouldn't do at all!"

" Never mind, Grandma, when you are at home alone, I will come over and paint you; I will do it for your children's sake, I know they will be delighted."

" Since your Grace desires it, I cannot object, but, I beg of you, nobody must know anything about it; they would say I am becoming vain. While I am with them, they need no picture; but when I am gone, — let it be as you say!"

The Countess was satisfied.

" But where did your Grace learn this? In all

my life I never heard of women painters," said Grandmother, turning over another leaf.

"Among our class of people we must learn a great many things that we may know how to pass away our time, and I took a fancy to painting," replied the Countess.

"It is an excellent thing," remarked Grandmother, looking upon a picture that was loosely placed in the album. In the foreground of the picture was a rock overgrown with shrubbery, its base washed by the waves of the sea. A young man stood upon the rock, holding a rosebud in his hand, and gazing out over the sea, upon whose bosom were seen in the distance several ships with outspread sails.

"Did your Grace paint this, too?" asked Grandmother.

"No, the artist from whom I took lessons gave that to me," replied the Countess in a low voice.

"That perhaps is himself?"

The Countess did not at once reply; her face turned crimson; she arose. "It seems to me that the Princess is coming," she said.

Grandmother took the hint; she now understood what ailed the Countess.

The Princess was not coming. The young lady sat down again, and after several attempts Grandmother succeeded in turning the conversation upon Christina and Milo; she confided to the Countess her intention of speaking to the Princess about it. The young lady approved of the plan, and promised to intercede for them.

The Princess returned through the path, while the empty carriage was taken along the road. She greeted Grandmother very heartily, and brought a bouquet for Hortense, saying: "You are very fond of wild pinks! I gathered these for you along the way."

The Countess bowed, kissed the hand of the Princess, and put the pinks in her belt.

"These are tears," said Grandmother, looking at the bouquet.

"Tears?" wondered both the ladies.

"Yes, the tears of the Virgin. That's what these flowers are called. When the Jews led Christ to Calvary, the Virgin Mary followed, although her heart was breaking with grief. When she saw on the way the bloody tracks of Christ's wounds, she wept bitterly, and from those tears of Christ's mother and the blood of her son sprang forth, along the way to Calvary, such flowers as these," said Grandmother.

"Then they are the flowers of grief and love," said the Princess.

"Lovers never pick them for each other, lest they should bring them tears," returned Grandmother, at the same time offering the Princess a glass of cream and humbly begging her to partake of her hospitality.

The Princess did not refuse. Grandmother continued: "Indeed, they have enough to weep for, even if they gather no tears, for there is always much grief as well as joy. If they are happy in each other's love, envious people are sure to pour in some wormwood."

"Dearest Princess, Grandmother wants to intercede for two unhappy lovers. I beg you to listen and, dearest Princess, help!" The Countess clasped her hands and looked up imploringly into the face of her guardian.

"Speak, my good woman, you know I told you once that if you should come to me for help, I would gladly grant your request; I know you would not beg for any one who is unworthy," said the Princess, smoothing the glossy hair of her ward and looking kindly at Grandmother.

"I should not presume to come to your Grace, if I thought they were unworthy."

Then she told about Christina and Milo, and how he came to be taken into the army, keeping back only the poor girl's persecution by the steward. She did not want to injure him any more than was necessary.

"That is the same girl whose lover had that quarrel with Piccolo."

"The same, your Grace."

"Is she so pretty that all the men fight for her?"

"A girl like a strawberry, your Grace; at the harvest festival she will present the wreath, so your Grace can see her. To be sure, sorrow doesn't add any beauty; when a girl grieves for love, her head droops like a faded flower. Christina is now but the shadow of herself, but one word will restore her, so that she will soon be as before. Her Grace, the Countess, is also very pale; but when she sees her old home and what is dear to her heart, her cheeks will blossom out like rose petals," added Grandmother giving the words, "dear to her heart," such an emphasis that the young lady was startled. The Princess cast a keen glance first upon the Countess then upon Grandmother, but the latter acted as if nothing had happened; she wanted to give a hint, that was all. She thought: "If the happiness of that child lies near her heart, she will seek further."

After a moment of silence the Princess arose, placed her hand upon Grandmother's shoulder, and said in a pleasant voice: "I'll care for those lovers. But you, my good woman, come to me about this time to-morrow."

"Dear Princess," said the Countess, placing the book under her arm, "Grandmother has consented that I shall paint her picture, but wants it to remain a secret while she lives. How can we do it?"

"Come to the castle, Grandmother; Hortense can paint you there. While you live, I shall keep the picture. She will paint your grandchildren, too; but that picture will be for you, so that when they are grown up you can see how they looked when they were small."

Thus speaking, the Princess bowed, entered the carriage with the Countess, and rode toward the castle.

Grandmother went into the house, her heart overflowing with joy and thankfulness.

CHAPTER XVI.

THE morning was hot and sultry. Everybody, old and young, worked in the fields so as to get in at least what grain was already cut. The householders were obliged to put in a good part of the night, so that they might be able to keep up with their own work and the socage required by their manor lords. The sun shone scorchingly hot, and the baked ground cracked beneath its burning rays. People panted with heat, the flowers wilted, the birds flew near the ground, the animals sought the shade. From early dawn clouds gathered here and there above the horizon; at first small and gray or white. As the day advanced they grew more numerous, collected in heaps, rose higher, clashed and rifted, leaving long dark fissures. Their color grew darker and darker, till by noon the whole western sky was enveloped in a heavy, black cloud, which was drawing toward the sun. The reapers looked upon the sky with fear. Although they were panting from exhaustion, each redoubled his exertions, not waiting to be urged on by the overseer's imprecations and curses. This was his custom in order that the people might not forget that he was their master and had a right to demand due respect for his authority.

Grandmother sat upon the doorsill; she was watching with great anxiety the clouds, which were already above the house. Adelka and the boys were playing in the yard, but were so warm that they would have gladly taken off their clothes and jumped into the stream, if Grandmother had only given them permission. Adelka, who was always bright and active as a linnet, was gaping; she did not feel like playing; and finally her eyes closed and she was asleep. Grandmother, too, felt her eyelids growing heavy. The swallows flew low, and at last hid in their nests; the spider that Grandmother had watched that morning, as he decoyed and devoured several flies, concealed himself in his den; the poultry in the yard gathered in groups; the dogs lay stretched at Grandmother's feet, and with their tongues drawn out as if they had come from some wild chase, panted for breath. The trees stood perfectly quiet; not a leaf stirred.

Mr. and Mrs. Proshek came home from the castle. " My dear people, a terrible storm is coming on, is everything safe at home?" called Mrs. Proshek from afar. The linen bleaching on the grass, the poultry, the children, — everything was attended to and put out of the way of danger. Grandmother placed a loaf of bread upon the table and got ready the " blessed " storm candle. All the windows were closed. The air was sultry, the sun was covered by a dark cloud. Mr. Proshek stood in the road, looking in all directions. In the woods he saw Victorka standing under a tree; a brisk wind came up, the hollow rumbling of thunder was heard, streaks of lightning shot through the dark clouds. "Heavens, that woman stands under a tree!" said Mr. Proshek to himself and began to call and motion to Victorka to go away. She, however, did not notice him, and at each flash of lightning clapped her hands and laughed aloud.   Great drops of rain began to fall, zigzag lightnings gleamed through the black clouds, the thunder roared, and the storm burst forth in all its fury.   Mr. Proshek hastened into the house.   Grandmother had the blessed candle lighted; she was praying with the children, who turned pale every time the lightning struck.   Mr. Proshek went from window to window, looking outside.   The rain came down in torrents, and the sky was a continuous sheet of lightning; peal after peal of thunder was heard, as if the furies were flying through the air.   A moment of silence, — then again the bluish yellow light gleamed in the windows, two fiery snakes crossed each other in the sky, and — crash! crash! came two explosions in quick succession, directly above the house.   Grandmother wanted to say: "God be with us!" but the words died upon her lips; Mrs. Proshek took hold of the table, Mr. Proshek turned pale, Vorsa and Betsey fell upon their knees, and the children began to cry.   With that last stroke the storm seemed to have spent its wrath, and now began to pass away.   The rumbling of the thunder grew lower and lower, the clouds gradually scattered, they changed color, and already the blue sky was seen behind the gray curtain. Lightnings gleamed only now and then, the rain ceased, — the storm was over.

What a change outside! The earth rested as if she were weary; her limbs still trembled, and the sun looked down at her with a tear-stained, but glowing eye, though now and then clouds were seen over his face, the remaining signs of the recent tempest.   The grass and the flowers were beaten to the ground; streams of water were flowing along the sides of the road; in the river the water was muddy; the trees shook off thousands of glittering drops from their bright green foliage; the birds again swept through the air; the geese and ducks were enjoying the pools of water that the rain had made for them; the chickens were running about seeking worms which were seen squirming in great numbers on the ground; the spider came out of his den. All creatures seemed refreshed and hastening out to new enjoyment of life, to new struggles and conquests.

Mr. Proshek went outdoors, walked around the house, and behold! the old pear tree, whose branches for so many years had sheltered the house, was split from top to bottom by the lightning! half of it lay on the roof, the other half was bent to the ground. That old wild pear tree had not borne fruit for many years; still they loved it, for with its wide branches it had shaded the house from spring to winter.

The rain had done some damage in the fields, but the people were thankful that it was no worse; they had all feared that a hail storm was coming up. In the afternoon the roads began to dry, so that the miller could go, as was his custom, to the lock in his slippers. As Grandmother was going to the castle she met him; he told her that the heavy rain had done some damage to his fruit trees. Then he asked her where she was going and offered her a pinch of snuff; when she told him, they bade each other good day, and went their several ways.

Mr. Leopold must have received orders to take Grandmother to the Princess without any announcement; for as soon as she appeared at the entrance, he opened the doors to her without any delay or ceremony and showed her into a small parlor where the Princess was sitting. She was alone and bade Grandmother to be seated beside her.

"Your simpleheartedness and sincerity please me greatly; I place entire confidence in you, and think you will tell me honestly what I ask you?" began the Princess.

"How could I do otherwise, your Grace? only ask, I shall be too glad to reply," said Grandmother, wondering what it could be that the Princess wanted to know.

"You said yesterday that when the Countess reaches her native land and sees what is dear to her heart, her cheeks will regain their color. You placed such emphasis upon those words that my curiosity was aroused. Was I mistaken, or did you do it intentionally?" Thus speaking, the Princess looked keenly upon her visitor.

Grandmother was not confused. She considered a moment, then said candidly: "I said it intentionally; what was in my mind came to my tongue. I wanted to give your Grace a hint; sometimes a word spoken in season is profitable."

"Did the Countess confide in you?" questioned the Princess further.

"Heaven forbid! Her Grace is not one of those that parade their grief before the whole world; but when we have suffered ourselves, we are quick to understand others."

"What did you understand? What did you hear? Tell me all about it; it is not curiosity, but anxiety for my child, whom I dearly love, that impels me to want to know all", said the Princess much disturbed.

"I can tell you all I heard, for it is nothing wrong, and I did not promise on my soul not to tell," replied Grandmother, and began to relate how she had heard of the betrothal and illness of the Countess. "One thought suggests another," she said; "and it often happens that one can judge better of a thing when seeing it from a distance than when observing it close at hand; reflection, too, brings wisdom. Thus, your Grace, it occurred to me that, perhaps, the Countess did not like to marry that nobleman, and only consented because she knew it would please your Grace. Yesterday, as I observed her so pale and wan, I could have wept; we were looking at those beautiful pictures that she painted, — it is wonderful, — and then we came to a picture, which, as she told me, her teacher painted and gave her. I asked her if that handsome gentleman was the painter himself, — an old person, like a child, wants to know everything. She blushed, arose, made no reply, but her eyes filled with tears. That was enough for me, and your Grace can tell best, whether the old woman was right."

The Princess arose, paced the floor several times, and then said as if speaking to herself: "I observed nothing; she was always cheerful and submissive. She never spoke of him."

"Well," replied Grandmother to these audible thoughts, "natures differ. One would not be happy if he could not set up every joy, every sorrow for the wonder of the world; another carries them hidden in his bosom all his life, and takes them with

him to the grave. It is hard to win such people, but
love begets love. People seem to me like plants; for
some we need not go far,— we find them in every
meadow, in every hedge; for others we must go
into the forest's deep shade, we must search for them
under the leaves, must not be discouraged if we
climb over hills and rocks, or if brambles and thorns
obstruct our way. But our labors, in this case, are
rewarded a hundred fold. The old herb woman
that comes to us from the mountains always says
when she brings us fragrant moss: ' I must search
long before I find it, but it pays.' That moss has
the odor of violets, and its fragrance reminds one of
spring. But pardon me, your Grace, I always
wander away from the subject. I was going to
say that perhaps the Countess was happy because
she had hope; and now, when she has lost that,
she realizes her grief. How often is it that we do
not value our blessings until we have lost them."

"I thank you, Grandmother, for your suggestion," said the Princess. "I fear I shall not be the
gainer by it, but what care I, if she is only happy.
She will have you alone to thank, for without you
I never should have guessed the truth. I will keep
you no longer. The Countess is preparing to paint;
so to-morrow come here with the children."

With these words she dismissed Grandmother,
who went home happy that with a good word she
had contributed to the happiness of another human
being.

Approaching the house, she met the gamekeeper;
he was excited, his step was quick. "Listen, hear
what has happened!" he said to Grandmother in a
voice full of sorrow.

"Do not frighten me, but tell me quickly, what is it?"

"Victorka was struck by God's messenger!"

Grandmother clasped her hands. It was some time before she could utter a word, then two great tears rolled down her cheeks. "God loved her, let us be glad that he has called her home!" she said quietly.

"Her death was easy," said the gamekeeper.

Just then the children and Mr. and Mrs. Proshek came out, and hearing the sad news stood mute with grief. At length Mr. Proshek said: "I was greatly concerned about her before the storm, when I saw her standing under the tree. I called, I motioned, but she only laughed. I saw her then for the last time. It is well."

"Who found her, and where?"

"After the storm I went into the woods to see if much damage had been done; I reached the top of the hill where those united fir trees stand, as you know, just above Victorka's cave. I saw something lying under some green fir branches and called, but there was no reply. I looked up to see where the branches came from. Both the firs, on the sides next to each other had their branches and bark torn off from top to bottom. I raised the branches; beneath them lay Victorka—dead. I shook her, but she was already cold. From her shoulder to her foot, on the left side, her clothes were scorched. I suppose she was pleased at the storm,— she always laughed when it lightened,— and ran up on the hill,— there is a fine view from that fir, and there death overtook her."

"As it came to our pear tree," said Grandmother. "And where did you put her?"

"I had her carried to our house; it was the nearest. I am going to take charge of the funeral myself, although her relatives object. I've been to the village to announce it. I did not think we should lose her so soon. I shall miss her," said the gamekeeper.

The tolling of the bell was now heard from Zernov. They signed themselves and began to pray; they knew it was for Victorka.

"May we go to see her?" begged the children.

"To-morrow you may come, when she is laid out!" said the gamekeeper, taking his leave.

"Poor Victorka won't come to our house any more; we shall never again hear her singing above the dam; she has gone to heaven!" said the children returning to their tasks without even asking Grandmother about the Countess.

"Certainly she is in heaven, for she suffered enough upon earth," thought Grandmother.

The news of Victorka's death spread quickly over the whole neighborhood; every one who knew her pitied her, and was glad, therefore, that death found her, especially such a death, they said, "as God sends to but few people." They had always pitied her, but now that pity was joined with reverence.

The next day, when Grandmother and the children went to the castle to be sketched and painted, the Princess spoke of Victorka. The Countess, hearing how the unfortunate girl was loved both at The Old Bleachery and the gamekeeper's, promised that she would paint for them copies of the picture that she had shown to Grandmother, in which Victorka was seen standing under a tree.

"She wants to do something for everybody, before she leaves; she would like to take all of you with her," smiled the Princess.

"What is better than to be among those that love us, what greater happiness than to make others happy?" said Grandmother.

The children thought it was a grand thing to have their pictures painted, — no one knew anything about Grandmother's,—they also looked forward with great eagerness to the gifts the Countess promised them, if they would sit very quiet. Grandmother watched how under the skillful hand of the artist the features of her loved ones appeared clearer and clearer, and reproved the children whenever they indulged some foolish habit. "Johnny, do not stand upon one foot, you will be lopsided! You, Barunka, don't wrinkle up your nose like a rabbit, how you would look! Willie, don't raise your shoulders all the time as a goose raises her wings when she loses a quill!" But when Adelka forgot herself so far as to put her index finger into her mouth, then Grandmother scolded: "Are you not ashamed, a maid big enough to cut her own bread!* Some day I must sprinkle some pepper upon it."

The Countess enjoyed her work very much and had many a hearty laugh at the children's expense. Indeed, she seemed to grow brighter every day, so that Grandmother remarked that she appeared to her not so much like a rose as like the buds of an

---

* Among the country folk of Bohemia, bread is baked once in two or three weeks. The loaves are very large, and at the end of two weeks are so hard that it is quite a feat for a child to cut them.

apple tree just before it blossoms. She was happier, her eye was clearer and sparkled with a new light; she had a pleasant smile for everyone, and spoke only of those things that she knew interested others. Sometimes she fixed her eyes upon Grandmother, tears seemed to gather in them, she cast aside her brush, put her arm around her neck, kissed her wrinkled forehead, and smoothed her white hair. Once she bent down and kissed her hand.

Grandmother had not expected this; she was startled, turned red, and then said: "What is your Grace doing? Such honor does not belong to me!"

"I know what I am doing and for what I have to thank you. You were my good angel!" she said as she knelt at Grandmother's feet.

"Then may God bless you and grant you all the happiness you desire!" said Grandmother, placing her hands upon the forehead of the kneeling girl, a forehead white and clear, like the petals of a lily.

"I shall pray for you and for the Princess, she is a good lady."

The gamekeeper stopped at The Old Bleachery the day after the storm to let them know that they could now come to take a last look at Victorka and to bid her farewell. Mrs. Proshek did not like to look at a corpse, so she remained at home; the miller's wife had the same excuse, but the miller declared that she was afraid lest Victorka's ghost should appear to her in the night. Christina was in the manorial harvest field, so nobody went with Grandmother and the children except Manchinka. On their way they gathered flowers to make a wreath, together with the mignonette which they brought from home. The boys carried consecrated pictures, which Grandmother had brought them from the Svatonovitz shrine; Grandmother had a rosary, and Manchinka, also, some pictures.

"Who would have thought that we were to have a funeral?" said the gamekeeper's wife, meeting them at the door.

"We are all here for a time; we arise in the morning, but know not what the day will bring to us," replied Grandmother. The fawn came and pushed her head against Adelka's lap and the boys and dogs surrounded the new comers.

"Where have you laid her out?" asked Grandmother, entering the hall.

"In the garden house," replied the gamekeeper's wife, taking Nannie by the hand and leading the guests into the garden.

The garden house, — or rather a sort of arbor, — was lined inside with evergreens. In the middle of the room upon a bier of rough birch wood stood a plain coffin; in it lay Victorka. The gamekeeper's wife had dressed her in a white shroud. Her fore-head was covered with a wreath of wild pinks, and her head rested upon a pillow of moss. Her hands were folded upon her breast as she was wont to carry them when she was alive. The coffin and the cover were trimmed with evergreens, a lamp burned at her head, and at her feet was a small vase with holy water, in which was a sprinkling brush made of ears of rye. The gamekeeper's wife had done everything, seen to everything herself; many times a day she had been in the little arbor, so that the sight had become familiar to her; but Grandmother stepped to the coffin, made the sign of the cross over the body, knelt down, and began to pray. The children followed her example.

"Now tell me, are you satisfied, have we arranged everything as it should be?" asked the gamekeeper's wife anxiously, when Grandmother arose from prayer. "We did not give her any more flowers or pictures because we knew that you, too, would want to put some little gifts into the grave."

"Everything is well done, very well, indeed," replied Grandmother.

The gamekeeper's wife took the flowers and pictures from the children and placed them around the body of Victorka. Grandmother twined the rosary around her stiff hands, and looked long and lovingly into her face. The wild expression was gone! The black, burning eyes were closed, their light had died out. The black, tangled masses of hair were smoothly combed out, and around the forehead, cold as marble, was wound a red wreath, like the band of love. The distortion of features which had made her hideous in wrath was not seen; the muscles of the face were relaxed in calm repose; but upon her lips lay her last thought, as if in her surprise she had died with it, — a bitter smile.

"What was it that grieved thee, thou poor heart? what did they do to thee?" said Grandmother in a low voice. "Alas! no one can atone to thee for thy sufferings. God will judge the guilty one. Thou art in eternal light and peace."

"The blacksmith's wife wanted us to put shavings under her head, but my husband would have moss; I am afraid the people, and especially her relatives, will say that we took charge of her funeral and then disposed of her as if she were a pauper."

"My dear woman, let the people say what they will! After a person is dead, they would wrap him in cloth of gold, but while he lives they do not ask: 'Poor soul, what aileth thee?' Let her keep that green pillow; for fifteen years she has slept on no other." And Grandmother took the rye brush, sprinkled Victorka from head to foot three times, made the sign of the cross over her, bade the children do likewise, and then without a word all left the garden house.

Behind Riesenburg, in a romantic little valley where stands the chapel that the Lord of Turyn built out of gratitude for the recovery of his deaf daughter, is a graveyard; there they buried Victorka. Upon her grave the gamekeeper planted a fir tree. "That is green both summer and winter, and she always loved it," said Grandmother, when they spoke of it.

Victorka's lullaby was heard no more by the dam; the cave was empty, the fir above it cut down; still she was by no means forgotten. For many years her unhappy fate resounded through the neighborhood in a sad song, composed by Bara of Zernov.

The Countess kept Grandmother's picture as had been agreed, bringing her only that of the children. The father and the mother were delighted, but Grandmother's joy knew no bounds. "The Countess knew how to put a soul in those faces," she said, showing the picture to everybody who came into the house; and everybody agreed with

her when she declared that they looked as if they
could open their lips and speak.

When years had passed and the children had
left home, Grandmother often said: " Although it
is not the custom among the common people to
have their pictures painted, nevertheless it is a good
custom. For my part, I remember each face well;
but years will pass away, the memory will fade,
the image will grow dim, and then what a comfort
it will be when I can look at this picture."

The last sheaves were taken in from the manorial fields. Since the Princess was anxious to hasten
her departure to Italy, the steward ordered that the
harvest festival should be held at the end of the
wheat harvest.

Christina was the most beautiful maiden in the
whole neighborhood, and therefore everybody was
pleased that Grandmother selected her to present
the harvest wreath to the Princess.

There was a large open place behind the castle
covered partly with grass and partly with straw
stacks. In the middle of this space, the young
men set up a long pole decorated with red handkerchiefs, ribbons, evergreens, wild flowers, and
ears of grain. Benches were put around the straw
stacks, booths were built of evergreens, and the
ground was trampled down to make a dancing
floor.

" Grandmother, Grandmother," said Christina,
" you have fed me on hope, I lived on your words,
sent armfuls of comfort to Jacob; and behold! the
harvest festival is here, and still we know not what
to expect. Tell me, dearest Grandma, was it only
the apples of promise that you showed us, to keep

up our hearts until we should become reconciled to our lot?"

"My dear girl, it would have been very unwise to comfort you in that way. I meant what I said. To-morrow put on your best, the Princess will be pleased. If I am alive and well I shall be there, too, and then if you ask me, I will tell you all," replied Grandmother, while her face beamed with a hidden joy.

She knew well what had been done for Milo, and had she not promised the Princess to be silent, she would not have delayed a moment to remove all anxiety from Christina's mind.

The next day all the socagers, together with the young people from the manor, dressed up in their holiday attire, gathered together in one of the fields to celebrate the harvest festival. A wagon was partially loaded with sheaves; the horses, upon one of which was mounted the driver, were trimmed with gay streamers. Christina with several other girls took their places upon the top of the sheaves, while the others, old and young, ranged themselves in couples about the wagon. The reapers carried scythes and sickles, the women sickles and rakes; each one had a harvest bouquet in her corsage, and the young men had their hats trimmed with corn flowers and other field blossoms.

The driver cracked his whip, the horses started, the reapers sang and the procession moved to the castle. As soon as they reached it, the girls dismounted, Christina placed the wreath upon a red kerchief, and the young people, ranging themselves in couples behind her, began to sing, and thus the procession entered the hall. The Princess entered at the same time from the opposite direction. Christina, trembling, blushing, and with downcast eyes, stammered through the recitation, wishing their mistress a successful and abundant harvest and rich crops for the coming year. She then laid the harvest wreath at the feet of the Princess. The reapers waved their hats and shouted long life and health to their mistress. She thanked them and referred them for food and drink to the steward. Then turning to Christina, she said: " To you, my dear girl, I am especially grateful for the beautiful wreath and wish that you have given me; I see that all the rest are in couples, but you are still alone; perhaps I shall please you best if I furnish you with a partner!"

She smiled, opened the parlor door, and there stood Milo,— and dressed in a peasant's garb!

" Holy Virgin! Jacob!" exclaimed Christina, and would have fallen down, overcome with surprise and joy, had not one of the company caught her.

The Princess quietly left the hall. " Come, come," cried Milo, " the Princess doesn't want any thanks," and when they were outside he raised a full purse saying: " The Countess gave me this to distribute among you. Here, comrade, take it and distribute it yourself!" he added giving the purse to Tomesh, who like the rest was staring at Milo, unable to say a single word. When they were out of the castle they raised a wild shout. Milo embraced his loved one fervently and then told the company that all gratitude for his deliverance was due to the Princess.

"And to Grandma," added Christina, "if we did not have her, we should have nothing."

All went to the dance. The officers of the castle, together with their families, mingled among the reapers, and so did Proshek's family, the miller's and the gamekeeper's; but Grandmother was the first. Joy at the meeting of two persons who were so dear to her urged her to go. Christina and Milo could hardly refrain from embracing her.

"Do not thank me; I spoke but a word, the Princess helped me, and God gave his blessing."

"But, Grandmother," said Christina, shaking her finger at her, "You knew yesterday that Jacob had come and that he was hidden at Vaclav's, and you wouldn't say a word."

"Because I was not at liberty to do so. Besides, you should have trusted me when I promised that you should see each other soon. Remember, my child, that all things come round to those who will but wait in patience."

Around the decorated pole the air resounded with music, laughter, and song. The attendants from the castle danced with peasant maidens, and their daughters were not ashamed to step into the circle with peasant youths, both being well pleased with their partners. The spirits of all became so excited by the abundance of beer, the sweet mixed drinks, and the dance, that when the Princess came with the Countess to look at them, and the young people went through a national dance, their joy reached the highest pitch, all restraint ceased, caps flew into the air, and shouts were heard of "Long live our gracious Princess!" and cup after cup was drained to her health. The ladies were

much pleased and had a kind word for every one.
When Christina came to kiss the hand of the
Countess, that young lady congratulated her; she
spoke to the miller and the gamekeeper, and then
turned with loving familiarity to Grandmother, at
which the stewardess and her daughter turned
yellow with envy; they could not endure Grandmother,— she brought to naught all their plans.
But when the fathers seated at the table,
with their heads quite full, began to rail at
the secretaries and the steward, and when one of
them seized the beaker to pass a drink to the
Princess, and was only restrained by Tomesh, that
lady suddenly disappeared.

Several days after the harvest festival she
started with the Countess, for Italy. Before their
departure the young lady delivered into Grandmother's hands a beautiful garnet necklace, a wedding present for Christina.

Grandmother was satisfied; everything had
turned out according to her wishes. But one thing
was still on her mind, and that was a letter to her
daughter, Johanna. Mrs. Proshek would have
attended to this, but then it would not have been
as Grandmother wanted it. One day she called
Barunka into her room, closed the door, and pointing to the table, upon which lay ready a sheet of
paper, pen and ink, she said: " Be seated, Barunka,
I want you to write a letter to Aunt Johanna."
Barunka sat down; Grandmother seated herself
beside her so as to overlook the work, and began
to dictate:

" Praised be our Lord Jesus Christ! "

" But, Grandma," said Barunka, " We do not

begin a letter that way; we must write at the top
'Dear Johanna.'"

"Not so, my little girl; your great-grandfather
and your grandfather always wrote in that way,
and I never wrote to my children in any other way."
Therefore begin:

"Praised be our Lord Jesus Christ! A thousand
times I greet and kiss you, dear daughter Johanna,
and let you know that I am, thank God, in good
health. My cough troubles me somewhat, but that
is no wonder, for soon I shall count my age by
eight crosses. It is a good age, dear daughter, and
one must feel thankful to God when one enjoys
with it such good health as I have; I hear well and
see well, I could still mend my clothes if Barunka
did not do it for me. As for my feet, they are still
quite spry. I hope that this letter will find you in
good health, and Dorothy, too. From your letter
I learned that Uncle is ill, but I hope that he will
recover soon. He is often ailing, and they say:
'Often unwell doesn't bring the bell.'*

"You also write to me that you want to get
married, and you ask my consent. My dear
daughter, since you have already chosen according
to your heart, what can I say but this: Máy God
grant you happiness and bless you both; may you
live to the honor and glory of God, and be useful
to the world. Why should I object, when George
is a worthy man and you love him; it is not
I but you that will live with him. I had hoped,
indeed, that you would choose a Bohemian,—those
of the same nationality are best adapted to each
other,—but it was not your fate; I do not blame

* The funeral bell.

you. We are all the children of one father, one mother* nourishes and sustains us, and therefore we should love each other, though we be not from the same country. Give my greeting to George, and when you have your business established and nothing to hinder you, come and make us a visit. The children already talk of your coming. May God bless you and keep you in good health. I bid you good-bye."

Barunka read the letter through again, then they folded it, sealed it, and Grandmother put it away in the side drawer of her chest till she should go to church, when she herself would take it to the post office.

---

* A figurative expression for the earth.

CHAPTER XVII.

ONE afternoon, several days before St. Katherine's, the young people were gathered at the inn. The whole house, inside and outside, shone; around the doors were garlands of evergreen, a branch of greens was behind every picture upon the wall, the curtains were white as snow, and the floor was like chalk. The long basswood table was covered with a white cloth, and upon it were bunches of rosemary, white and red ribbons, and around it blushing maids like roses and pinks. They had come together to make the wedding wreaths for Christina's wedding. She sat behind the table in the corner, the handsomest maid of them all. She was excused from all household duties, and placed under the charge of the spokesman and the wedding matron, which honorable offices were filled, the first by Martin, the leader of pilgrimages, and the second by Grandmother. She could not refuse this to Christina, although she usually avoided such public duties. The miller's wife took the place of Christina's mother, who, on account of lameness in her feet, could not take charge of the housekeeping. Cilka and her mother helped. Grandmother sat among the girls, and although she had nothing to do, her advice was constantly needed. The bride was fastening long pieces of ribbon upon beautiful sprays of rosemary for the bridesman and the spokesman. The

335

younger bridesmaid was to weave the wreath for
the bride, the older the one for the groom; the
others, one apiece for their partners. The rosemary that was left was made into wedding favors
for all the guests. Even the horses that were to
take the bride to church had their harness trimmed
with ribbons and rosemary. The eyes of the bride
beamed with joy and love, whenever she glanced at
the stalwart form of the groom. He was standing
among his friends, each of whom had more liberty
to speak with his own love than he had to address
his bride, upon whom he could only cast a longing
glance. The bridesman waited upon the bride, and
the groom was obliged to give his attention to the
first bridesmaid. Every one, except the bride and
groom, had full liberty to be gay, to joke, to make
witty remarks; the last, however, was expected of
the spokesman especially. Christina spoke but
little; with downcast eyes she sat behind the rose-
mary-covered table. When the younger and older
bridesmaids began to weave the wreaths, and all
joined in singing:

> "Where, white dove, hast thou flown,
> Aye flown,
> That thy snow-white plumage is soiled,
> Is soiled?'

the bride covered her face with her white apron and
wept.

The groom looked at her anxiously and asked
the spokesman: "Why does she weep?"

"You know, groom, that joy and grief are bed-
fellows, and thus it happens that the one often
wakes the other. Never mind. 'To-day weeping,
to-morrow rejoicing.'"

Here followed song after song, both gay and sober; they sang the praises of youth, beauty, and love, of the happiness of a bachelor's life; but at last the youths and maidens began to sing the joys of married life, when two hearts love each other like two turtle-doves, when they live in harmony like two grains of corn in one ear. They were, however, constantly interrupted by the mocking voice of the spokesman. When they sang of marriage, harmony, and concord, he announced a solo by himself, saying that he would sing them a brand-new song.

"Then crow, to show what you know," cried the company.

The spokesman took his stand in the middle of the room and began in a mocking tone, which was as natural to him at a wedding as the serious one was at a pilgrimage:

> "Oh, wedded bliss!
> There's naught so delightful as this.
> If I bid her cook pease,
>   She'll only cook barley,
> If I ask her for meat
>   For pastry she'll parley.
>   Oh, wedded bliss!
> There's naught so delightful as this."

"Both the song and the singer are not worth a broken penny!" cried the girls, and immediately began to sing so as to spoil the pleasure of the young men who wanted to hear the rest of the song. With constant singing and joking the bouquets and wreaths were finished; then the girls arose, joined hands, and, dancing around the table, sang:

22

> " All is now finished,
>   The prize is won;
> The kolaches are baked
>   The garlands are done."

At this point the door flew open, and the miller's wife, with several other women, came hurrying in with their hands full of food, the miller and the bridesman bringing the drinks. The company sat down again to the table, which was now covered with various dishes instead of rosemary. The groomsmen sat next to the bridesmaids, the groom between the first bridesmaid and the wedding matron, the bride between the younger bridesmaid and the bridesman. The spokesman went around the table, allowing the bridesmaids to feed him, and at times to rate him soundly; for this privilege, however, they were obliged to receive every jest in good humor, though sometimes it was quite pointed. When the table was cleared, the spokesman brought in three dishes as presents for the bride. In the first was wheat, which he gave her with the wish that she should be fruitful; in the second, ashes mixed with leek seeds, which she was obliged to pick out to show her patience; the third dish was the one with the " secret " in it, and was covered up. The bride was expected to receive this dish without looking into it. But how could she endure that? When no one observed her, she carefully raised the corner of the cloth that covered it, and f-r-r-r—the sparrow hidden there flew up to the ceiling.

" You see, dear bride," said Grandmother, giving her a tap upon the shoulder, " that is what happens to the inquisitive. Some persons would rather die than not try to find out what is hidden from them, and when the cover is raised, they catch nothing after all."

The young people remained together till late at night, for dancing followed the feasting. The groom and the bridesman escorted the wedding matron home, reminding her at parting, that they were to meet early the next morning.

The whole neighborhood of Zernov was up early the next day. Some were to accompany the bride to church, some only to attend the wedding at the house, and those who were not invited could not overcome their curiosity to see the procession about which everybody had talked for several weeks. It was to be so grand; the bride was to ride in a carriage drawn by horses from the manor; she was to wear a costly garnet necklace, a white embroidered apron, a rose-colored taffety jacket, and a sky-blue skirt; the Zernov gossips knew all this, probably before Christina herself had thought of it. They knew all the details as to the quantity and kinds of food that would be prepared for the wedding feast, and in what order the guests were to come to the table; what kind of furniture the bride was to have for her outfit, how many feather beds and how many pieces of underwear. They knew all as well as if she had given them a written statement of it. Not to go to look at such a wedding, not to see how becoming the wreath was to the bride, how much she wept, how the guests were dressed, would have been so great a negligence that it could never be pardoned. This was an epoch in the history of Zernov, this furnished material for conversation for at least half a year. How, then, could they miss it?

When the guests from The Old Bleachery and the mill came to the inn, they were obliged to push their way through a large crowd of people that had assembled in the yard. The guests on the bride's side had already arrived. The miller was dressed in his best, his boots shone like a mirror, and to-day he held a silver snuff box. He was the bride's witness. The miller's wife was dressed in silk; beneath her double chin glistened strings of pearls, and upon her head was a golden cap. Grandmother also had on her wedding dress, and a Sunday cap with the dove knots. The bridesmaids, the groomsmen and the spokesman were not at the inn; they had gone to Zernov to fetch the groom. The bride also was not to be seen; she was hidden in her chamber.

Suddenly a great commotion was heard in the yard: "They're coming, they're coming!" and from the mill were heard the sounds of the violin, flute, and clarionet. They were bringing the groom. The spectators whispered: "Look, look! Milo's sister is the younger bridesmaid, and Tichanek's daughter the elder one. There is no doubt that if Tomesh's wife were still single, she would have filled that place."

"Tomesh is the groom's witness!"

"And where is his wife? She is nowhere to be seen."

"She is helping the bride to dress."

"And see! there comes the squire, too; what a wonder that they invited him, for he alone was to blame for Milo's conscription!"

Everybody marveled.

"The squire himself is not so bad; Lucie made him start the fire, and the steward added fuel. No wonder that he acted as he did. Milo did well to invite him; that was the best punishment he could mete out to him, and especially to Lucie. She will turn yellow with envy."

"Why she is betrothed," said another.

"How can that be?" exclaimed a third, "I have not heard of it."

"It took place only day before yesterday,— with Joseph Nitlovitz."

"He had been waiting upon her a long time."

"Yes indeed, but she would not have him as long as she had any hope of getting Jacob Milo."

"What a beautiful handkerchief the groom has, it must have cost the bride no less than ten guilders!" said some of the women. "What a dashing figure he cuts. His like is not seen every day!"

These and similar remarks were made by the lookers-on while the groom was approaching the house; he was greeted at the door by the innkeeper with a full beaker. The groom went at once to look for the bride, and found her, as was expected, weeping in her chamber. He led her into the room where the parents of both were waiting for them, to give them the blessing. They knelt before them, and the spokesman began his speech, as is the custom on such occasions; he spoke long in behalf of the couple, thanking the parents for all they had done for their children and asking their benediction. Everybody in the room was moved to tears. The blessing having been given, the company prepared to start for church. Christina was led between the

bridesman and the first bridesmaid; then came
Milo with the second bridesmaid; they were followed by the others arranged in couples, except the
spokesman, who went at the head of the procession.
When they entered the carriages and wagons which
were waiting for them, the girls waved their handkerchiefs and sang, being soon joined by the young
men; but the bride wept silently, at times casting
a wistful glance upon the second carriage, where
the groom rode with the witnesses and the matron.

The spectators scattered to their respective
homes, and for a while the inn was empty, save
that at one window sat the old mother watching
the procession and praying for her child, who for
so many years had filled her place, and endured all
her moods with gentle patience, attributing them
to her long and severe illness. Soon the women
came to arrange the tables. Wherever one turned,
a cook or one of her assistants was to be seen.

The young Mrs. Tomesh had charge of everything. She assumed the responsibility gladly, as
the miller's wife had done the day before at the
weaving of the wreaths.

When the wedding party returned from church,
the innkeeper, as before, met them at the door with
a full beaker. The bride changed her dress and
they went to dinner. The bride and bridegroom
sat at the head of the table; the bridesman waited
upon the bridesmaids, who laid aside a part of their
viands for him and from time to time passed to him
the nicest bits from their plates. The spokesman
declared he fared "like God in Paradise." Grandmother, too, was gay, and with many a witty
remark answered the spokesman, whose ears were

everywhere and whose large, angular person was in everybody's way. At home she would not have allowed a single pea to be thrown upon the floor, but when the guests began to throw handfuls of peas and wheat at each other, she herself threw some at the groom and bride, saying: "May God so shower his blessings upon you." But the peas and wheat were not trampled upon; Grandmother had noticed how the tame pigeons were picking up everything from the floor.

Dinner was over; many a heavy head swayed from side to side; each one had before him a generous allowance of food to take home, and if he was not able to take care of this himself, Mrs. Tomesh saw to it that he fared no worse than the rest. It would have been considered a disgrace to come home from a wedding empty handed. There was an abundance of everything, so that whoever went past the inn got as much to eat and drink as he wished; and the village children who came "hanging about" got their aprons full of buns and kolaches. After dinner they gave the bride money "for the cradle," and she was not a little astonished to see silver pieces falling into her apron. The grooms-men brought bowls of water and towels to the bridesmaids to wash their hands, for which service they were expected to throw a piece of money into the water. As each girl wished to be thought liberal, nothing but silver gleamed at the bottom of the dishes; this was spent the next day by the young men in dancing and drinking with their partners.

The bride and bridesmaids went to change their dresses again, for the dancing was now to begin.

Grandmother embraced this opportunity to take the children home; they had been feasting in Christina's room. She herself was obliged to return, because later in the evening would occur the unwreathing of the bride, at which ceremony the presence of the wedding matron was indispensable. She also brought the cap which, with the help of Mrs. Proshek, she had selected and bought for the bride. This was also one of the duties of the matron. When all had danced as much as they liked, and the bride was almost breathless from the exercise,— every one wanted to dance with her, even if he took but one turn,— Grandmother beckoned to the women and whispered that it was after midnight, and that now the bride "belonged to the wives." They began to quarrel about her, the groom and the bridesman refusing to give her up to be deprived of her beautiful wreath; but it was of no use. The women got possession of her and led her off to her chamber. The girls stood behind the door singing to her in a sad voice, not to let them take away her green wreath, for once laid aside she would never find it again.

All in vain! The bride was seated upon a stool, Mrs. Tomesh unbraided her hair, the floral coronet and the green wreath were laid aside, and Grandmother replaced them with a cap, having long strings. The bride wept constantly; but the women sang and shouted, and only Grandmother remained serious, though sometimes a smile passed over her face and her eye grew moist as she thought of her daughter Johanna, who also celebrated her wedding at this time.

The bride's cap was quite becoming to her, and

the miller's wife declared that she looked like a "Meissen apple" in it.

"Now to the groom! Which one of you will go to tease him?" asked Grandmother.

"The oldest," said the miller's wife.

"Wait, I'll bring him one," quickly cried Mrs. Tomesh. She ran out and brought the old washerwoman, who was helping in the kitchen. They threw a shawl over head, and the wedding matron took her by the arm and led her out to the groom to see if he would "buy her." The groom walked about her and examined her till he had an opportunity to raise the shawl; underneath he saw an old wrinkled face soiled with ashes. All laughed. The groom did not want to claim such a bride, so the matron hurried with her out of the room. A second one was brought out. Both the groom and the spokesman thought she looked more like a bride; at first they thought they would buy her, but the spokesman said: "Indeed, we won't buy a hare in a bag!" he raised the shawl and they saw the fat face of the miller's wife, whose small black eyes laughed mischievously.

"Buy her, buy her; I'll sell her cheap!" laughed the miller, turning his snuff box in his fingers, but slowly, either because it was heavy or his fingers were stiff.

"Hush, hush, Father," laughed his wife, "today you would sell, to-morrow you'd be glad to buy back."

The third was the tall, slender form of the bride. The spokesman offered an old kreutzer for her, but the groom emptied the silver from his purse and won her. The women came rushing into the room, joined hands, put the groom in the circle, and sang:

> "All is now finished,
>   The unwreathing is done;
>   The kolaches are eaten,
>   The bride is won."

The bride now belonged to the groom. The money which the women received for her was spent the next day in feasting, when they came "to make the bed," at which ceremony there was again much singing and joking. The spokesman declared that a well-ordered wedding ought to last eight days, and this was usually the case with grand weddings. The weaving of the wreaths before the wedding, the wedding itself, the making of the bed, the reunion at the home of the bride's parents, a second reunion at the groom's house, the meeting at the inn of all the young friends: thus the whole week was spent before the newly married couple had any rest, before they could say: "Now we are alone."

A few weeks after Christina's wedding, Mrs. Proshek received a letter from the first chambermaid, who wrote that Countess Hortense was to celebrate her marriage with a certain artist, her former teacher, that she was perfectly happy, that she was again like a rose, and that the Princess rejoiced at her happiness.

Grandmother hearing this good news, nodded her head saying: "Thank God; all has turned out well."

    *   *   *   *   *   *   *

It is not the purpose of this little book to describe the life of the young people that grew up around

Grandmother; neither do I wish to weary the reader by leading him from the gamekeeper's to the mill and back again, through the little plain in which life was always the same. The young people grew up; some remained at home, married, the old people giving up their places to them, just as upon the oak the old leaves fall away when the young ones begin to bud. Some left this quiet region to seek their fortune elsewhere, like seeds which are blown away by the wind, or carried far away by the waters, that upon new shores they may find better soil in which to strike their roots and grow.

Grandmother never left the place where she had found a second home. With a quiet, happy heart she saw how everything about her prospered; she rejoiced at her neighbor's good fortune, she comforted the sorrowing, she helped, when it was possible for her to do so, and when, one after another, her grandchildren left home, she followed them with tearful eyes, and with the wistful sigh: "God grant that we may meet again." And they did meet again. Year after year they returned to visit their home, and Grandmother's eyes brightened as she listened to the descriptions which the young men gave of the great world; she encouraged their brilliant plans for the future, she excused the shortcomings of youth, which they did not conceal from her. They, on their part loved to listen to her advice, even though they did not always follow it; they honored her words and her virtuous life. The grown up girls made Grandmother their confidant. She knew all their secrets, their dreams, their hopes and fears; for with her they were always sure of sympathy and love. Thus Manchinka from the mill sought refuge with Grandmother when her father forbade her to love a poor but handsome youth. Grandmother knew how to "set the father's head upon the proper handle," as the miller himself declared; and when in after years his daughter was happy and the business, under the management of an industrious and enterprising son-in-law, prospered, the miller would say: "Grandmother was right; God follows the poor with his blessing."

The children of the young women loved Grandmother as if they were her own grandchildren; they knew her by no other name than Grandma. When, two years after Christina's wedding, the Princess returned to the castle, she sent at once for Grandmother and showed her a beautiful boy, the son of the Countess, who, a year after her marriage, had died, leaving the bereaved husband and the Princess this child. Grandmother took it in her arms, and her tears fell upon its silken robe as she thought of the young, good, and beautiful mother; but laying it again in the arms of the Princess, she said in a low tone: "Let us not weep. She is in heaven; the world was not for her. God loves those the most whom he calls away when they are the happiest, and your Grace is not left desolate.

People did not know how Grandmother was failing; she alone felt it. She would often say to Adelka, pointing to an old apple tree that year by year grew dryer and put on its green foliage more sparingly: "We are alike; we shall probably go to sleep together." One spring, when all the other trees were clad in their green livery, the old apple tree stood there alone, without a single leaf. It was dug up and used for fuel. The same spring, Grandmother coughed severely; she could no longer walk to the village to "God's dear church." Her hands withered more and more, her hair was like snow, her voice grew weaker and weaker.

One day, Mrs. Proshek sent letters in all directions urging the children to come home. Grandmother had taken to her bed, she could no longer hold the spindle. From the gamekeeper's, from the mill, from the village, messengers came several times a day to ask how Grandmother was; she was no better. Adelka often prayed with her; she was obliged to tell her every morning, every evening, how the trees were growing in the orchard, how the vegetables were thriving in the garden, how the poultry was doing, how Spotty was; she had to reckon in how many days Mr. Beyer would probably be with them. "Perhaps John will come with him," Grandmother would add. Her memory began to fail. She often called Barunka instead of Adelka, and when the latter reminded her that Barunka was not at home, recollecting herself she would say, sighing deeply: "No, no, she is not at home, I shall not see her again. Is she happy?" And yet she saw them all again.

Mr. Proshek came, and with him Willie and Johanna; her son Caspar came, and from the Riesengebirge mountains came Mr. Beyer, bringing with him his sturdy apprentice, John; Orel came from the school of forestry, where the Princess, discovering his talents, had placed him. Grandmother counted him, too, among her grandchildren, for she had observed the growing attachment between him and Adelka, and approved of it, knowing his nobleness of character. All gathered around Grand-

mother's bed. The first of all was Barunka,
came with the nightingale. He came back to his
by Grandmother's window, and Barunka foun
old place in Grandmother's room. There her bec
to stand, there she used to listen to the music c
sweet singer, there, rising up and lying down, G
mother used to bless her. They were tog
again; the same voices were heard around
these were the same stars upon which the
gazed together, the same hands rested upon B
ka's head. It was the same head, but difi
thoughts crowded in it, and the tears which G
mother saw rolling down the cheeks of her be
grandchild were different from the tears of
hood, which a pleasant smile dried from the
cheeks, when, as yet a little girl, she slept ii
little bed in Grandmother's room. Those
bedewed, but did not dim the eyes.

Grandmother knew she had not many da
live; therefore, like a good housewife, she se
house in order. First she made her peace with
then she distributed her little property. Eac
received a keepsake. For all who came to se
she had a kind word, and when they left, her
followed them till they were out of sight.
the Princess, with the son of Hortense, came
her, and when they were leaving, she looked
after them; for she knew she should never see
again. Even those dumb brutes, the cats and
were not forgotten. She called them to her
caressed them and allowed Sultan to lick her
" See to them." she said to Adelka and the ser

Vorsilka,*— I know my time is near at hand, for I dreamed last night that George came for me,— when I die do not forget to tell it to the bees, so that they shall not die out! The others might forget." Grandmother knew that Vorsa would do it; for the others did not believe as she did and, therefore, might neglect to do it in time, even though they were willing to fulfill all her wishes.

Towards evening of the day following the children's return, Grandmother was quietly passing away. Barunka read to her the prayer of the dying, she repeating the words after her. Suddenly the lips ceased to move, the eye was fixed upon the crucifix hanging over the bed, the breathing stopped. The flame of life went out like a lamp in which the oil has been consumed.

Barunka closed her eyes. Christina opened the window "so that the soul might have freedom to fly away." Vorsa, not lingering among the weeping, hastened to the hive which the miller had set up for Grandmother some years before, and rapping upon it called three times: "Bees, bees, our Grandmother is dead!" and then she sat down upon the bench under the lilacs and sobbed aloud. The miller went to Zernov, to have the bell tolled. He himself offered to do this service; he felt oppressed in the house; he wanted to go outside so that he could weep and ease his grief. "I missed Victorka; how, then, can I forget Grandmother!" he said on the way. When the tolling of the bell was heard, announcing to the people that Grandmother was no more, the whole neighborhood wept.

"The third day, when the funeral procession,

* The diminutive of Vorsa.

composed of a great company of people, was passing the castle,— for everyone who had known
Grandmother wanted to follow her to her last
resting place,— a white hand pushed aside the
heavy curtains, and the Princess appeared between
them. Her sad gaze followed the procession as
long as it was in sight, and then dropping the curtains and sighing deeply, she whispered:

"Happy woman!"

Made in the USA
Lexington, KY
18 August 2015